ROUTLEDGE LIBRARY EDITIONS:
THE NINETEENTH-CENTURY NOVEL

Volume 10

CLASS IN TURN-OF-THE-CENTURY NOVELS OF GISSING, JAMES, HARDY AND WELLS

CLASS IN TURN-OF-THE-CENTURY NOVELS OF GISSING, JAMES, HARDY AND WELLS

CHRISTINE DEVINE

Routledge
Taylor & Francis Group

LONDON AND NEW YORK

First published in 2005 by Ashgate Publishing Ltd.

This edition first published in 2016
by Routledge
2 Park Square, Milton Park, Abingdon, Oxon OX14 4RN

and by Routledge
711 Third Avenue, New York, NY 10017

Routledge is an imprint of the Taylor & Francis Group, an informa business

British Library Cataloguing in Publication Data
A catalogue record for this book is available from the British Library

ISBN: 978-1-138-67777-7 (Set)
ISBN: 978-1-315-55928-5 (Set) (ebk)
ISBN: 978-1-138-67591-9 (Volume 10) (hbk)
ISBN: 978-1-315-56035-9 (Volume 10) (ebk)

Publisher's Note
The publisher has gone to great lengths to ensure the quality of this reprint but points out that some imperfections in the original copies may be apparent.

Disclaimer
The publisher has made every effort to trace copyright holders and would welcome correspondence from those they have been unable to trace.

Class in Turn-of-the-Century Novels of Gissing, James, Hardy and Wells

CHRISTINE DeVINE

ASHGATE

Published by
Ashgate Publishing Limited   Ashgate Publishing Company
Gower House   Suite 420
Croft Road   101 Cherry Street
Aldershot   Burlington
Hants GU11 3HR   Vermont, 05401-4405
England   USA

Ashgate website: http://www.ashgate.com

British Library Cataloguing in Publication Data
DeVine, Christine
   Class in Turn-of-the-Century Novels of Gissing, James, Hardy and Wells –
   (The Nineteenth Century Series).
   1. Gissing, George, 1857–1903. Nether world. 2. James, Henry 1843–1916. Princess Casamassima. 3. Hardy, Thomas, 1840–1928. Tess of the d'Urbervilles. 4. Wells, H. G. (Herbert George), 1866–1946. Tono-Bungay. 5. Social classes in literature. 6. English fiction – 19th century – History and criticism. 7. English fiction – 20th century – History and criticism. I. Title
   823.8'09355

US Library of Congress Cataloging in Publication Data
DeVine, Christine
   Class in turn-of-the-century novels of Gissing, James, Hardy and Wells / Christine DeVine
      p. cm. – (The Nineteenth Century Series)
   Includes bibliographical references and index.
   1. English fiction – 19th century – History and criticism. 2. Social classes in literature. 3. Literature and society – Great Britain – History – 19th century. 4. Wells, H. G. (Herbert George), 1866–1946 – Political and social views. 5. Gissing, George, 1857–1903 – Political and social views. 6. Hardy, Thomas, 1840–1928 – Political and social views. 7. James, Henry, 1843–1916 – Political and social views. I. Title. II. Series: Nineteenth century (Aldershot, England)
   PR878.S6D485 2005
   823.8'09355–dc22   2005001824

ISBN 0 7546 5150 9

Printed and bound in Great Britain by
Antony Rowe Ltd, Chippenham, Wiltshire

For my parents, Peggy and Stan Hawthorne

Contents

Illustrations

Acknowledgements

I am grateful to friends and colleagues who have read drafts of chapters and discussed my ideas during the writing of this book. Special thanks go to Joseph Wiesenfarth (University of Wisconsin-Madison), Pierre Coustillas (University of Lille), Gert Buelens (University of Ghent), Simon J. James (University of Durham) and Kristine Ottesen Garrigan (DePaul University).

A Research Grant from the University of Louisiana at Lafayette helped me to finish this project, and the College of Liberal Arts at the University of Louisiana helped financially with obtaining the illustrations. My thanks go to Leslie Donahue Schilling of the Humanities Resource Center at UL who expertly produced the camera-ready copy for this book and to Doris Meriwether for her patient and invaluable editorial assistance.

Portions of Chapter 1 appeared previously in *The Gissing Journal* and a version of Chapter 2 was first published in the *Henry James Review* (The Johns Hopkins University Press). I would like to thank the editors of these journals.

Introduction

Oliver Twist (1838) begins with a young mother dying in utter poverty in a workhouse immediately after the birth of what the narrator describes on the novel's first page as "the item of mortality whose name is prefixed to the head of this chapter" (17)— to wit, Oliver Twist. The good-looking girl wearing no wedding ring had been found lying in the street, her shoes worn to pieces, about to give birth. She does so, in the workhouse, attended by a parish surgeon and "a pauper old woman, who was rendered rather misty by an unwonted allowance of beer" (18). Oliver's mother dies shortly after he is born. "It's all over, Mrs. Thingummy!" the surgeon informs his tipsy helper. Despite the sad fact that such circumstances must have been none too uncommon in the 1830s, the first chapter of the novel is full of Dickensian humor and wit. While the narrator's sense of injustice is clear, his sardonic but lively tone intervenes between the reader and the scene itself, helping us to feel more comfortable about the death while appreciating its pathos.

Defending himself in his 1841 preface to *Oliver* against those who criticized the "lowness" of his subject matter, Dickens compares his own realistic depiction of the criminal world to its romanticized portrayal in earlier works: Gay's *Beggar's Opera* (1728) and Edward Bulwer-Lytton's *Paul Clifford* (1830). "Here are no canterings upon moonlit heaths," he writes, "no merry-makings in the snuggest of all possible caverns, none of the attractions of dress, no embroidery, no lace" (5). He points out the effectiveness of showing crime in all its ghastliness: "[t]he cold, wet, shelterless midnight streets of London; the foul and frowsy dens, where vice is closely packed and lacks the room to turn; the haunts of hunger and disease, the shabby rags that scarcely hold together," render the criminal world less tempting to his readers (5).

Despite his claims to verisimilitude and the fact that *Oliver* was both praised and criticized by contemporary critics because it was so realistic in its portrayal of poverty and vice, Dickens had presented his middle-class readers with disturbing material in a reassuring way. As we have seen with regard to the first chapter of *Oliver*, the humorous if indignant tone of the narrator tends to mitigate the realism. Many of Dickens's criminals in *Oliver* are comedic, in part because most of them are merely children. Nancy, prostitute though Dickens claims her to be, is never seen "at work," and she displays loyalty and self-sacrifice to her man, those over-sentimentalized and idealized virtues usually attributed to nineteenth-century fictional heroines of a higher social standing. What Dickens labels "the foul and frowsy dens" and "haunts of hunger and disease" are not *real* locales, despite his recourse to specific London street names, so much as evocations of what his middle-class readers might imagine criminal haunts to be. In addition, the teleological format of *Oliver*, a convention of the traditional Victorian realistic novel, is well known to the reader, who anticipates a happy ending, enabling her to face the story of crime and poverty along the way. We suspect that Oliver is a fine little gentleman no matter how ragged he may appear, and that despite all the ups and downs, he will triumph in the end. As George Gissing writes, Dickens is a novelist "who would on no account bring a blush to the middle-class cheek; who at any moment tampers with the truth of circumstance that his readers may have joy rather than sorrow" (*Critical Study* 59).

The working classes and the poor became topical in novels during times of social unrest and during political debates about enlarging the franchise or changing the laws that dealt with the poor. But though they purported to give a realistic picture of the poor, such novels were generally written by middle-class authors for middle-class readers and so the depiction of the working classes was manipulated to serve the political purpose of the author, and the solutions they created were idealized.[1] Like many novelists at the time, Dickens was critical of certain facets of the middle-class-led society in which he lived—he wrote *Oliver* to protest the effects of the Poor Laws. But his protest stemmed from a middle-class world-view, and so did his fictional creations. Gissing, when writing about his famous predecessor—who had himself seen some hard times as a child—perceives Dickens's sympathy for the poor: "he is incapable of speaking and thinking of the poor as from a higher place" (*Critical Study* 168). Ultimately, however, he admits that Dickens's position is a middle-class one:

> Dickens, for all his sympathy, could not look with entire approval on the poor grown articulate about their wrongs. He would not have used the phrase, but he thought the thought, that humble folk must know "their station." He was a member of the middle class, and as far from preaching "equality" in its social sense as any man that ever wrote. Essentially a member of the great middle class, and on that very account able to do such work, to strike such blows, for the cause of humanity in his day and generation. (*Critical Study* 171)

Towards the end of the nineteenth century realist novelists took up the poor once again. But an evolution had taken place between what Dickens saw as his realistic depictions of the poor and working classes and those which appeared later, especially in the novels of George Gissing. Many have compared the two writers because they both wrote about the London poor, and in his later years, Gissing was considered something of a Dickens expert.[2] But as the later writer recognized, there is not much similarity in approach; he writes, "[s]o great a change has come over the theory and practice of fiction in the England of our times that we must needs treat of Dickens as, in many respects, antiquated." He goes on, "theoretically, he had very little in common with the school of strict veracity, of realism" (*Critical Study* 59).

This "school of strict veracity" was a new version of realism that came into being, this book argues, due to political and ideological shifts in the last decades of the nineteenth century. This new realism was facilitated by an alignment of concurrent and interconnected historical changes, in particular increasing literacy rates, the rapid commercialization of publishing, and changes in the political power base.[3] Exemplified by the novels I examine in this study, it was a fiction not centered in the middle-class ethos predominating earlier in the century.

The late-century writers I focus on in this study had a view of issues of class that is not merely part of a social protest; it expresses a new way of experiencing the class system that no longer sees it as the natural order of things. This view was afforded them, in part, by their own "outsider" position in society: Gissing, Hardy and Wells were educated, but lower-middle-class, and James, of course, was American. Not only did these writers recognize the need for a new kind of realism, but they were writing from a world-view which was not limited by a middle-class English consciousness, and which expressed therefore a more skeptical view of the social class system.

Unable to accept the social class system as it stands, each of these writers implicitly asks the question: What is class? In addition, they interrogate history by disrupting traditional literary conventions in an attempt to reveal the ideology of the historical moment in which those conventions obtained. This suggests to me not only that they each see a reciprocal relationship between history and fiction, but that they want to manipulate that relationship. The most important difference between Gissing, James, Hardy and Wells and most earlier writers, however, is their unwillingness to accept the class system as a natural phenomenon; instead they see it as a social construction.

II

Social class is difficult to discuss with any precision and without feeling as though one is using stereotypes and making sweeping statements. There is, in fact, no exact definition of social class; it appears to be recognized by all, but completely understood by none. Part of the problem is that class labels describe relationships between groups almost as much as they describe the groups themselves. And while there are only a few labels—working class, middle class, upper class—there are unlimited divisions within these groups.

The two most frequently used terms in discussions of class, *middle class* and *working class(es)*, each stem from a different view of the system. The term *middle class* suggests a hierarchy and fits more comfortably with *lower class*, which it implies. *Working class* was a term originally imposed from above by those to whom leisure time was a status symbol, and then adopted by those it labeled because it points up a useful productiveness, implying perhaps a slur of uselessness on other classes (Williams 55). Despite having newly come to power, the flourishing bourgeoisie of the mid-nineteenth century benefited from an ideology that saw the middle class as part of a hierarchy, a thinking more suited to the older system of rank. Conversely, it would not benefit those in the lower strata of society to see themselves as part of this age-old hierarchy and therefore permanently exploited. They preferred to see themselves as part of a system newly created by the growing power of capitalism and as the most useful, that is, working members of society. Furthermore, if these divisions had only recently been created by society, they were not natural and God-given and could therefore be changed.

In his discussion of class in *Keywords*, Raymond Williams argues that older terms such as *degree* and *order*, widely used before the nineteenth century, were replaced after 1800 by *class* more frequently because of "a new sense of a society or a particular *social system* which actually created social divisions, including new kinds of division" (52), whereas degrees and orders were based solely on birth. However, the middle-class hubris of the Victorian realistic novel seems to regard even these new divisions as permanent and fixed.

In comparing the approach of late-century writers with the mainstream Victorian novelists, I am not suggesting a teleological view of history, in which later writers necessarily see more clearly merely because they came later. If this were so, writers would by now have an all-comprehending view of the world. Nor am I claiming that that all earlier writers were blind to class issues. As we know, most innovations in the arts are a reaction to the stance of a previous generation, and this is true of the writers I study here. Furthermore, I am not arguing for a clear division between all earlier writers and Gissing, James, Hardy and Wells, for some earlier writers showed signs of breaking away from the solidly middle-class stance of the typical Victorian realistic novel. Wilkie Collins, in *The Woman in White* (1860), manipulates class issues, using an impecunious lower-middle-class man to reinstate Laura Fairlie to her original class status. However, the idealized ending that brings Laura into her true social position with Walter Hartright as her husband seems to validate the middle-class ideology, suggesting that the upper classes—here represented by Laura's sickly uncle—need some good healthy middle-class blood to keep them from the road to ruin. Collins, then, while stirring up some questions about class, arguably comes down on the side of the status quo. Thackeray's *Vanity Fair* (1848) mercilessly satirizes the emptiness of upper-class society and the social ambition of the wealthy bourgeoisie. But the fate of Thackeray's Becky represents, in the end, a cautionary tale.

Even fiction that criticized the system—like the social protest novels of Dickens and Gaskell—was reacting with middle-class values from within a middle-class frame of reference. It may seem simplistic to pack up in one bundle the work of such disparate writers as Dickens and Gaskell and claim their novels as bastions of the bourgeoisie. However, in novels such as *Oliver Twist*, *Hard Times*, *Mary Barton* and *North and South*, while displaying great sympathy for the ("deserving") poor and while clearly and stridently protesting the suffering occasioned by urbanization and industrialization, these writers sought to find some solution to these problems, rather than protesting the class system itself. From their middle-class world-view, neither writer could possibly see the class system as intrinsically oppressive and exploitative, a social construction that might need deconstruction. Instead, despite their realistic approach, they both created utopic visions of a reformed system in which members of the existing classes, *while accepting their position*, showed sympathy for those of other classes, thus creating a harmonious whole.

It must be remarked here that while I use Dickens's *Oliver Twist* as an example of the earlier world-view, Dickens's later work moves towards a more complex depiction of class. *Our Mutual Friend* (1865), for example, trenchantly satirizes both the self-serving established middle class and class climbers in the form of the Podsnaps, the Lammles and the Veneerings, while it idealizes the good-hearted but hopelessly lower-class Boffins, Lizzie Hexam, Jenny Wren and Betty Higden. But Dickens's point here is more the comparison of the good-hearted with the money-grubbers. He objects to society's focus on wealth to give itself meaning, and his analogy between wealth and refuse reduces that meaning to absurdity. I would say, therefore, that Dickens was wrestling with society's problems, but he was not ready to risk alienating his readers by going too far.

Some sensation fiction writers, in the 1860s, to an extent critiqued the social class system: Mary Elizabeth Braddon's *Lady Audley's Secret* (1862) suggests that class is mere performance. Lady Audley is apparently able convincingly to *perform* the role of governess and then of Lady Audley. Even though she, as the supposed villain of the piece, is locked up in the end—because she is mad, as a punishment for her crimes, or because she *has* been convincingly playing the part of an upper-class woman—the ironic tone of the idyllic ending undercuts the notion that all is well with the system. Ultimately, sensation fiction writers like Braddon were attacking the system from the viewpoint of subversives. This is the reason for my emphasis on world-view; because a different world-view creates a possible trend, whereas earlier writers like Braddon were exceptions to the norm. [4]

What I have aimed at identifying in this study is a trend in which mainstream writers reversed or worked against the techniques and visions of earlier writers, developing a new realism through their depictions of class. However, it must be recognized from the outset that despite Gissing's claim to a "school of strict veracity," his novels and those of Hardy, James and Wells are no more a window onto life as it was experienced in the nineteenth or early twentieth century than had been earlier depictions. Their realism, too, is a literary construction built from a set of literary conventions; they, too, represented people and places in a way which suited their own purposes.

My purpose in choosing the writers I study here—both earlier and later writers—was to focus on those who now form our canon, despite the fact that working-class writers had their own vision, fictionalized their own lived experience. There is an implicit class system in the very notion of a canon, of course. Therefore, for lower-middle-class writers like Gissing, Hardy and Wells (and for James, from the upper middle class, but American) who questioned the class system so profoundly—for them now to be considered canonical, is in itself important. That their more radical critique of the class system has, to a great extent, been overlooked by critics who have canonized them is significant also, keeping in mind the fact that critics' own class prejudices have played a large role in canon formation. This has kept these writers, who were popular during their own era, out of the canon during much of the twentieth century, and has kept James—in the American academy at least—confined mainly to the purview of Americanists.

III

The Victorian realistic novel, then, was a decidedly middle-class genre with decidedly middle-class concerns and attitudes. In *The English Common Reader*, Richard Altick describes its readers—"the people whom writers like Macaulay, the Brontës, Meredith, Eliot, Mill had in mind"—as "[t]he relatively small, intellectually and socially superior audience […] the readers of the quarterly reviews" (6). For the most part the working classes—lacking time, money and education—were excluded from the reading and writing of mainstream novels.[5] It was mainly the middle classes who could afford time to write and money to buy books or borrow them from the circulating libraries (Cross 6). Many critics have noted that a hegemony of the middle class had dominated the literary field for much of the nineteenth century.[6] Not only did this class have physical control over the means of publishing, but their monopoly helped to bolster middle-class ideology, to consolidate power and increase confidence within the bourgeoisie even if, given the assumption that the chief audience for the mainstream novel was itself middle-class, social control could not thereby be exerted over the working class.

But a gradual change was taking place throughout the century as regards both readers and writers. For one thing, their numbers were growing. The Forster Act[7] in 1870 extended state education at the primary level, encouraging a continuation of the already steadily increasing literacy rates, even amongst those who were hardest to reach, such as the urban poor. It also helped to equalize basic primary education between girls and boys. After the Forster Act, the literacy rate increased from 80.6 per cent of men and 73.2 per cent of women in 1871 to 93.6 per cent of men and 92.7 per cent of women by 1891 (Cross 206).[8] Cheap mass-circulation newspapers and magazines had been gaining strength since the fourpence newspaper tax had been lifted in mid-century. So that while cheap newspapers and periodicals flourished at century's end, they were not a new phenomenon. But the development of the suburbs and the resulting necessity for train commuting, towards the end of the century, created more and more need for reading materials of all kinds, both for the working classes and for the growing number of lower-middle-class readers (all included in what Gissing calls "the quarter-educated"). The term "railway literature" came into being in the middle of the century, and Altick claims that "[p]erhaps no other single element in the evolving pattern of Victorian life was so responsible for the spread of reading [as the railway]" (80). The number of novels published in England grew by leaps and bounds, especially in the last two decades of the century: in 1880, the year Gissing published *Workers in the Dawn*, the total number of novels published was 380. By 1891, the year *New Grub Street* came out, 896 novels were published, and this number increased to 1,315 by 1895 (Cross 206). The number of periodicals and newspapers produced for the new readers grew and a new outlet for fiction appeared in the form of newspaper syndication. The controlling influence of the circulating libraries over the writing, production and marketing of books was finally dissolved around 1894, ending high prices and the need for the "respectable" three-volume novel. This change freed writers from the length requirements of Mudie's and other libraries, and allowed for more one-volume, cheap editions, increasing the accessibility of books. "Never before in English history had so many people read so much" (Altick, *Common Reader* 4). These changes encouraged an expansion of the pool of writers, allowing writers from the lower middle classes—such as Gissing, Hardy and Wells—to join the profession.

A definite movement towards democratization had become apparent in England during the nineteenth century, nurtured and spurred on by this spread of reading throughout the classes.[9] In the last decades of the century, such events as the Reform Act of 1884, which expanded the franchise, speeded up the trend toward democracy—except, of course, among women.[10] At this time trade union membership swelled, ensuring that workers had a further voice in ordering their own lives. One of the interesting contradictions of the period, however, is that while there were democratic trends, by 1900 English society had become even more divided along class lines. All aspects of people's lives—their choice of clothes, area of residence, their choice of vacation spot, and the focus of the education they received—were ruled by their social status (Dentith 4). (Wells's *Tono-Bungay*, which describes efforts at class climbing at the turn of the century, emphasizes this contradiction.) In addition, while the lower middle class especially were benefiting from the increased accessibility of education and reading materials, reading and writing became yet another means of class division. But, of course, this increased sense of class division at century's end gave an additional spur to the nascent democracy movement and to working people's sense of class identity.

Although this outline of historical changes is necessarily incomplete, it gives some idea of the forces culminating at this time and of the tensions which were influencing novelists. The late century, then, is a period in which the world-view of both readers and writers was shifting gradually, destabilizing the previously dominant attitudes and value system and allowing for new depictions of the social class system, and consequently a new kind of realism. This book examines the relationship at the end of the century between fictional realism and social class.

The chapters that follow read the work of novelists who wrote from a world-view that was outside the middle-class world-view most often expressed in mainstream nineteenth-century fiction, and who thus were able to ask previously unasked questions about class in their work. Most importantly, they question whether the class system is a "natural" one. While I situate these novelists within their historical context by relating each to a specific moment within that context, I also examine how they each take up, in some way, earlier writers in order to show that their depictions of class are not only a reflection of their historical circumstances, but also form a part of literary history. My point, then, is one of literary history—that is, a change in realism—but this point cannot be made without reference to the socio-historical circumstances within which the literature was written. There is a reciprocal relationship between history and literature, and there is a sense in which each of the writers in this study interrogates history by disrupting traditional literary conventions in an attempt to reveal the ideology within his historical moment.

Of the various phenomena associated with social class in Victorian England, poverty is the most obvious, and so I begin in Chapter 1 with George Gissing's *The Nether World*, a novel that focuses on London's poverty problem. The poor became a reality for late-Victorian readers through the publication of investigations into the poverty problem such as Charles Booth's *Life and Labour in London*. Beginning publication in 1889, *Life and Labour* finally filled seventeen volumes, the result of a massive collection of data by a volunteer team. Booth also published a series of maps color-coding the streets of London according to degree of poverty. Like Booth, Gissing wants to expose the evils of poverty. But his purpose also includes a recognition of the dangers of representation and an acceptance of the fact that the class system helps to increase those dangers by blaming the poor for their own situation, for example. I argue that while Gissing's depictions of poverty in *The Nether World* evoke the Boothian investigative method (Gissing gives details of real locales—though in Clerkenwell rather than the East End), he critiques Booth's approach by chronicling far more than dry statistics. Yet, at the same time, the novelist presents a picture that neither melodramatically calls for sympathy proposing some idealistic solution nor creates a sense of the exotic. In other words, in his novel, Gissing walks a fine line avoiding both claims of "objective" reporting and exploitation of the poor through romanticizing or exoticizing. Gissing exposes the middle-class ideology behind the sociological movement, espoused by some, that brought classifications, explanations and unrealistic solutions. He critiques previous literary modes because of the inherent danger in representing the poor in literature and takes a narrative approach that attempts to avoid a class-based, class-affirming ideology.

In Chapter 2, I examine the way in which the *Times* employed the same authoritative narrative tone used in the traditional Victorian realistic novel, a voice which, by associating democracy, protest over the Irish question, unemployment unrest and international terrorism, attempted to scare its readers into a lack of sympathy for those protesting domestic problems by associating them with foreign anarchy. In the 1880s, the various mass marches and strikes, and frequent terrorist acts—including bombings and assassinations at home and abroad—seemed to confirm suspicions amongst the prosperous middle class that the comfortable and safe world to which they had grown accustomed would soon be destroyed. The rhetoric of fear promulgated in public discourse, such as that of the *Times* in its reporting of these events, is what James addresses in *The Princess Casamassima* (1886*)*. James is working against the all-knowing, middle-class, admonitory voice that the *Times* uses to report terrorist acts and that is typical of the omniscient narration in many

Victorian novels. By undermining this voice of authority, founded in the assumption that the social class system is "natural," James is questioning the class system itself. By exposing the apparatus of narration in such discourse as that of the *Times*, James also exposes the social class system as in part a rhetorical construction. In wrestling with that narratorial authority, he writes a fiction that embodies a more democratic world-view.

Chapter 3 examines the relationship between class and gender in Thomas Hardy's *Tess of the d'Urbervilles* (1891). Hardy writes *Tess* in the moralizing atmosphere of the late nineteenth century in England when the social purity movement was strong. The movement cohered around the fight to pass the Criminal Law Amendment Bill, and was prompted by groups of reformers, drawn mainly from the middle classes, who banded together demanding state intrusion into matters of morality. By adding the subtitle "A Pure Woman" to his novel's title in the first three-volume edition of *Tess* in 1891, Hardy set the tone for his surprisingly revolutionary depiction of working-class women. Hardy's novel flies in the face of middle-class moral superiority.

Debate over the Criminal Law Amendment Bill came to a climax with W.T. Stead's sensational campaign in the *Pall Mall Gazette* headlined "The Maiden Tribute to Modern Babylon" (1885), a publicity campaign to end the traffic in young English women who were sold into Continental prostitution. Even after passage of the Criminal Law Amendment Act, and after the excitement over the "Maiden Tribute" campaign had died down, Stead continued to emphasize sexual crimes in his paper and to depict morally deficient working-class girls as the sexual victims of upper-class men. Gender, class and morality were often combined in the discourse of novels and newspapers, for the social class system was seen as inextricably linked in the middle-class mind with issues of morality, and morality was always a gendered concept.

Many novelists had used the combination of gender and morality to reinforce and strengthen the concept of social class as a natural and fixed system. Hardy brings them together to question the system, and in so doing, he exposes the deployment of gendered morality as a way to reinforce a middle-class identity. For writers like George Eliot and Elizabeth Gaskell, the power provided to the male seducer by the class system is abused; Hardy questions why that power exists at all.

As the twentieth century dawned in England, important changes were taking place in the class ordering of the country. At the time of Queen Victoria's death, the great British country house system, relic of feudal times, which both represented and constituted the power and wealth of the ruling elite, was about to collapse. The third Reform Act in 1884-85 had expanded the franchise even further, and during the reign of Edward VII the landed elite were under siege both politically and financially. Democracy was becoming a reality; the class system itself was under pressure.

Anxiety caused by this state of affairs precipitated depictions of social class in novels of the era. In Chapter 4, I focus on Wells's novel *Tono-Bungay* (1909) as it chronicles the changes taking place in the English class system in the last decades of the nineteenth century and the first years of the new one. But though England may have had a different monarch and a whole new look during the Edwardian era, this novel suggests the class system was still strongly embedded, and its strength now came from the nouveau riche who fought to sustain the class hierarchies for their own ends.

Far from disappearing in the early twentieth century, with the beginnings of democracy, the advent of the new monarch and the commercial boom bringing with it the rise of the plutocracy, the class system was still very powerful and perhaps more pernicious because ostensibly unacknowledged. Like Gissing, James and Hardy, Wells cannot accept class as a natural and inevitable organizing principle, a fixed frame. He questions the version of class depicted and embodied in the Victorian novel, and implicates the novel itself as a tool and supporter of the class system.

What this book foregrounds, then, is an alternative vision, a view of class through the eyes of writers other than those slightly uncomfortable middle-class Victorian novelists such as Dickens, Gaskell, and even Eliot. It examines depictions of class by those who had a different perspective in the late nineteenth century, a perspective previously incompatible with the genre of the realistic novel. And even though this world-view, too, represents "an ideologically constituted experience of real history" (Boumelha 6), it helps to illuminate the relationship between fiction and history in late nineteenth- and early twentieth-century fiction, and especially the relationship between changing depictions of class and the development of realism.

Notes

[1] P.J. Keating makes this point in *The Working Classes in Victorian Fiction*.
[2] Gissing was modest about this, writing to his agent, James Pinker, on 13 Oct. 1901: "I am not at all a Dickens specialist—though people seem to be regarding me in that light"(*The Collected Letters of George Gissing*, ed. Paul F. Mattheisen, Arthur C. Young and Pierre Coustillas, Athens, Ohio: Ohio UP, 1990-1997, VIII, p. 261). His *Charles Dickens: A Critical Study* was published in 1898, and between August 1898 and February 1900 he completed prefaces for the Rochester edition of Dickens's work published by Methuen. Only six of the eleven prefaces written were used due to the lack of success of this edition, but they were then published in 1925 as a volume entitled *The Immortal Dickens* (in America: *Critical Studies of the Works of Charles Dickens* [1924]). He also revised and abridged Forster's *Life of Dickens* in 1903.
[3] While I recognize the vast influence of Britain's international status (not only as empire builder, but also as financial center) on life at home, these concerns are not the focus of this study, and the effects of domestic changes on the fiction of the period (whether or not those changes were brought about in part by Britain's global role) are sufficient justification for this study.
[4] The term *world-view* is used in this study to denote a whole value system and way of comprehending the world, including conscious and unconscious attitudes, expressed in fiction intentionally and unintentionally. Although one's world-view may be influenced, even produced by prevailing ideologies, the term as I use it here more specifically addresses issues of epistemology. One's world-view, in other words, encompasses what it is possible to see and know in viewing the world at a specified historical moment, and what, therefore, it is possible

to depict in a novel, in spite of *and* because of prevailing ideologies. Fiction is necessarily written from a specific world-view born of the historical moment, and necessarily partaking of, reflecting and therefore often bolstering that moment's ideologies. For a fuller explanation of how "world-view" differs from "ideology" and "hegemony," see *Keywords* by Raymond Williams.

[5] The term "mainstream" is used here to denote the majority of novels published by established publishing houses, reviewed in established journals and whose popularity is demonstrated by their selling reasonably successfully, especially to the circulating libraries.

[6] See for example P.J. Keating, T.B. Tomlinson, D.A. Miller and Marxist critics such as Mary Eagleton and David Pierce, among others

[7] Altick writes: "the act's importance can easily be exaggerated. [...] The Forster Act did not significantly hasten the spread of literacy. What it did was to insure that the rate at which literacy had increased in 1851-71 would be maintained." He goes on to say that this Act "was responsible for the mopping-up operation by which the very poor children, living in slums or in remote country regions, were taught to read" (171).

[8] What constitutes literary in such statistics is a basic writing skill.

[9] While the total population of England and Wales had grown during the century from about 8.8 million in 1801 to about 32.5 million in 1901, in 1900 only about 2,000 persons in Britain held a title of any kind and there were only 522 British peers. Thus the Reform Acts of 1832, 1867 and 1884 were gradually affecting more people and a larger percentage of the population. Yet, paradoxically, economic historians see the last three decades of the century as "marking the zenith of income inequalities" despite government reform (W.D. Rubinstein, *Britain's Century: A Political and Social History, 1815-1905*, New York: Oxford UP, 1998). While democratization was occurring (trade unions, for example, gained power during this period) "politicians and social observers spoke and behaved as though they believed that the British political system was much more broadly democratic than it actually was." José Harris, *Private Lives, Public Spirit* (Oxford: Oxford UP, 1993).

[10] To many in the nineteenth century, the idea of democracy meant "rule by the mob." It is not until the end of the century that the idea of democratic government as we understand it today—that is, a representative democracy—began to be widely accepted in England (see Raymond Williams, *Keywords*).

Chapter 1

"We are the working classes": The London Poor in Gissing's *The Nether World*

> East London lay hidden from view behind a curtain on which were painted terrible pictures:—Starving children, suffering women, overworked men; horrors of drunkenness and vice; monsters and demons of inhumanity; giants of disease and despair. Did these pictures truly represent what lay behind, or did they bear to the facts a relation similar to that which the pictures outside a booth at some country fair bear to the performance or show within? This curtain we have tried to lift.
> (Booth, *Life and Labour* 1:172)[1]

Thus, with a somewhat literary flair, writes Charles Booth at the end of the nineteenth century in *Life and Labour in London*. The problem, according to Booth, is not that the poor and needy are overlooked, go unnoticed, but that they are over-painted, overdetermined one might say, by all the different parties working to represent them, bring attention to their problems and, in many cases, offer up some unrealistic solution. In fact, his analogy with the booth at the country fair suggests that the denizens of the East End have been intentionally misrepresented and sensationalized by the discourse of philanthropists, reformers, journalists and novelists in pursuance of their own agendas. Booth, through *his* series of investigations, was out to "lift the curtain," as he says, to tell the truth by turning the East Enders into numbers, into statistics that could not lie. He writes of his "resolution to make use of no fact to which [he] cannot give a quantitative value," even though "the materials of sensational stories lie plentifully in every book of [his] notes" (1:6).

In his 1889 novel, *The Nether World*, George Gissing, too, focuses on the poverty of Londoners and attempts to lift the curtain that hides through misrepresentation the lives of the London poor. He too aims at accuracy in his depictions of the poorer areas of the city and defies those who offer comforting solutions to the problem. By using a specific London location with real street names in his novel, Gissing evokes the Boothian investigative method. But in his fictional realism the extent of the poverty and hardship suffered by the people of London is far more than dry statistics and yet is not sensationalized. But more than describing the plight of the poor in *The Nether World*, Gissing also exposes the middle-class, self-serving ideology behind the sociological climate of his day that brought classifications (such as Booth's), explanations and idealistic solutions (such as those of the East End university settlements, the People's Palace, those in non-fiction accounts of "explorations" of the slums, and in the "slum" fiction of the day). Gissing thus engages with literary, sociological and philanthropic misrepresentation.

In the late nineteenth century, the London poor became the focus of much political and literary activity. A flurry of investigations was going on in the slums, especially in the East End, often focusing on the poorest people who were variously labeled the "residuum," the "hopeless classes," "the unfit," "the abyss," the "quagmire," the "pauper Frankenstein" and the "submerged tenth" (Harris, "Residuum" 68). And this attention to the conditions of the poor had helped to spur on the trend for the so-called "slum novels" of this period, a genre that includes *The Nether World*.

A large-scale transformation had taken place in nineteenth-century England. At the beginning of the century, roughly seventy-five per cent of the population lived in rural areas, with only twenty-five percent living in cities; by the beginning of the twentieth century, these numbers had been reversed. This rapid change caused a crisis of overcrowding in some of England's cities, leading to unemployment and lack of adequate sanitation and housing. Earlier in the century, Victorians had felt confident in their ability to approach social problems both philanthropically and legislatively. And despite the major problem that urban poverty represented in the late nineteenth century, many still had confidence in organized charities. Philanthropists such as Octavia Hill, and Helen and Bernard Bosanquet were trying to solve the poverty problem one family at a time. Toynbee Hall and Oxford House were attempting to bring university-educated men and women into the East End to live in settlement houses to effect a change, and the People's Palace was offering education and culture to the poor, paid for by the rich.[2]

But the very magnitude of the problem posed by large-scale urbanization and the shift towards a belief in the efficacy of science, including the new social science, that had occurred during the Victorian era, meant that some now felt the need to leave behind the Christian-based belief in philanthropic solutions. As Booth himself says, "mere giving as a remedy for poverty no longer holds the field" (1:163).

Robert Owen, Auguste Comte, the researchers of the Social Democratic Federation, and Charles Booth—to name just a few—were taking a scientific approach to the investigation of the problem of poverty and social reform. One of the most ambitious studies was that of Booth, a wealthy ship-owner from Liverpool who, like many in his class, felt something had to be done about the growing problem of poverty in England's industrial urban centers. A great believer in civic responsibility, but not in out-and-out charity, Booth tried to effect change through education in the north of England. When he moved to London, and became involved in the Royal Statistical Society, he became convinced that the scientific collection of data and the objectivity of statistics were the only ways to bring some order to the overwhelming disorder with which London's poorer classes seemed to threaten society.

Booth's monumental study of the conditions of the London poor, which began as a study of the East End and Hackney, eventually filled seventeen volumes. Raymond Williams says that Booth's work "belongs to a way of seeing which the new society itself was producing [...] a necessary response to a civilisation of this scale and complexity" (*Country* 222). His work certainly tried to encompass a great deal. His first series focused on poverty—he later studied employment and the influence of religion—and began publication in 1889, the same year that Gissing's *The Nether World* appeared. Booth found that thirty-seven per cent of the population of East London and Hackney lived below what he had designated as the line of poverty,[3] while more than fourteen per cent were "very poor." His method was to use a team of investigators who conducted hours of interviews with school board visitors, rent collectors, officers of the Charity Organization Society and others.[4] He categorized eight classes of people "according to Means and Position of Heads of Families," and then divided those again into forty sections "according to Character of Employment of Heads of Families."[5] Booth's work also included the production of *Descriptive Map of London Poverty, 1889*, a huge project which color-coded the streets of London according to the income and living conditions of the inhabitants.

While Booth makes it clear that the groups he classifies are not necessarily homogeneous, and that the distinctions between groups are not rigid, still an approach such as his to the problem, an approach which includes classifying and color-coding the population of London, encourages ways of thinking about "the poor" which, though supposedly scientific, can objectify large segments of the population—and, in many ways, this is his point. Pages of statistics bear witness to the countless hours of work Booth and his team devoted to this project. For example, he offers a two-page table of family expenditures identifying families by type of employment. One can find out from this table that a casual worker and his wife and three children spends 3 3/4*d*. on potatoes in a five-week period, whereas a policeman apparently buys none, though he does spend a lot on liver. Booth details the expenditures of thirty families; items listed include fish, bacon, eggs, cheese, suet, bread, flour, sugar, milk, tea and coffee. The number of purchases of tea is recorded and Booth notes that the very poor buy tea each time they want to brew it rather than spending ahead. His analysis of this table reads as follows:

> The amount spent by Class B on meat [...] varies from 3*s*. to 5*s*. per male adult for 5 weeks; the amount spent in Class D varies from 3*s*. to 8*s*., and in Class E from 3*s*. 6*d*. to 10*s*. The minimum amount in each class is about the same, being 1*d*. per day for each male adult, or 1*d*. for men, 3/4*d*. for women, and from 1/4*d*. to 3/4*d*. for children. (1: 134)

My point in quoting this is to show the way in which Booth tries to nail down the facts and only the facts in minute detail so that he cannot be accused of misrepresenting life in East London.

In choosing the East End to begin his study, he was choosing an area that, in the last decades of the century, seemed to many as alien and unknown as Africa. One of the poorest areas in London, the East End was geographically and symbolically the opposite of the wealthy West End. It was home to many immigrants, especially Jews, and was a place that seemed threatening to the middle classes. Williams describes the porblem thus:

> A social division between East End and West End, which had been noted by some observers from early in the century [and even before], deepened and became more inescapably visible. Conditions in the East End were being described as "unknown" and "unexplored" [...] and by the 1880s and 1890s "Darkest London" was a conventional epithet. [...] A predominant image of the darkness and poverty of the city, with East London as its symbolic example, became quite central in literature and social thought. (*Country* 221)

The East End, through its representation in fact and fiction alike, became a symbol of all that was poor, dirty, immoral and marginalized in London, a stigma from which it has difficulty recovering more than one hundred years later. Booth's representation of the East End's population in a series of letters, numbers and colors on tables, charts and maps appears to bring the whole matter within reach, to reduce the threat to a numerical problem, to transform it into something one can know and control. He claims to have proved by his investigation that "the hordes of barbarians of whom we have heard, who, issuing from their slums, will one day overwhelm modern civilization, do not exist. There are barbarians, but they are a handful, a small and decreasing percentage: a disgrace, but not a danger"(1: 39). While Booth's characterization of a segment of the population is disturbingly judgmental, this revelation must, indeed, have been a comfort to those who had been frightened by characterizations of poor areas as "darkest England," as General William Booth of the Salvation Army was to phrase it in the title of his 1890 book.[6]

It is significant that, rather than the East End, Gissing sets his novel in Clerkenwell, an area in north London shown on Booth's map to be fairly heavily populated with the "Very Poor" and the "Poor."[7] By doing so, he disrupts the East End/West End binary. And because his working-class characters are not in a metonymic relationship with the East End, they escape being lumped together as the lumpen proletariat or the residuum.

Despite his statistical approach, Booth was not immune to what appeared to be the exotic flavor of the unfamiliar territory he studied—perhaps enhanced for him by reading about this area in recent novels. In his account of East London he writes, "The neighbourhood of old Petticoat Lane on Sunday is one of the wonders of London, a medley of strange sights, strange sounds, and strange smells" (1: 66). And he describes another East End market with enthusiasm:

> Brick Lane should rightly be seen on Saturday night, though it is in almost all its length a gay and crowded scene every evening of the week, unless persistent rain drives both buyers and sellers to seek shelter. But this sight—the "market street"— is not confined to Brick Lane, nor peculiar to Whitechapel, nor even to the East

Fig. 1.1 Clerkenwell and St. James's Parish, from Charles Booth, *Map Descriptive of London Poverty*, 1888-9 (Reproduced with permission of the Library of the London School of Economics and Political Science)

End. In very poor quarters of London it is to be met with—the flaring lights, the piles of cheap comestibles, and the urgent cries of the sellers. (1: 68)

Booth's determination to remain statistical has been undermined by the excitement of these urban scenes:

> In the streets the love of dancing bursts out whenever it has a chance; let a barrel organ strike up a valse at any corner and at once the girls who may be walking past, and the children out of the gutter, begin to foot it merrily. Men join in sometimes, two young men together as likely as not, and passers-by stand to enjoy the sight. A couple of ragged, perhaps even bare-footed children, dancing conscientiously the step of the latest *trois-temps*, are a pleasant sight to see. (1: 117)

Booth's knowledge of the street life of the East End comes from short periods of "slumming." Three different times he took lodgings there for several weeks and appears to have believed that his identity and purpose remained unknown to those around him while he observed their lives. Those with whom he lived he classifies as belonging to Classes C, D and E,[8] and it is this group whose lives appear to him as more appealing than the lives of the wealthy. On a rather plaintive note he writes, "I perhaps build too much on my slight experience, but I see nothing improbable in the general view that the simple natural lives of working-class people tend to their own and their children's happiness more than the artificial complicated existence of the rich" (1: 160). There is something particularly disturbing about Booth, with his fixation for numbers and facts, seeing the lives of those he studies as "simple natural lives." That he does not see these lives as complicated—even if only by what must have been an ongoing anxiety about money—after pouring over his own statistics, demonstrates a singular lack of perception in Booth. And the idea that he sees the poor as living more *natural* lives echoes a romantic-era idealization of the rustic.

At the same time that he sees the life of certain classes as colorful and appealing, Booth does not disguise the blame he places on many of the objects of his study. And while he writes, "My object has been to show the numerical relation which poverty, misery, and depravity bear to regular earnings and comparative comfort" (1: 6), the very idea that depravity is associated in his mind with poverty and misery suggests much about his objectivity. It could suggest, for example, that Booth has a tendency to believe that depravity is not an innate characteristic, but something that happens to people who are poor and miserable—that is, that poverty causes it. On the other hand, this association implies that wherever Booth sees poverty, he also sees depravity.

It was typical of many social reformers of the time to equate lack of money with lack of morals, and to see reform as an effort to teach the poor to behave properly. Booth hardly tries to hide his judgmental tone as he describes Class B:

> [T]here will be found many of them who from shiftlessness, helplessness, idleness, or drink, are inevitably poor. The ideal of such persons is to work when they like and play when they like; these it is who are rightly called the "leisure class" amongst the

poor—leisure bounded very closely by the pressure of want, but habitual to the
extent of second nature. They cannot stand the regularity and dulness of civilized
existence, and find the excitement they need in the life of the streets, or at home as
spectators of or participators in some highly coloured domestic scene. There is
drunkenness amongst them, especially amongst the women. (1: 43)

While this diligent and hardworking investigator claims objectivity, wants to
rely only on statistics, and verifies his numbers in several ways in order to ensure
their accuracy, because of his own values and beliefs, those statistics clearly speak to
him of behaviors that bring with them poverty and unemployment instead of the
other way round. In other words, out of the dry numbers he and his team report,
Booth weaves a fiction to suit his own purposes and class loyalties. His own views
tend to support those of the Poor Laws: "the difficulty lies solely in inducing or
driving these people to accept a regulated life" (1: 167). And so his statistics tell
him the story he wants to hear. The numbers do not shake his faith in the class
system; they simply verify his need to organize the classes in more detail.

Interestingly, at times Booth conflates fiction with facts. He writes, "Of
Shoreditch, or rather Hoxton [...] I am tempted to recall a description by Mr. Besant,
which will be remembered by all who have read 'The Children of Gibeon.'[9] There is,
he says, nothing beautiful, or picturesque, or romantic in the place, there is only the
romance of life in it" (1: 72). And Booth goes on to mention Gissing:

> It is not easy for any outsider to gain a sufficient insight into the lives of these
> people. The descriptions of them in the books we read are for the most part as
> unlike the truth as are descriptions of aristocratic life in the books they read. [...]
> something may be gleaned from a few books, such for instance as "Demos."[10] (1:
> 157)

The man of statistics, member of the Royal Statistical Society, classifier of people,
believer in the reliability and truth of facts, at times turns his readers to fiction to
find out about life in East London. And while his reference here to Gissing's 1886
novel is evidence perhaps of the radical difference Gissing brings to his realism,
Booth's narrative voice, with its moralizing viewpoint, is suggestive of those Victorian
novels whose narrators enable the reader to discern the difference between the
deserving and the undeserving amongst the "lower" classes.

In *The Nether World*, Gissing dismisses the possibility of the scientific objectivity
of an approach such as that of Charles Booth, as well as the efforts of philanthropist,
church and state. He also shows the ways in which the traditional Victorian middle-
class novel, through its depictions of the class system told from the middle-class
world-view, produces limited ways of thinking about the other classes.[11] Indeed, it
produces the misrepresentation figured by Booth as the curtain at the country fair.

Booth may have divided his classes by sections according to the seemingly objective
criterion of occupation, but the labels he places on those classes are evaluative.
While East Enders were classified by Booth as "Higher Class Labour," "the poor"

or "the Lowest Class," the denizens of Gissing's Clerkenwell claim another designation: Sidney Kirkwood in *The Nether World* insists, on several occasions, "We are the working classes." This self-labeling is important. For while the nether world of this novel is shown to be just as full of minute class distinctions, based on very little actual difference, as had been the middle-class world portrayed in novels earlier in the century, for Sidney it is work and the need for work that holds them together as a group. The nether world as depicted by Gissing is not an area at the other end of London, seen from the comfort of middle-class homes in the West End or from a few weeks of slumming. For its inhabitants, it is the whole world. The middle classes depicted in fiction may see whatever is beyond the boundaries of their world as alien, but then so do the nether-world folk in this novel. Gissing's fictional depiction of Clerkenwell may be a world of slums and poverty, but it is still a world full of characters for whom this poor section of London sets the boundaries of their thinking.

I am not suggesting that Gissing's new version of realism should be read as "true history." As Penny Boumelha writes, "The 'history' of the text is not a reflection or a doubling of real history, but it represents an ideologically constituted experience of real history" (6).[12] What I am arguing, however, is that the texts of "objective" investigators such as Booth, like other accounts of the poor, are also an ideologically constituted experience of real history. In *The Nether World* Gissing points to the dangers of distancing hidden within the seductions of the scientific approach and the inherent difficulties in representing others in literature or, indeed, in any discourse.

"The accursed social order"

Set almost entirely in Clerkenwell, *The Nether World*[13] tells the story of Jane Snowdon, a pathetic creature described by the narrator as the "thrall of thralls." Treated as the family slave by her foster mother and sister, she lives in fear of being beaten and is always hungry and cold. Her wealthy grandfather, returning from Australia, finds and rescues her. He wants to leave her all his money—not so that she can raise herself up from the working classes, but so that she can use it to help the poor. Jane is in love with Sidney Kirkwood, who, after much mooning over Clara Hewett, realizes he loves Jane. However, once he finds out about the inheritance, Sidney feels he cannot marry Jane because it would look as though he is after her money. He ends up married to Clara—and supporting the whole pathetic Hewett clan in Crouch End, a new London suburb where "poverty tries to hide itself with venetian blinds," and where "[w]hatever you touch is at once found to be sham" (364). Clara is now not only bitter, but disfigured from vitriol thrown on her beautiful face by a rival at the moment when she might have made a success of her career in the theater. Her disfigurement is a visible sign of the degradation of her position.

This novel portrays only the working classes; no middle-class or upper world is visible. And while Sidney and Jane are in many ways superior to many of their neighbors, they are also firmly identified with their class. They remain within that class. Jane undergoes no miracle transformation; she does not turn into a wealthy, well-educated, middle-class lady once her rich grandfather appears. In other words, there is no happy ending or comforting middle-class solution even for these deserving representatives of the working class.

As do the other authors in this study, George Gissing (1857-1903) has the ability to stand outside the middle-class world-view, a world-view shared by Booth and others depicting London's poverty at this time. He is able to do this in part because of his own lack of strong class identification. Though merely the son of a Wakefield shopkeeping chemist, Gissing had managed to get into Owens College in Manchester due to his academic talents. He was an outstanding student, winning many prizes, and was expected to go on to London University in order to prepare himself for a full academic career. However, he was caught stealing from fellow students in order to provide for a young prostitute named Nell, whom he had met and fallen in love with on the streets of Manchester. He was dismissed from the college, given one month of hard labor, and then shipped off to America by his family. Upon his return to England, he went to London to seek his fortune, and once there he married Nell.[14] Unlike Dickens's Nancy, Nell was not the devoted "whore with the heart of gold"; she was an alcoholic, and despite her husband's efforts to get her off the streets, she continued to use her old profession in order to get money for her drinking habit.

Though Gissing always provided her with money out of the little he had, at the time of her death she and Gissing had not lived together for some five years. Nell died at the age of thirty, and Gissing gives an account in his diary of the scene he found when he went to identify her body in what he calls "a wretched, wretched place" (22):

> Let me describe this room. It was the first floor back; so small that the bed left little room to move. [...] On the door hung a poor miserable dress and a worn out ulster; under the bed was a pair of boots. Linen she had none; the very covering of the bed had gone save one sheet and one blanket. I found a number of pawn tickets, showing that she had pledged these things during last summer,—when it was warm, poor creature! [...] I drew out the drawers. In one I found a little bit of butter and a crust of bread,—most pitiful sight my eyes ever looked upon. There was no other food anywhere. [...] Came home to a bad, wretched night. In nothing am I to blame: I did my utmost; again and again I had her back to me. [...] But as I stood beside that bed, I felt that my life henceforth had a firmer purpose. Henceforth I never cease to bear testimony against the accursed social order that brings about things of this kind. [...] Poor, poor thing! (22-3)

Amid the desolation of Nell's poverty-stricken room Gissing found a photo of himself and many of the letters he had sent her, going all the way back to his time in America. For his part he took the pawn ticket he found and redeemed her wedding ring for 1*s*.9*d*. and also noted in his diary: "Cut a little hair from the poor head,— I scarcely know why, alas!" (23). For all the sordid and insoluble problems of their relationship, a glint of affection had apparently somehow survived.

This diary entry shows the sort of close-up experience Gissing had of the poor and how he sees them as victims of a class-based society. Nell's death spurs the author into action: henceforth he wants to "bear testimony against the accursed social order." Gissing had viewed Nell's body on 1 March 1888. He spent two weeks of misery following this depressing experience, noting in his diary that he is in "wretched spirits," and that he is taking Cod Liver Oil. On 19 March, believing that the Cod Liver Oil has helped him, Gissing feels "greatly better, in body and mind," and notes, "Began a novel to be called "The Nether World", and wrote six pages, which satisfy me" (24). His solution to the problems caused by "the accursed social order" is to write a novel.

Critics have been quick to paint Gissing as a reactionary novelist who was obsessed with writing about class relations because, as Williams claims, he had "fallen foul of [...] the social standards of his own class" (*Culture and Society* 176), and therefore despised the lower classes with whom he was forced to live. Because of Nell, the story goes, he had forgone all chance of a respectable academic career. He was thus obliged to earn his keep by his pen. Writing feverishly through hunger, cold and horrible conditions, Gissing was paid little for the constant stream of prose he produced. Unable, therefore, to rise above his lower-class position, Gissing made another disastrous marriage to a woman he considered beneath him.

All this has become part of the legend which surrounds Gissing's life and seems to explain the resentment towards the lower classes critics see in his work. Yet a fairly cursory reading of the diary entry quoted above sheds doubt on this explanation. No resentment can be found in this entry, except towards "the accursed social order that brings about things of this kind." His demeanor in the scene described above is one of empathy for Nell's plight, despite the difficulties she had brought to his life, and his redemption of her wedding ring, his cutting the lock of hair, and his "wretched spirits," which he reports in his diary in the days following, bear witness to the fact that his feeling was not a momentary one.

While I feel that critics have relied too easily on Gissing's so-called "fall," or what Jameson describes as "that incurable wound of social and class humiliation" (203), to explain his dislike of the lower-classes, Gissing's own ambivalent class position and therefore lack of secure class identity does help to create the attitude towards class relations which is in evidence in *The Nether World*. This attitude emphasizes the dehumanizing effects of the social class system itself—including the problem of inveterate poverty—and questions whether this system is a "natural" one.

Gissing sees the class system as man-made. When *The Nether World*'s narrator refers to Mrs. Candy's visits to Mrs. Green's beer shop on Rosoman Street, he says, "For many years, that house, licensed for the sale of non-spirituous liquors, had been working Mrs. Candy's ruin [...] under the approving smile of civilisation." He goes on: "The struggle was too unequal between Mrs. Candy with her appeal to Providence, and Mrs. Green with the forces of civilisation at her back" (76). It is "civilisation"—that great middle-class, capitalist civilisation—that supports Mrs.

Green in her undertaking. The narrator shows his sympathy for Mrs. Candy, unsympathetic character though she is: "Poor, poor creature!" he calls her, echoing his diary comment about Nell on the day he viewed her dead body.

Gissing's perspective was, no doubt, affected by his own ambivalent class status (John Goode calls him "the lower middle-class *arriviste* who never makes it to the elite" [*Ideology and Fiction* 202]): he had an unlooked-for close-up view of the poor, in addition to glimpses of that upper, richer world where some other authors bathed in the sunlight of popular success and financial stability. Resentful Gissing may have been, but this does not make him entirely out of sympathy in representing the poor. In fact, in Gissing's realism depictions of the poor are far more nuanced than had been those of the realism earlier in the century. This nuance derives not *only* from Gissing's personal world-view; at century's end, owing to the democracy movement, education, and changes in publishing and reading practices, the world-view of both writers and readers was gradually shifting.

"The growing good of the world"

Like Dickens, Gissing wants to use the realistic novel as a weapon against the evils of society. But he does not believe, as did his novelist forebears, in the "growing good of the world." He does not believe in religious, philanthropic or political solutions. Who, then, is Gissing's imagined audience? For if fiction is to be an *exposé* of social evils, any exposing that is to be done is not only *of* something, but *to* someone. Clearly for Dickens and other novelists earlier in the century writing about poverty, the *to whom?* question was easily answered: they wanted to influence their middle-class friends and neighbors, the philanthropists and the voters who could change things. (Although in the case of Dickens, who didn't seem to have much faith in the political system as a force for good, "His saviour of society was a man of heavy purse and large heart, who did the utmost possible good in his own particular sphere" [Gissing, *Critical Study* 167].) But for Gissing, middle-class philanthropists and politicians are part of the problem. P.J. Keating claims that Gissing's novels were "almost entirely ignored by the general reading public," but "were praised by a small group of London intellectuals" (*Working Classes* 4). To whom, then, is Gissing's complaint about society aimed? Is Gissing's fictionalized reader, to use Walter Ong's phrase,[15] a poor person, perhaps someone in Gissing's own circumstances—educated, lower-middle-class,[16] but constrained to live amongst the poor?

Though *The Nether World* was first issued by Smith, Elder in 1889 in three volumes, and only five hundred copies were printed, it was quickly reissued in cheap editions. The following year, a one-volume edition came out, and in the same year, reissues appeared selling at 2*s*.6*d*. and 2*s*. (Collie 48). While a fairly small audience was expected for the three-decker edition, a wider, more varied audience could have been expected for the cheaper edition. At this time, not only was the world-view of readers shifting, but the make-up of the reading public was changing. For, as Richard

Altick points out in *The English Common Reader*, not only was there a growing number of readers at century's end among "the ever expanding bourgeoisie," but the group below this, the lower middle class, was expanding, too, and it was this group which benefited most from board schools, mechanics institutes, public libraries and, above all, cheap books (6). Gissing, therefore, may well have imagined, and even appealed to, a different audience from the one Dickens had in mind.[17] Although we don't know the makeup of the readership for this novel, we do know that it would have been harder for writers, towards the end of the century, to envisage their readers. They were no longer what Altick describes as "the relatively small, intellectually and socially superior audience for which most of the great nineteenth-century authors wrote—the readers of the quarterly reviews, the people whom writers like Macaulay, the Brontës, Meredith, George Eliot, and John Stuart Mill had in mind" (6). Envisioning a more socially diverse group of readers must surely have given Gissing the freedom to take a different stance *vis-à-vis* social class from that which novelists earlier in the century had taken. Gissing is also free to criticize the church, the state and the middle-class philanthropist.

In *The Nether World*, there is no Christian master-narrative of fall, growth and eventual redemption. Mad Jack's is the lone religious voice in this novel. He is a strange, seemingly allegorical character who plays no obvious role in the plot. The population of Clerkenwell revile and ridicule him. In a dream, an angel tells Jack that the people around him were once rich, but behaved so poorly that they are now suffering in Hell. "This is Hell-Hell-Hell!" (345), he cries, a claim with which many in Shooter's Gardens—the worst of the slums in Clerkenwell—would have to agree. It is indeed an irony that the poor people of Clerkenwell should be accused of formerly being mean rich people. Mad Jack symbolizes the madness of the world around him and the irrelevance of the Church when speaking to this world.

For despite the looming presence of St. James's church from the first page of the novel on, it does not seem to exert much influence over its parishioners. The bells are sometimes to be heard, "their music, like the rain that fell intermittently [...] flung westwards by the boisterous wind [...] until the notes failed one by one, or were clashed out of existence by the clamour of a less civilised steeple" (120). The bells are emblematic of the Church of England's lack of influence or effect in Clerkenwell. The church bells are "flung westwards," towards the West End where their influence is stronger. A "less civilised steeple" presumably would be that of a Roman Catholic church, perhaps St. Peter's on Clerkenwell Road, or the Church of the Holy Redeemer on Exmouth Street. The other steeple is less civilized, Gissing ironically notes, but is apparently more powerful.[18] The narrator gives us a clue as to why St. James's is irrelevant: "just now the bells were playing [within hearing of the House of Detention] 'There is a happy land, far, far away,' and that hymn makes too great a demand upon the imagination to soothe amid instant miseries" (120). The Church of England offers platitudes—not help. St. James's Church looks along Clerkenwell Close the short distance to Clerkenwell Green where, the narrator tells us, on Sunday evenings, "fervent, if ungrammatical, oratory was to be heard [...] and participation [...] was open to all whom the spirit moved" (53). It is, then, the political oratory that takes the place of Evensong in Clerkenwell on Sunday evenings. And it is, in Victorian novels, the middle classes represented by the gentleman, whose character is constituted by Christian values (Young 48-9). Gissing's reaction against religion is therefore not only a reaction against a certain theology, but a reaction against a class symbol.

Neither does Gissing put faith in middle-class philanthropy—a point which is clear from his depiction of the mishandling of the soup-kitchen in *The Nether World*. When Miss Lant and her fellow do-gooders are indignant because the recipients of their philanthropy show no gratitude, the narrator, addressing the philanthropic ladies, says, "Have you still to learn what this nether world has been made by those who belong to the sphere above it?—Gratitude, quotha? Nay, do *you* be grateful that these hapless, half-starved women do not turn and rend you" (252).

Political solutions are anathema to Gissing; even the radical impulse of John Hewett is seen as ineffectual; no one takes him very seriously, especially not the working people. And Gissing's narrator becomes highly ironical at the end of the chapter entitled "Mad Jack's Dream," in speaking of "Law and Society." Pennyloaf, whose child has just died and who has been nothing but submissive all her life, is huddled in the bare room in Shooter's Gardens with her abusive husband and her alcoholic mother. Bob Hewett, who has been trapped by the police, is now scared and dying. The police are banging on the door, insisting it be opened, and Pennyloaf, in her first-ever act of resistance, says to her mother, "No—no! [...] They shan't come in! don't stir" (347), as if this could save them all. "Useless, Pennyloaf, useless," says the narrator, sympathetically sizing up the pathetic nature of Pennyloaf's stand. "That fierce kick, making ruin of your rotten barrier, is dealt with the whole force of Law, of Society" (347). Law and Society bring to bear the force against which Pennyloaf is, for once in her life, fighting hopelessly. It is, of course, the same Law and Society that allows landlords to take away even Mrs. Candy's bedding, leaving her and her son Stephen with nothing but a bare room: "Yes; they can take everything. How foolish of Stephen Candy and his tribe not to be born of the class of landlords!" (341) comments the narrator wryly.

It seems clear that Mrs. Candy would have been grouped in Booth's Class A, the class of whom Booth says, "They render no useful service, they create no wealth: more often they destroy it. They degrade whatever they touch, and as individuals are perhaps incapable of improvement" (39). But while Gissing's narrator might agree that Mrs. Candy is, at this point, beyond hope, he does not attempt to blame her own "low character" for her troubles in order to mollify middle-class readers. Instead, this novel is full of bitter outbursts of irony aimed at the Law and Society: "For, work as you will," the narrator tells us, "there is no chance of a new and better world until the old be utterly destroyed" (109).

"I want to take no side at all"

Gissing saw himself not only as part of a new generation of realist novelists, but as an innovative member of that new generation who must push the possibilities of the genre to the limit. He was creating a fiction which he said was "to be judged by the standard of actual experience" ("Oliver Twist" 92). The question is whether it is possible for Gissing, with his new realism, to write a novel which will "bear testimony against the accursed social order"—the purpose he claimed on the day of Nell's death—with no recourse to a middle-class frame of reference, no middle-class yardstick against which to make value judgments. Can he, in other words, write a novel containing only characters such as those from Class A and B, victims of the accursed social order, who have already been corrupted? Is it possible to imagine a novel written with Clem Peckover as its heroine, a character who sees violence and cruelty as the norm? Or with John Hewett as its hero—a character who would see frustration and defeat as the norm? Would these characters, in the end, "expose" the evils of the social order? Or would they represent a kind of Biffenlike[19] realism, a realism which is ultimately unreadable? Unlike Booth, Gissing has understood the impossibility of achieving complete objectivity, absolute realism, a goal he would gently mock when he wrote *New Grub Street* (1891):

> 'I want to take no side at all; [says Biffen] simply to say, Look, this is the kind of thing that happens.'
> 'I admire your honesty, Biffen,' said Reardon, sighing. 'You will never sell work of this kind, yet you have the courage to go on with it because you believe in it.' (*New Grub Street* 175)

Biffen's work, he himself admits, will be "unutterably tedious"—something like Booth at his driest, his endless tables and charts. In the end, then, Gissing's goal is *not* complete objectivity. He, like the novelists before him, creates characters who, while they coincide with much that is real, are created for his own purpose. And much like Booth, Gissing wants to record the depth of poverty some Londoners experience. But Gissing's purpose also includes a recognition of the dangers of representation and the fact that the class system helps to increase those dangers by blaming the poor for their own situation.

For example, Booth and others in the nineteenth century felt that lack of hygiene, lack of thrift and other failings of character were the cause of poverty. But in *The Nether World*, Mrs. Hewett's, and indeed her baby's, constant ill health seem to result from a poor environment and indeed to explain the lack of cleanliness in their living conditions—what strength has she to clean?—thus reversing the expected cause and effect.

Gissing firmly believes that poverty and a mean environment corrupt, unlike Booth, who suggests that bad character brings poverty, or the author of *Oliver Twist*, of whom Gissing writes, "[Dickens] takes no due account of the effect of conditions upon character" (*Critical Study* 165). His narrator describes the process of corruption *because of* poverty in relation to Clara Hewett thus:

> The disease inherent in her being, that deadly outcome of social tyranny which perverts the generous elements of youth into mere seeds of destruction, developed day by day, blighting her heart, corrupting her moral sense, even setting marks upon the beauty of her countenance. (86)

The results of this corruption are the Peckovers and the Hewetts, the Candy family and the other inhabitants of Clerkenwell. While there is much pseudo-scientific talk in the last two decades of the nineteenth century of degeneration and Darwinian hereditary traits, Gissing is not claiming that these characters are the result of any biological process of degeneration. Despite this passage's use of the word "inherent," in this fictional Clerkenwell, degeneration is caused by poverty and all of its concomitant problems.

Wanting fame and an audience (and above all a reliable income), Gissing well knew that he was unable to have "sympathy with his readers," as Dickens had. "Only one way," he writes, "can the public evince its sympathy with an author—by purchasing his books" (*Critical Study* 62), and this Gissing knew was a difficulty for him. For while he recognized the impossibility, even undesirability of a Biffenlike absolute realism, one "without one single impertinent suggestion of any point of view save that of honest reporting" (*New Grub Street* 174), Gissing was heroic in a Biffenlike way in that he was unwilling to compromise his art even though he knew his novels did not sell well, at least compared with such popular writers as Walter Besant. Gissing, among others, felt that the level of popularity Dickens had enjoyed was no longer possible for the true artist. He writes, "[T]he novelist's first duty is to make us see what he has seen himself, whether with the actual eye or with that of imagination" (*"Oliver Twist"* 93), and this Gissing knew he could do, whether popular or not.

"Gold, Pennyloaf, real gold"

Gissing uses a somewhat sardonic and often ironic omniscient narrator in order to make his readers "see what he has seen himself." An omniscient narrator replicates in many ways a subject position, and is constructed in a partly conscious and partly unconscious way.[20] Arlene Young makes a relevant point about the omniscient narrator in *Middlemarch*:

> The narrator of *Middlemarch*, while dis-embodied, has so distinct a personality that one critic has been prompted to attribute the pervasive wisdom and discernment of the narrative voice to middle-aged sagacity rather than omniscience.[21] More fundamental, but perhaps less obvious, is that narrator's middle-class sensibility. It is indeed the unobtrusiveness of his/her class position that makes the narrator

undeniably middle-class; the narrator in *Middlemarch* is the normative voice *par excellence* of the nineteenth-century British novel, the classic bourgeois genre. (45)

It is this normative quality of the omniscient narrator in the Victorian novel that caused critics (especially Marxist ones) in the twentieth century to critique this genre as hegemonically bourgeois. Because of the constellation of changing historical circumstances (which I have outlined more fully in my introduction), *The Nether World*'s narrator was not only an expression of Gissing's conscious and unconscious attitudes towards social class and poverty, but embodied to a great extent the new view of social class which became possible in late-Victorian society itself (though writers such as Gissing were in the vanguard). And so we find in Gissing a variance from this traditional omniscient narrator's normative bourgeois stance.

Gissing's narrator has an ambivalent attitude towards issues of class which seems to create a double vision for the reader, one which, rather than confirming a complicity between the narrator and the middle-class reader, disrupts it. In *The Nether World*, Gissing is able to depict the poor, working-class inhabitants of Clerkenwell as though from the "inside," while his narrator simultaneously remains aloof *and* passes judgment. It is a rhetorical balancing act: the narrator refuses to privilege either sympathy for the working classes ("Poor, poor creature!" [76] the narrator says of the battered, alcoholic Mrs. Candy), or judgments against them ("they came to love vileness" [74]). And he demonstrates this further when he addresses the reader concerning Clara Hewett, saying, "Yes; but you must try to understand this girl of the people" (79). While his description of Clara as a "girl of the people" suggests a distancing of the reader from the girl and the people, at the same time, the narrator's use of the second person is an attempt to lure the reader into a close-up view of the working-class Clara, who is a sort of anti-heroine in Victorian novel terms. This manipulation helps effect a double vision for the reader; at the same time as seeing Clara as a member of a different group whom we cannot understand, we are drawn into collusion with the narrator who wants our sympathy for Clara.

While sensitive to the concerns of the working-class subjects he describes, the narrator of *The Nether World* sees himself as more educated and therefore on a different intellectual plane. His use of French phrases evidences this, as well as the fact that he labels one chapter "Io Saturnalia!" Knowledge of the Saturnalia, and therefore of Roman customs, implies that the narrator is an educated individual using what might be seen as elitist concepts. And yet the Saturnalia was a carnival which specifically dispensed with class distinctions. In fact, the Saturnalia was a festival at which slaves and masters ate at the same table. Schools and courts were closed and the population indulged in unbridled merrymaking of much the sort engaged in by the merrymakers from Clerkenwell, who make an excursion to the Crystal Palace for the August Bank Holiday. And as with the Roman festival, when Bob Hewett and his new bride, Pennyloaf, board the train at Holborn Viaduct for the "Paliss," as Gissing's narrator points out, there is "[n]o distinction between 'classes' to-day" (105). The Saturnalia, then, has been precisely chosen by Gissing for its double-edged implications.

It is on this day of festival that Bob Hewett marries Pennyloaf Candy. Pennyloaf advertises by her very name her lack of education and therefore her social inferiority. The idea of being named after a penny loaf—something mundane, cheap, bland, a mere necessity of life—damns the poor girl from the beginning. And the fact that she is labeled Pennyloaf, without objection by her, when her real name is Penelope, shows that the Candy family is unable to pronounce the name of their own child, affording educated readers the opportunity to smirk at the joke in a superior fashion. This makes us—as readers—participants in the book's acting out of class relations. By smirking at Pennyloaf we show our own sense of class superiority towards a girl, merely sixteen years old, who has seen much hardship and who is entirely sympathetic and blameless. As always in his dealings with Pennyloaf, the narrator encourages us to laugh at her and, then, by making her sympathetic instead of truly comical, makes us feel mean-spirited for doing so.

He describes for us how, on the day of her wedding, "Pennyloaf shone in most unwonted apparel. Everything was new except her boots" (105). What we are being told here is how ridiculous Pennyloaf looks rather than how beautiful: "Her broad-brimmed hat of yellow straw was graced with the reddest feather purchasable in the City Road; she had a dolman of most fashionable cut, blue, lustrous; blue likewise was her dress, hung about with bows and streamers" (105). There is a decided contrast between this description of Pennyloaf's wedding outfit, and that of the clothing worn by Clara Hewett earlier in the book:

> [I]ts peculiarity (bearing in mind her position) was the lack of any pretended elegance. A close-fitting, short jacket of plain cloth made evident the grace of her bust; beneath was a brown dress with one row of kilting. She wore a hat of brown felt [...]. Her gloves, though worn, were obviously of good kid; her boots [...] were both strong and shapely. This simplicity seemed a declaration that she could not afford genuine luxuries and scorned to deck herself with shams. (26)

In the narrator's view, Pennyloaf dresses vulgarly; Clara does not. Yet there is sympathy for Pennyloaf, and in the same paragraph as the description of her clothing: "How proud she was of her ring! How she turned it round and round when nobody was looking! Gold, Pennyloaf, real gold! The pawnbroker would lend her seven and sixpence on it, any time" (105). We see Gissing's irony at work here,[22] but it is a sympathetic irony. As soon as Pennyloaf has anything of symbolic value, because at the same time it has real monetary value, she can see nothing but a pawnbroker's price. It says much about the struggle Pennyloaf and her family have had to survive. And at the end of the chapter, on her wedding night, her clothes ripped and torn from a fight with Clem Peckover, her husband drunk and injured from a fight with Jack Bartley, Pennyloaf lies in bed "thinking all the time that on the morrow it would be necessary to pawn her wedding ring" (113). Again, the narrator evinces open-eyed sympathy; he does not idealize. But despite his insistence on her colorful clothing, the narrator lets us know that a woman like Pennyloaf has no illusions, and that even in a novel, romance and marriage are not going to bring a happy ending.

"A great review of the People"

Half-way through "Io Saturnalia," as though sickened by the vulgar behaviour of the rival groups from Clerkenwell—the newly married Bob Hewett and his hangers-on versus the jealous Clem Peckover and her satellites—the narrator interjects a paragraph of sarcasm wrought of frustration: "Well, as every one must needs have his panacea for the ills of society, let me inform you of mine," he says, referring to those other novelists, such as Walter Besant, who find easy solutions in their fiction. "In the first place, you must effect an entire change of economic conditions [...] then you must bring to bear on the new order of things the constant influence of music" (109). Gissing points a satirical finger at his successful rival. In *All Sorts and Conditions of Men* (1882), that wildly popular novel which resulted in the building of the "People's Palace" on the Mile End Road, Besant offers up culture as a solution to the problems of the East End.[23] It must have struck Gissing, that adherent to the "school of strict veracity," which was to be "judged by the standard of actual experience," as bitingly ironic that Besant's unrealistic fantasy had become a reality. For Gissing's new style of realism produces characters who, given an August Bank Holiday filled with the pleasures of the Crystal Palace, will get drunk and brawl—both men and women—while Besant's East End working girls, given a nice room in which to listen to music and read, and an open space in which to play tennis, will start to imitate their middle-class betters. No wonder then that Gissing's narrator claims that "there is no chance of a new and better world until the old be utterly destroyed" (109).

　　It is after this outburst that the narrator begins to use the first person plural in his narration. The narrator is split between identifying with the revelers and judging them, creating a disturbing, unstable position for the reader:

> [H]ere by good luck we find seats where we can watch the throng passing and repassing. It is a great review of the People. On the whole how respectable they are, how sober, how deadly dull! See how worn-out the poor girls are becoming [...] the stoop in the shoulders so universal among them merely means over-toil in the workroom. Not one in a thousand shows the elements of taste in dress; vulgarity and worse glares in all but every costume [...]. They are pretty, so many of these girls, delicate of feature, graceful did but their slavery allow them natural development [...]. (109-10)

At first the narrator's use of the first person plural here suggests that he is inviting the reader into a position of observation with him from which we can pass judgement together on the vulgar crowd. But he unexpectedly begins by criticizing the respectability and sobriety of those who pass before us. And his criticisms here, of the taste in dress, for example, are continually opposed by his sympathetic understanding of the poor environment from which these people come, the "slavery" which forms them. Some of the narrator's most blighting judgments are expressed in this paragraph: he calls the middle-aged women "animal, repulsive, absolutely vicious in ugliness" (109), but goes on to explain of the men that "their legs are twisted out of shape by evil conditions of life from birth upwards" (109). We are unable to rest comfortably in our smug superiority.

"A great review of the People," the narrator concludes. "Since man came into being did the world ever exhibit a sadder spectacle?" (110). At this point he seems to have written off this crass crowd of merrymakers, but immediately falls into identification with them again:

> Away to the west yonder the heavens are afire with sunset, but at that we do not care to look; never in our lives did we regard it. We know not what is meant by beauty or grandeur. Here under the glass roof stand white forms of undraped men and women—casts of antique statues—but we care as little for the glory of art as for that of nature [...]. (110)

The position of the reader has subtly changed. We realize that we are no longer united with the (highly educated) narrator in simply observing the crowd go by. We are all, in fact, part of the crowd here. Gissing's narrator constantly plays with his relationship with his readers in this way, ensuring that, if they are middle-class, they are not allowed to sit back comfortably in their well-padded West End interiors and view the world safely as though through a stereoscope. And if they are, like Gissing, well-educated but lower-middle-class, they recognize, in reading this novel, the ongoing problem of class identification. Because of lack of money, they are a part of this crowd, yet their education sets them apart and they feel like outsiders.

"We're working people, we are"

Not only does Gissing's narrator represent a departure from the conventional Victorian novel, so does his insistence on class distinctions within the nether world. As Keating points out, earlier Victorian novelists incorporate a cast of stock working-class characters used to further the author's purpose: the respectable skilled artisan, for example, deserving recipient of middle-class philanthropy, or the poor, illiterate character who is the object of social pity (*Working Classes* 26-7). But Gissing's purpose in *The Nether World* does not fit with that of his predecessors. That is, his purpose is not to elicit pity from the middle-class philanthropists, or gain a change in the laws, since, as we have already discussed, he saw no hope in such solutions. Accordingly, his working-class characters do not fit with these previous categories.

In fact, the narrator expresses a certain nicety in explaining the nuances of the social class system within the working-class world of Clerkenwell. This represents a sort of parody of the Victorian novel considering that *The Nether World* is confined almost exclusively to an area which in the early twenty-first century is a fashionable quarter of London, but in the late nineteenth century was equivalent to—though not a part of—the notorious East End in its slum housing, hopeless poverty and precarious employment.[24]

The Hewetts and their relationships with other characters demonstrate these class nuances. John is a man who has had some good luck and some bad; twice he has tried to start his own business but failed. Now in his fifties, he is reduced to dyeing his hair because he feels that, due to his age, he is being refused employment. There is something infinitely poignant about the idea of a rough, outspoken, hard-up working-man, who lives in two shabby rented rooms with his wife and many children, dyeing his hair in order to look younger. It is this kind of detail that gives one the impression that Gissing's story is told from the "inside." Yet John Hewett, despite his difficult circumstances, "had his ideas of decency, and stuck to them" (21). For example, he says: "I won't have my girl go for a barmaid, so there's an end of it" (23), feeling that this would be beneath his daughter's dignity. And while he, his wife, three small children, the baby and the seventeen-year-old Clara all live in two rooms, the family goes to extra expense so that Bob, the grown son, can share "the bed of a fellow-workman upstairs" (21). This is done, we assume, in order that Clara and Mrs. Hewett (who is the step-mother of Clara and Bob) may have a modicum of privacy. One is reminded of a similar circumstance in Émile Zola's *Germinal* (1885). But *chez les Maheu*, at number sixteen of the second block of Village Two Hundred and Forty, Catherine who is fifteen must share a bedroom with Zacharie (twenty-one), Jeanlin (eleven), Alzirée (nine), Lénore (six) and Henri (four). Meanwhile the parents sleep in a passageway with their three-month old baby. When Étienne Lantier, who is almost a complete stranger, is lodged at the house, he too shares the room with Catherine and the children. Therefore the only way for Catherine to have privacy for dressing is in the darkness. It is, of course, such details as this from Zola's great novel that provide the *choc* to the middle-class sensibility (even in France); for while it shows the shocking extent of the family's poverty, it also delivers a *frisson* because it evokes the idea of sexual intimacy. To some extent, Zola reinforces middle-class stereotypes of the working classes here. This scenario confirms that they have no sense of respectability.

In the description of the Hewett family's conditions, Gissing deliberately avoids sexual overtone. Is Gissing following in Dickens's footsteps, refusing to fly in the face of his middle-class readers? In *Charles Dickens: A Critical Study*, Gissing claims that "the artistic generation of to-day" criticizes Dickens for this very reason:

> What!—they exclaim—a great writer, inspired with a thoroughly fine idea, is to stay his hand until he has made grave inquiry whether Messrs. Mudie's subscribers will approve it or not! [...] what is the use of work, meant to be artistic, carried on in hourly fear of Mrs. Grundy? (61)

While deftly ventriloquizing the voice of "the artistic generation of to-day" in this way and expounding at great length on Dickens's "sympathy with his readers,"

Gissing is able to step aside himself from a position critical of Dickens and claim that "[a]s regards Dickens, it is irrelevant. Dickens [...] never desired freedom to offend his public" (61). Gissing thus makes his point and yet does not seem guilty of defaming the ever-popular Mr. Dickens.

But is Gissing himself refusing to adhere to what he describes as "our school of strict veracity"? (*Critical Study* 59). Is Gissing siding with Dickens, Mrs. Grundy and respectability, or with "the artistic generation of to-day"? In assigning "ideas of decency" to the character of a poor man like John Hewett, is he assigning middle-class attitudes where none exist?—respectability, of course, being the great middle-class virtue. In other words, is Gissing dividing his poverty-stricken characters—as Keating suggests earlier novelists had done—between those who are worthy of middle-class sympathy because they aspire to middle-class notions of respectability, and those who are not? Gertrude Himmelfarb and others have argued that "[t]he historian who belittles the idea of respectability by relegating it to the realm of 'middle-class' values does justice neither to the facts of history nor to the working classes who struggled so hard to attain what the middle-class historian finds it so easy to deride" (9). And historian Brian Harrison agrees:

> Respectability was never cramped within any clearly distinct status-group or occupation; it was an attitude of mind which deeply influenced those who rose, remained stationary, or fell. It impinged on groups of working men of every political opinion and religious denomination, in every region, and at every status-grade within their class, at whatever stage they had reached in their progress towards self-improvement. It was an anxious state of mind. (qtd. in Himmelfarb 9)

In other words, it is not necessarily an indication of a middle-class world-view to recognize that the Hewett family adheres to some small standards of decency despite their financial difficulties and despite their living conditions. It suggests a sympathy with such poverty-stricken members of the working class rather than an imposition of middle-class values. There are, after all, seven members of this family sharing two rooms for all activities, including washing, cooking, eating, sleeping, recreation and the receiving of guests. When Mrs. Hewett is too ill to get up, she receives Sidney Kirkwood while still in bed, evincing not much pretense at middle-class respectability. And while some members of the Hewett family (John and Bob) have "fancies," and Clara is taught piano and sent to a church school, the Hewett family as a whole is not shown as aspiring to the middle classes. The description of John Hewett's meal shows Mrs. Hewett lacking in middle-class cleanliness and other domestic virtues:

> It consisted of a scrap of cold steak, left over from yesterday, and still upon the original dish amid congealed fat; a spongy half-quartern loaf [...]. A shapeless piece of something purchased under the name of butter, dabbed into a shallow basin; some pickled cabbage in a tea-cup; and, lastly, a pot of tea, made by adding a teaspoonful or two to the saturated leaves which had already served at breakfast and mid-day. This repast was laid on a very dirty cloth. The cups were unmatched

and chipped, the knives were in all stages of decrepitude; the teapot was of dirty tin, with a damaged spout. (20-21)

This is, indeed, a poor excuse for a dinner to serve to a man who has spent the day walking around London searching unsuccessfully for employment. But in order to elicit our full middle-class sympathies, Gissing would have to have the dinner laid pathetically on a spick-and-span table cloth by a frayed, but spotlessly clean, wife.

Gissing describes this family as having a less-than-clean table, while at the same time having a sense of decency and even, in the case of John, being ambitious for his daughter in wanting her to learn the piano. An interesting question to ask of the passage quoted here is from whose point of view are we judging this table? Is the narrator judging the Hewett's table or is Sidney? It is not clear whether Mrs. Hewett herself notices or cares whether her cups are "unmatched and chipped"; we have been told, after all, that "the poor woman was, under any circumstances incapable of domestic management, and therein represented her class" (56). Are we seeing the table from Sidney's viewpoint? This would make the description a form of free indirect style: in other words, the narrator might be ventriloquizing Sidney's thoughts here. This could be the case for Sidney is, in some ways, a cut above the other working-class characters in the book. We are told, for example, that although "[t]here is not much in the room [Sidney inhabits in Tysoe Street] to distinguish it from the dwelling of any orderly mechanic" (59), there is one difference:

> The walls [...] were otherwise ornamented than is usual; engravings, chromo-lithographs, and some sketches of landscape in pencil, were suspended wherever light fell [...]. To select for one's chamber a woodcut after Constable or Gainsborough is at all events to give proof of a capacity for civilisation. (59-60)

We are also shown that Sidney is on a different level from Mrs. Hewett because his speech is not altered to approximate the London dialect, while hers, and even John's, is: for example, she says of Clara, "It 'ud a been better for her if she'd had a father like mine, as was a hard, careless man" (18). Sidney speaks in an English that is almost indistinguishable from that of the narrator, which causes it to be seen as the norm (although the narrator uses flourishes such as foreign phrases which are unknown to Sidney.) It is interesting to note, therefore, that the oft-repeated mantra, "We're working people, we are; we're the lower orders," is put into Sidney's mouth.[25]

It could be the case, then, that we see Mrs. Hewett's unmatched china through Sidney's rather meticulous eyes. But while we can see that Sidney appears to be on a level above the Hewetts, they consider themselves as superior to others: "Clara [...] looked down upon Miss Peckover as a mere vulgar girl," but all the same, "Clem had the obvious advantage of being able to ridicule the Hewett's poverty" (33). The complicated relations between the Hewetts and Peckovers are a good example of the nuances of class relations Gissing describes. For while the Peckovers are clearly wealthier than the Hewetts and own the house in which the Hewetts struggle to rent two rooms, Clara has been educated at a church school and taught to play the piano, and can look down on Clem as vulgar. We see that despite the paramount importance of money in the nether world, there are class distinctions even here that can be made, according to Gissing, without recourse to financial stakes.

One of the ways in which the Hewetts are able to exercise their sense of superiority is in objecting to Bob's marriage to Pennyloaf Candy, the daughter of an abused, alcoholic mother whose father frequently abandons them. Bob is, like Clara, on a slightly higher level than some of those around him. The narrator informs us with cutting irony that "In the social classification of the nether world [...] it will be convenient to distinguish broadly, and with reference to males alone, the two great sections of those who do, and those who do not, wear collars" (69). He goes on: "To John Hewett it was no slight gratification that he had been able to apprentice his son to a craft which permitted him always to wear a collar [...]. Bob was raised for ever above the rank of those who depend merely upon their muscles" (69-70). But while the father is aware of this minor elevation of his son, Bob "did not sufficiently appreciate social distinctions. He, who wore a collar, seemed to prefer associating with the collarless" (70-1). Because of this, "Bob, it seemed evident, was fated to make a *mésalliance* [...]. He might have aspired to a wife who had scarcely any difficulty with her *h*'s; whose bringing-up enabled her to look with compassion on girls who could not play the piano; who counted among her relatives not one collarless individual" (71). But Bob married Pennyloaf, and "John Hewett would have nothing to do with an alliance so disreputable; Mrs. Hewett had in vain besought her stepson not to marry so unworthily" (104). The narrator ironizes this snobbishness in the family of an unemployed man partly by the use of the French term *mésalliance*. We are reminded thus of similar circumstances in other Victorian novels: wasn't Fred Vincy destined for a more prestigious match than Mary Garth? And Rose Maylie could not think of wedding Harry with the "stain" she suspected existed in her background.

Great Expectations

Through the inversion of traditional novel plot conventions, Gissing launches a direct attack on the Victorian novel in another way. He alludes to novels which include a "rags-to-riches" pattern, not only encouraging the reader to anticipate the same teleological narrative in *his* novel, but to expect the same urge to social climbing as can be seen in the typical "rags-to-riches" plot. Yet the reader's expectations are not fulfilled.

As others have pointed out, the beginning of *The Nether World* consciously invokes *Great Expectations*.[26] On the first page we meet a traveler (who, we later discover, is back from Australia) loitering near a graveyard, and he turns out to be looking for a young person on whom he is intending to bestow his wealth. We even have the young person living with a (foster) sister[27] who is vicious and cruel, and who cuts the bread, we are pointedly told, by holding it under her arm, in much the same fashion as Mrs. Joe when cutting the bread for Pip's supper. However, Gissing carefully contradicts the details of the Dickens story: the traveler is looking for a girl, not a boy, and once he finds her, even though he wants to bestow his wealth upon her, he wants her to use it for philanthropy. The one thing that he insists upon is that she not become a gentlewoman; she must remain a woman of the people if she is to help them. Here Gissing would appear to be consciously inverting Dickens's plot with motives in Jane's grandfather that are far more philanthropic than those of Dickens's convict. But, of course, in true Gissing fashion, Jane's grandfather is shown to be a little crazy and controlling in wanting to direct Jane's life in this way, and his philanthropy poisons her life and Sidney's.

Another similarity between Dickens's and Gissing's novels is that for Pip, in his childhood misery, there is Joe Gargery, that natural gentleman who, though uneducated, always behaves decently. He does so especially with regard to Pip, even when that young man does not behave at all decently to him. Joe is a Christlike figure against whom we can measure the vanity and superficiality of Pip's aspirations to become a gentleman. For Gissing's Jane Snowdon, there is Sidney Kirkwood, who offers words of kindness in her misery. Like that of Joe Gargery, Sidney's kindness is well-meant, a balm to wounds, but ultimately ineffectual. Whereas Joe is faithful to Pip always, Sidney must abandon Jane for the sake of his own sense of self-worth. In Dickens's original ending to *Great Expectations*, he leaves Pip a wiser but happier man for not having gained his expectations. In *The Nether World*, the wisdom achieved by both Jane and Sidney makes them sadder for not having gained their expectations, but their wisdom teaches them resignation in the face of a hopeless world.

It is *Great Expectations'* second ending to which *The Nether World* responds, the ending which Dickens wrote because of Edward Bulwer-Lytton's entreaties.[28] This second ending has Pip and Estella heading towards marriage.[29] Their marriage, though superficially satisfying for the reader, is out of keeping with the main thrust of Dickens's story. For if Pip, as the adult narrator, is indeed wiser than he had been as a boy—and we are led to believe this by the older Pip's ironical and judgmental attitude towards his younger self—then he would have learned that his yearning for Estella was part of his ambition to be a "gentleman," one who displays all the appropriate trappings, including a beautiful wife. If one meditates for a moment on how a marriage between these two would turn out after all the unhappiness they have shared in the past, one cannot but predict a very somber partnership.

Gissing's novel roundly critiques Dickens's apparently happy ending. His hero and heroine, though they have been in love for much of the novel, do not end up together. Instead, Sidney *does* achieve one of his expectations—he finally marries Clara, his original love. But that is *not* the telos towards which this plot has been heading. The reader is treated to a detailed look at the dreary and blighted lives of the erstwhile lovers once they are married. At the end of *The Nether World*, Sidney Kirkwood, now married to Clara Hewett, lives in Crouch End, one of the new London suburbs where he struggles to support and keep together the ragged remnants of the Hewett family. But removing this family to a suburb away from the dirt and crowd of Clerkenwell does not transform them into respectable middle-class or even lower-middle-class citizens. The narrator tells us that "the kitchen [...] was disorderly [...] and spoke neglect of the scrubbing brush. As for the table, it was ill laid and worse supplied" (364). The children, too, are disorderly; the ten-year-old boy is "a very ill-conditioned youngster [...]. His clothes were dusty, and his hair stood up like stubble" (365). The corrupting effects of the Clerkenwell environment are not so easily discarded, and Sidney must continue to battle them. Even removing slum dwellers to model housing or the suburbs does not solve the problem, and Gissing's readers cannot expect to be lulled into security by a fictional happy ending either.

Again, Gissing is rebelling against these earlier literary conventions, urging his reader to recognize that even romantic love, that healer of all wounds, is not a match for poverty, for poverty is the result of an inhuman but overwhelming social system.[30] Money, that other great reward in the traditional Victorian novel, is the cause of the breakdown of romantic love in Gissing's book, for Jane's inheritance becomes the obstacle barring the way for Sidney's proposal of marriage. It is the lack of money in Clara's life before marriage which causes her to become bitter and eventually physically scarred as though the vitriol thrown in her face were an expression of the bitterness she feels inside. And, to a great extent, it is the grinding poverty of Sidney and Clara's life together, shared with her ne'er-do-well family, that makes their marriage painful. With his inveterate irony Gissing allows neither Sidney nor Jane, the novel's two most sympathetic characters, to end up with the inheritance, and causes Jane's father, that most unsympathetic character, who *does* snag the money, eventually to lose it through his own stupidity.

As the idea of "great expectations" reverberates through Dickens's novel—that is, all have their own expectations—so the same idea reverberates through Gissing's. Mrs. Peckover, Clem, Bob Hewett, John Hewett, Clara, Pennyloaf, Jane's father, Scawthorne, all of these characters have their own great expectations which, in the end, are failed expectations. Strikingly, none of their hopes (except perhaps in the case of Scawthorne) depend on the "upper world" (and in Dickens almost everyone's expectations depend on Pip's supposed upper-class benefactor). Even in the throes of their greatest expectations, the denizens of the nether world expect little from the world above.

Jane Eyre is another "rags-to-riches" novel invoked by Gissing in *The Nether World*. He repeats the plot of the sad little girl named Jane who is ill-treated by her foster family. The scene in which Clem tries to force Jane to sleep in the back parlor with the dead body, which is laid out for burial, is reminiscent of the scene in Brontë's novel in which Jane is locked in the red room. Jane Eyre is *so* overcome by fear during her experience in the red room where her uncle has died that she finally summons up one of her fits of spunk and finds the courage to tell her aunt exactly what she thinks. Jane Snowdon, however, is simply made ill by the fear of the dead body, and it is only through the intervention of her long-lost grandfather that she is rescued from the clutches of the Peckovers. And whereas Jane Eyre, despite the inferior position she was reduced to as a child and the cruelties she suffered with her foster family and at Lowood, grows up to be a self-willed, self-confident, capable young teacher, Jane Snowdon is forever handicapped by her unfortunate childhood. Even after three years of living with her kindly grandfather, Jane Snowdon is still affected by her childhood experiences:

> Though nature had endowed her with a good intelligence, she could only with extreme labour acquire that elementary book-knowledge which vulgar children get easily enough; it seemed as if the bodily overstrain at a critical period of life had affected her memory, and her power of mental application generally. In spite of ceaseless endeavour, she could not yet spell words of the least difficulty; she could not do the easiest sums with accuracy; geographical names were her despair. (135-6)

Jane Snowdon has also been affected emotionally:

> The second point in which she had suffered harm was of more serious nature. She was subject to fits of hysteria, preceded and followed by the most painful collapse of that buoyant courage which was her supreme charm and the source of her influence. Without warning, an inexplicable terror would fall upon her; like the weakest child, she craved protection from a dread inspired solely by her imagination, and solace for an anguish of wretchedness to which she could give no form in words. (136)

Brontë's focus for her novel differs from that of Gissing and therefore requires a different approach. Gissing wants to underscore the point that an upbringing filled with physical hardship and cruelty, along with emotional and physical starvation, cannot be overcome simply by the application of a good deal of money.[31] This observation on Gissing's part, which would be fairly commonplace one hundred years later, was an innovative one at the end of the nineteenth century. And it has deeper ramifications for Gissing's attitude towards the class system as expressed in his novels, and the ways in which Gissing's view of social class differs from that of writers earlier in the century. In addition, Gissing's emphasis on the effects of environment—while not disregarding the concept of heredity—sets him apart from the great European naturalist models of the time such as Emile Zola. It was Zola's contention that the novelist, much like the scientist, is a mere observer and recorder of phenomena, and the phenomena which Zola wished to record were the inescapable effects of heredity on his characters. These characters could be affected by their environment, but not to the exclusion of hereditary traits. While Gissing recognized some effects of heredity (he says, for example, that Clara is rebellious because she takes after her father), it is the brutalizing effect of the environment—that is, the social system, and specifically the class system—which makes brutes out of human beings. It can be seen, then, that inherent in Gissing's position is some blame assigned to the social system and therefore some hope—though he is loath to attach that hope to any specific remedy such as religion, philanthropy or politics.

Invoking and overturning earlier Victorian novels not only situates his novels within the literary history of his century, but shows his disagreement with the implicit message these earlier works often carried. And his use of the "rags-to-riches" motif suggests that it is on the specific issue of class that Gissing wants to intersect with these earlier novels. For this motif carries two important messages, both comforting thoughts to the Victorian middle-class reader. The first is the "cream-rises-to-the-top" theory: it holds that the deserving, clean and moral working-class character—however low he or she has been brought—can, in the end, become middle-class (Pip, for example). The second is based on the "truth-will-out" theory: if a middle-class person should happen to fall on hard times, eventually the truth will out and his or her genuine middle-class status will be recognized (Oliver Twist and Jane Eyre are examples here). Neither of these messages rings true with Gissing; he therefore thwarts the reader's expectations, unhinging the middle-class narrative patterns established earlier in the century.

"Eloquent, unflinching, and without hope"

Slum novels, popular at the end of the nineteenth century, typically adhered to comforting narrative patterns similar to those seen in the social protest or condition-of-England novels of the 1840s and 1850s inasmuch as they worked to ease middle-class fears about the rising power of the working classes. Besant's *All Sorts and Conditions of Men*, for example, suggests that exposing the poor and overworked classes to culture will encourage them to be clean and instill them with middle-class values. His *Children of Gibeon*, the story of two girls (one from a rich family and one from a poor) brought up as sisters in wealth, and between whom no one can tell the difference, flirts with the idea that all are born equal. However, despite this liberal view of the class system, Besant's novel cannot help returning to the notion that neatness and cleanliness, and a less vulgar way of dressing the hair will turn a girl who wanders the streets until midnight into one who imitates middle-class behaviour. For example, when Valentine (the wealthy sister) is trying to show how much she loves Melenda, a working-class sibling of Violet (the poor sister), Melenda says: "oh! what's the use? [...] Look at your clothes and look at mine" (279). Melenda is right, of course, for while clothes are merely a surface indication of class, they symbolize much. Undaunted, Valentine responds: "My clothes! What have clothes to do with it?" (279). She wants to impress on Melenda that, even if they aren't related by blood, they are sisters under the skin, under their difference in clothes. But interestingly, as soon as Melenda succumbs to her entreaties and agrees to regard her as a sister, Valentine says: "First, I am going to dress you [...]. Everything has got to be changed [...]" (280). With that she runs off to find clothes of her own in which to dress Melenda, and then changes Melenda's hairstyle so that it looks less working-class: "Now sit quite steady, my dear, and I will dress [your hair] for you nicely, so as to hide the nasty fringe" (280). It would seem important to look the part of the middle-class character in order to appeal to the reader of that class. Appealing working-class characters are those who aspire to middle-class values and who therefore wish to constrain their very bodies to fit the middle-class mold. While slum novelists depicted some of the horrors of later-nineteenth-century poverty, therefore, their ideological message seemed to be based in a more traditional middle-class world-view.

Gissing manifests a world-view not based in these middle-class values, one which can both identify with and judge the working classes, and one which enables the author to unsteady any middle-class assumptions brought to the novel by his readers. The ending of *The Nether World* evidences this. In rather sentimental fashion, Sidney and Jane meet each year, on the anniversary of her grandfather's his death, at his grave, a fitting symbol of their blighted love, but also the resting place of the blighter of their love. The scene raises echoes of the meeting of Pip and Estella in the garden of Satis House. The last paragraph of the novel begins with these words about Sidney and Jane:

> In each life little for congratulation. He with the ambitions of his youth frustrated; neither an artist, nor a leader of men in his battle for justice. She, no saviour of society by the force of a superb example; no daughter of the people, holding wealth in trust for the people's needs. (392)

It would seem that the two most sympathetic characters in the novel have not only lost one another, but the death of their respective hopes for bettering the world are symbolized by the grave by which they stand. Not surprisingly, in his introduction to the novel, Stephen Gill describes *The Nether World* as "eloquent, unflinching, and without hope" (xiii). It would seem so. But is Gissing's novel as hopeless as Gill suggests? There is none of the old novelistic, Dickensian optimism, none of the Christian master narrative that winds its way through Besant's *Children of Gibeon*, none of the old reliance on the philanthropic bourgeois heart. But the last paragraph does raise the specter of hope—and it is no more than a specter—by raising, oddly enough, the ghost of *Middlemarch*. The narrator echoes the somewhat intangible promise of the last lines of Eliot's novel. Eliot writes of Dorothea, in the last paragraph of her novel:

> [T]he effect of her being on those around her was incalculably diffusive: for the growing good of the world is partly dependent on unhistoric acts; and that things are not so ill with you and me as they might have been, is half owing to the number who lived faithfully a hidden life, and rest in unvisited tombs. (785)

Similarly, Gissing's narrator describes Jane and Sidney as "[u]nmarked, unencouraged." He goes on to say, "they stood by the side of those more hapless, brought some comfort to hearts less courageous than their own [...] at least their lives would remain a protest against those brute forces of society which fill with wreck the abysses of the nether world" (392). By raising the ghost of *Middlemarch*, Gissing does not commit himself to "the growing good of the world," but he does at least admit of the possible worth of an individual's protest against "those brute forces of society," while avoiding an optimistic palliative.

Gissing died at the age of forty-six after having written twenty-two novels, over a hundred short stories, his books on Dickens, and other miscellaneous work. And while admittedly he worked hard because he was in constant need of money and early on earned very little for his writing, his earnestness and shunning of easy popularity give the lie to the idea that he felt hopeless. Instead of hopelessness, we can see a different style of realism.

I want briefly to highlight an unusual storytelling scene from Gissing's *Demos: A Story of English Socialism* because it tells us a lot about why Gissing was writing novels in this new style of realism about social problems. Gissing uses this story within his story as a parable which encapsulates his own conflicted message about the value of literature as "protest against those brute forces of society."

The working-class protagonist in *Demos*, Richard Mutimer, a promising Socialist leader, cautions his sister about the reading of novels; he says, "don't go playing with that kind of thing; it's dangerous" (220). Gissing clearly wants to mark Richard Mutimer as lacking a creative imagination, his frequent critique of the English working classes. We can perhaps also see in Mutimer's comments Gissing's response to novels that offer easy solutions. Richard's erstwhile fiancée, the poor uneducated seamstress whom he has abandoned back in Islington, seems to have gauged the value of imaginative storytelling: while she sits at the machine sewing in the evening, Emma tells stories to her niece and nephew, the children of her alcoholic sister. "It was a way," we are told, "of beguiling the children from their desire to go and play in the street" (394). Like many of the novels in the Victorian era, her storytelling has a purpose, an improving, moral purpose; it saves the children from the temptations and dangers which are lurking in the evenings on the streets of Islington, temptations and dangers to which their mother has already succumbed.

Gissing's narrator goes on to describe Emma's stories:

> Unlike the novel which commends itself to the world's grown children, these narratives had by no means necessarily a happy ending; for one thing Emma saw too deeply into the facts of life, and was herself too sad, to cease her music on a merry chord; and, moreover, it was half a matter of principles with her to make the little ones thoughtful and sympathetic; she believed that they would grow up kinder and more self-reliant if they were in the habit of thinking that we are ever dependent on each other for solace and strengthening under the burden of life. (394)

Here Gissing is mocking not only those other Victorian novels with the happy endings, but the childlike readers who crave them. Emma is a new kind of realistic storyteller, and just as Emma wants the children to grow up without illusions, Gissing wants his readers to harbor no illusions either. "Emma had two classes of story," we are told, "the one concerned itself with rich children, the other with poor; the one highly fanciful, the other full of a touching actuality" (395). If we read Emma's stories as analogous to novels, then the "highly fanciful" story represents traditional Victorian fiction, mainly concerned with the rich, while the story which concerns itself with the poor is a stand-in for the "touching actuality" we see in Gissing's own work.

And Gissing's realism is even more effective when strategically contrasted to the traditional, "highly fanciful," Victorian novel. The narrator continues:

> The most elaborate of her stories [...] was called "Blanche and Janey." It was a double biography. Blanche and Janey were born on the same day, they lived ten years, and then died on the same day. But Blanche was the child of wealthy parents; Janey was born in a garret. Their lives were recounted in parallel, almost year by year, and there was sadness in the contrast. (395)

The young girls in Emma's story are named for the rich girl and the poor girl in *Jane Eyre*: Blanche and Jane. Despite his respect for Charlotte Brontë's writing, Gissing subverts her novel's ending. There is seeming justice in Brontë's disposal of her two women: she sends Blanche off in pursuit of a wealthier catch, duped by Rochester's rumor-mongering; for all intents and purposes she is a victim of her own greed and materialism. And Jane's "Reader, I married him" is a signal of her success. But Jane's final victory is, in fact, won through inherited money, not all her hard work and spunk, the qualities modern-day readers admire in her. Jane comes back to Rochester because she has been remade into a middle-class, propertied woman. But for Gissing (and therefore for his Emma) this will never do, for this is not life as he (or she) experiences it.

Emma ends her story thus:

> "Yes, they died on the same day, and they were buried on the same day. But not in the same cemetery, oh no! Blanche's grave is far away over there"—she pointed to the west—"among tombstones covered with flowers, and her father and mother go every Sunday to read her name, and think and talk of her. Janey was buried far away over yonder"—she pointed to the east—"but there is no stone on her grave, and no one knows the exact place where she lies, and no one, no one ever goes to think and talk of her." (395)

The implication here for Gissing's late-Victorian readers, raised as they were in fairly close proximity to the Bible, was that Heaven and Hell are merely worldly terms. Blanche, being rich, is buried in the west—which suggests the West End. For her, death seems almost as happy as life: her parents visit, they bring her flowers, she is the center of attention. The cemetery in which she is buried has "tombstones covered with flowers." The wealthy dead have their possessions, just like the wealthy living. Blanche's ending is a parody of the sentimentalized view of life proposed by traditional Victorian novels; it betrays the usual stolid, middle-class, materialistic world-view. In this scenario, it is not Jesus Christ, but wealth that overcomes even the pain of death.

Janey, by contrast must be buried in the East, or the East End, that metonym of the London poor. She was poor and therefore unimportant alive; dead, she is entirely forgotten. No one has even marked her grave. She is the heroine of the new realism, Gissing's "school of strict veracity" (*Critical Study* 59), "to be judged by the standard of actual experience" ("Oliver Twist" 92).

Emma's storytelling suggests where Gissing's hope may lie. Commenting on her story of Blanche and Janey, the narrator says, "The sweetness of the story lay in the fact that the children were both good, and both deserved to be happy; it never occurred to Emma to teach her hearers to hate little Blanche just because hers was the easier lot" (*Demos* 395). Like Emma, Gissing does not try to teach hate, except perhaps of the class system itself, and like Emma, too, he does believe in storytelling. Despite Gissing's lack of hope for religious, political or philanthropic help for the poor, the very act of telling his stories, writing his novels, is an act of hope. It is a way to inform his reader, to educate his reader, just as Emma does. Like Emma, he believes, if nothing else, in the power of narrative, narrative that attempts to avoid a class-based, class-affirming ideology.

Notes

[1] All Booth page references are to the five-volume edition of *Life and Labour of the People in London*. 1902. New York: Augustus M. Kelley, 1969.

[2] Toynbee Hall and Oxford House were residential settlements in the East End where university students lived and tried to help those around them. According to Booth, classes were offered at Toynbee Hall during one week on the following: Socrates, Normandy, Chemistry, Spinoza, Shorthand, Carpentry, beginners Latin, English literature, the "Age of Pope," Greek, Embriology, Botany, French, Plato, Italian, Bacon, German. Booth notes, "Something of this kind goes on every week. There are over 600 members on the register of classes, and 600 tickets were sold for the last course of University Extension lectures. In all about 1000 people come weekly to Toynbee Hall for concerts, lectures, classes, &c;. Outside of all this, the residents—20 members of the Universities living in Toynbee Hall—do what is recognized as their chief work in forming friendships with the people, and coming into touch with their needs in connection with school management, co-operation, local government, charity organization, and children's country holidays" (1: 124).

[3] Booth: "By the word 'poor' I mean to describe those who have a sufficiently regular though bare income, such as 18s. to 21s. per week for a moderate family, and by 'very poor' those who from any cause fall much below this standard. The 'poor' are those whose means may be sufficient, but are barely sufficient, for decent independent life; the 'very poor' those whose means are insufficient for this according to the usual standard of life in this country. My 'poor' may be described as living under a struggle to obtain the necessaries of life and make both ends meet; while the 'very poor' live in a state of chronic want" (1:33).

[4] Clara Collet, who worked on Booth's team collecting information and writing essays—especially about women's work—was one of Gissing's most loyal and helpful friends. He met her in 1903 after publication of *The Nether World*. Collet was said to have spent a great deal of time with Karl Marx's daughters when she was a young woman, and to have been involved in amateur theatricals with them at which Marx himself had been a frequent spectator. For more information on Collet see the recent biography by Deborah McDonald: *Clara Collet 1860-1948: An Educated Working Woman*. London: Woburn Press, 2004.

[5] Booth divides the classes as follows: "A. The lowest class, which consists of some occasional labourers, street-sellers, loafers, criminals and semi-criminals" (1: 38). He says of class A: "They render no useful service, they create no wealth: more often they destroy it. They degrade whatever they touch" (39). "Class B—Casual earnings—very poor" (39). "Class C—

Intermittent earnings." "Class D, Small Regular Earnings, poor." "E. Regular Standard Earnings." "Class F consists of higher class labour, and the best paid of the artisans." "G. Lower Middle Class.—Shopkeepers and small employers, clerks, &c. and subordinate professional men." He says of these people: "A hard-working, sober, energetic class." "H. Upper Middle Class.—all above G are here lumped together, and may be shortly defined as the servant-keeping class" (37-60). Note that within the process of objectification inheres a tendency to judgment.

[6] *In Darkest England and the Way Out.*

[7] Interestingly, it was near Clerkenwell Green that Mr. Brownlow had his pockets picked by the Artful Dodger, and where Oliver was subsequently arrested. Perhaps Gissing is evoking Dickens in order to point up their differences.

[8] See note 14.

[9] Walter Besant's *Children of Gibeon* published in 1886.

[10] *Demos: A Story of English Socialism* is George Gissing's 1886 novel.

[11] Arlene Young notes that although female authors (the Brontës, Elizabeth Gaskell, and George Eliot, for example) "are somewhat less constrained and attempt to create protagonists like Jane Eyre and Felix Holt, who rebel against accepted social norms [...] their stories ultimately conform to standard middle-class expectations of marriage and domestic felicity. In *Mary Barton*, Gaskell [...] comes closer to producing a convincingly working-class ethos. The dominant ethos of the nineteenth-century novel, however, remains middle-class, and is virtually indistinguishable from that of the typical protagonist" (46).

[12] Penny Boumelha. *Thomas Hardy and Women: Sexual Ideology and Narrative Form.* Madison, WI: U of Wisconsin Press, 1985.

[13] *The Nether World* (1889) is the culmination of Gissing's series of five novels that focus on working-class life: *Workers in the Dawn* (1880), *The Unclassed* (1884), *Demos* (1886) and *Thyrza* (1887).

[14] For a detailed discussion of this important episode in Gissing's life, see the biographies by John Halperin, Jacob Korg and Gillian Tindall. Gissing married Marianne Helen Harrison (Nell) in 1879. She and Gissing had lived apart for some five years at the time of her death. Gissing married Edith Underwood in 1891. They had two sons, Walter and Alfred. He left Edith in 1897. In 1902 Edith Underwood Gissing was sent to an asylum. She died there in 1917.

[15] Walter J. Ong, "The Writer's Audience is Always a Fiction." *Interfaces of the Word.* Ithaca, NY: Cornell UP, 1977.

[16] Lower middle class was a term, according to Raymond Williams, not used with much frequency until the twentieth century. Thus it is possible that this group—a group which is growing rapidly at the end of the nineteenth century—saw themselves as "lower-class" but struggling to move into the middle class. Gissing, of course, saw himself as one of the "unclassed," along with the poverty-stricken intellectuals he sometimes depicted in his novels, especially in his novel *The Unclassed*.

[17] Anne Pilgrim, in "Gissing's Imagined Audience: A Note on Style," argues that because Gissing sensed that he had "little in common with most members of the vast middle-class reading public," he simply *imagined* "a fit audience for his work" (18).

[18] Booth's investigation showed that Church of England churches in London had by far the most attendees even in the East End and Hackney.

[19] Biffen is a character in Gissing's *New Grub Street* who is devoted to a new kind of realism, "an absolute realism in the sphere of the ignobly decent" (*New Grub Street* 173). "The result," he says, "will be something unutterably tedious [...]. That is the stamp of the ignobly decent

life. If it were anything *but* tedious it would be untrue. I speak, of course, of its effect upon the ordinary reader" (174). His *magnum opus* is a book called *Mr. Bailey, Grocer.*

[20] Young writes, "[narrators] are not characters, they are nevertheless constructed fictional identities, albeit often incomplete ones" (45). And such "[f]ictional characters are [...] cultural constructions, shaped as much by the values and assumptions of the society for which they are created as by the author who creates them"(45).

[21] Young refers here to Kerry McSweeney's *Middlemarch* (London & Boston: Allen & Unwin, 1984), pp. 73-4.

[22] For a detailed analysis of irony in Gissing's work, see Brian Robert Walker's excellent article, "Gissing's Use of Irony."

[23] Walter Besant's novel, *All Sorts and Conditions of Men* (1882), was the inspiration for the People's Palace, a center built for the people of the East End on Mile End Road. It was opened by Queen Victoria in June 1887. The University of London's Queen Mary and Westfield College now stands on the site. It was intended as a cultural and recreational facility, as had been its prototype, the "Palace of Delight" in Besant's novel. However, middle-class funders of the project gradually turned its direction more towards education. "Sales of *All Sorts and Conditions of Men*, already strong in the first four years after publication, were boosted by the building of the People's Palace and continued at a rate of over 26,000 per year well into the 1890s [...]. A sixpenny edition eventually appeared in 1897 [...] and by the end of the First World War, the novel had sold well over a quarter of a million copies in Britain, while also going through numerous editions—many of them unauthorized—in the United States," writes Helen Small in the introduction to the Oxford Popular Fiction edition (xi).

[24] Williams claims that, in the 1880s and 90s, "the sense of the great city was [...] so overwhelming, that its people were often seen in a single way: as a crowd, as 'masses' or as a 'workforce.' The image could be coloured either way, for sympathy or for contempt, but its undifferentiating character was persistent and powerful" (*Country* 222). He argues that in *The Nether World*, Gissing "saw in the great majority of people this single quality or condition" (222). Williams's argument does not do justice to the nuanced depiction of class within the working-class world that Gissing achieves in this novel.

[25] It is notable, too, that Sidney works in St. John's Square, which had once been the courtyard of the Priory of St. John, the chief seat of the Knights of St. John of Jerusalem (*The Nether World* n. 51,). These Knights Hospitalers have an ambiguous history: they were originally primarily an order that tended the sick, but their military branch, the Knights of Justice, were nobly-born, wealthy and through the centuries suffered various military defeats. While such an association could suggest that within Sidney Kirkwood beats a noble heart, one willing to fight for justice, these knights were neither as victorious nor as virtuous as one might hope, adumbrating Sidney's eventual defeat, and conceivably perhaps casting a vague shadow over his apparently spotless character.

[26] See, for example, Stephen Gill's introduction to the Oxford edition of *The Nether World* (1992).

[27] Though Clem and Jane are not related, they are fairly close in age, and Jane was to be brought up as a foster-child of Mrs. Peckover. As it turns out, of course, she is more of a slave than a foster-child—not much fostering, except of fear and resentment, has taken place.

[28] In his 1903 abridgement of John Forster's *The Life of Charles Dickens*, Gissing writes of the ending of *Great Expectations*: "As the end of the story originally stood, Pip was left a solitary man. Most unfortunately Dickens yielded to a foolish objection of Bulwer Lytton, and substituted the final page which we now have. It is the only grave blemish on the book" (*Collected Works of George Gissing on Charles Dickens*, III, Ed. and introduced by Christine

DeVine, Grayswood, Surrey: Grayswood Press, 2004). (p.184) In his *Critical Study* he writes: "Rightly seen, is there not much pathos in the story of Pip's foolishness? It would be more manifest if we could forget Lytton's imbecile suggestion, and restore the original close of the story" (*Collected Works*, II, 144).

[29] It is assumed by most readers that marriage is what follows the "happy" second ending however ambiguous Dickens managed to make those few last words: "I saw the shadow of no parting from her" (484). He changed the last words in the one-volume edition published in 1862 to make them less ambiguous, writing: " I saw no shadow of another parting from her" (n. 2, 507)

[30] Stephen Gill notes in his introduction to the Oxford edition of *The Nether World*, "That [Gissing] refuses to privilege romantic love [...] is extraordinary [...] for it has always been the transhistorical power to which artists appeal as the one element in life which surmounts social and economic determinism" (xvii).

[31] Oliver Twist is the obvious example of a child who appears not to be scarred by his unfortunate upbringing. Though Pip has acquired the ambition to become a gentleman, it seems not to be directly related to his unhappy childhood. And once he is living with a decent income, his childhood problems seem to disappear. Though Jane Eyre does not inherit her money until the end of the novel, she has been able to retain her native intelligence throughout, and once living at Thornfield with far more ease of body and mind, she is able to recover from her previous troubles so effectively that having inherited the money, she is whole.

Chapter 2

"Is this democracy to prove fatal to England?": International Terrorism, the *Times* and James's *The Princess Casamassima*

On Saturday, 6 May 1882, at about 7:30 p.m., Lord Frederick Cavendish, the new Chief Secretary for Ireland, and Thomas Henry Burke, the Under Secretary, were walking together across Phoenix Park in Dublin to dine with the Lord Lieutenant at the Viceregal Lodge. Suddenly they were set upon by four men who stabbed them to death and then escaped, leaving the two victims lying in a pool of blood. In the midst of the quarrel over Home Rule, this brutal act was part of the ongoing fight by Irish nationalists against British domination. Ironically, Lord Cavendish, who had arrived and been sworn in as secretary that very afternoon, had brought with him news of hope: Parnell and Gladstone had reached a tentative agreement on steps to be taken towards conciliation (Fairhall 17).

The English press, quite predictably, expressed outrage at the murders. The *Pall Mall Gazette* noted that the reaction on both sides of the Irish Sea denounced the murderers and accused them of wanting to derail progress in Home Rule negotiations at a time when Parnell had just been released from Kilmainham gaol and conciliation seemed sure. While quick to lay blame at the feet of American Fenians, the *Pall Mall Gazette* linked the murders with those in other countries, hinting at connections with international terrorism: "The barbarity of Saturday night shows that Ireland, too, is at last involved in the cycle of political assassination which has within the last three years thrown its ghastly shadow over Berlin, St. Petersburg, Rome, and Washington" ("Assassinations" 1). Several Invincibles, a small band of Irish nationalists unconnected to the Fenians or other nationalist groups, were eventually hanged for the killings. It was, therefore, a crime not linked with international terrorism, nor indeed any widely organized effort to derail conciliation.

In its reporting, the *Times* emphasized the contrast between the butchered bodies of Burke and Cavendish, and the sumptuous surroundings in which the bodies had been laid for postmortem examination:

> The scene was one indescribably horrible. On a table at the window nearest the conservatory, the door of which was closed, lay the body of poor Mr. Burke, stark and ghastly, his finely-chiselled face [...] scarcely recognizable through the blood which filled his mouth, while his neck and chest bore gashes which looked as if inflicted by a butcher's knife. On a table at the other end of the room was stretched the body of Lord Frederick Cavendish, presenting an appalling spectacle, and the room, which recently had been full of life and gaiety, was now become a shambles, the sight being rendered more hideous by contrast with the associations of the place. The mirrors on the walls and the furniture which remained still in the room were suggestive of refinement, luxury, and social enjoyment, while the two mangled corpses, surrounded by a group of medical operators, with coats off, aprons on, and scalpels and saws in their hands red with the blood of the victims, presented a sight which even those familiar with the terrors of the battlefield could not look upon without emotion. ("Assassination of Lord F. Cavendish" 8)

The ghastly detail used in describing the corpses and the blood on the hands of the medical men is made far more shocking in contrast with Burke's "finely-chiselled face," and the "refinement" and "luxury" of the room, evoking the "social enjoyment" one might imagine occurring there. The *Times* is emphasizing, perhaps, that it is the well-off, refined classes that are under attack. For this attack came at a time when the middle classes felt they were threatened from all sides, not only by the Irish, but by organized working-class groups and by the growing push towards political reform. Not only did the Irish want to rule themselves, but the English working classes wanted a greater voice in government. Not only was conciliation in the air, but so was democracy. These were frightening prospects for some—especially since politically motivated violence at home and abroad had become a frequent topic in the press.

"Is this democracy to prove fatal to England?"

Whereas democracy had been seen as a positive concept in the United States in the nineteenth century, in England it was seen by many as unpalatable Jacobinism. In his speech on the Second Reform Act of 1867 intended to expand voting rights, Disraeli had expressed his hope that it would "never be the fate of this country to live under a democracy" (qtd. in Read 145). The 1867 bill had been seen as likely to usher in a new era in which working-class leaders would confiscate private property and anarchy would reign. However, in 1868, no working-class MPs were elected, and in 1874 only two, both miners, entered the Commons (Read 149). But despite fears and protests, the series of Reform Acts of 1832, 1867 and 1884-5[1] brought the country slowly and steadily towards an increased franchise and a more democratic form of government.

In the last decades of the nineteenth century, the idea of this changing balance of power still appeared ominous to those who stood to lose. Discussing democracy in 1885, Lord Randolph Churchill, who had advocated the so-called Tory Democracy in a bid to win support of new voters, nevertheless expresses fear of the coming change:

> Are we being swept along a turbulent and irresistible torrent which is bearing us towards some political Niagara, in which every mortal thing we know will be twisted and smashed beyond all recognition? (qtd. in Read 309).

In the same year, T.H.S. Escott, editor of the *Fortnightly Review*, questions the efficacy of democracy as a means of government:

> What productive forces are there inherent in the democracy? What power has it of implanting energy, and inspiring action, in individuals? How is the principle of authority at home and abroad to be maintained under its supremacy? How are its passions to be curbed or its inertness to be dispelled? Who or what will be adequate to its discipline? Or is this democracy to prove fatal to England as an imperial State, and as a pattern and mother of constitutions to the world? (qtd. in Read 309)

It seemed to those threatened, as it seemed to James's protagonist in *The Princess Casamassima*, that "the flood of democracy was rising over the world ... [and] would sweep all the traditions of the past before it" (478).

The flood of democracy was, in reality, more like a trickle in the 1880s. In fact, in many working-class constituencies, one in two adult males *still* lacked the vote—not to mention, of course, the exclusion of women. So that, despite the Third Reform Act, middle-class males carried probably *twice* the electoral weight they would have had under a "one man one vote" system (Read 302-3). At the same time, although socialism was attracting attention and was equated in the minds of many with democracy, the Social Democratic Federation was not gaining members in great numbers. Large groups of the unemployed had willingly attended socialist meetings and demonstrations looking for a solution to their problems, but few had become socialists. In 1886 the SDF had eleven London Branches with only 390 members. And although such organizations as the Social Democratic Federation *did* support home rule for Ireland, almost all of the terrorist explosions in London, and of course the Phoenix Park murders, protested British policy in Ireland and were not perpetrated by socialists or by international anarchist organizations.

But the balance of power in England was slowly shifting and the working classes were gradually acquiring more representation. For one thing, trade unions now had about 500,000 members (Read 325). Despite this, the rumblings of discontent among the working class were getting louder. The discontent came to a head in February 1886 when, after a particularly hard winter that exacerbated rising unemployment in London, the hungry and unhappy unemployed met in Trafalgar Square to protest their desperate situation. The gathering ended with the protesters heading for Hyde Park, but along Pall Mall some members of the gentlemen's clubs for which that street was renowned shouted abuse at the marchers. At this point the march turned into a riot; windows were broken and shops were looted. For the next several days rumors spread of a mass of angry marchers from the East End heading towards the West End destroying property along the way. No such marchers materialized, but the fact that these rumors had been believed suggests the extent of the fear.

Henry James had written in September of 1884, "Nothing *lives* in England today but politics. They are all-devouring, their mental uproar crowds everything out […] the air is full of events, of changes of movement (some people wld. say of revolution, but I don't think that)."[2] Marx's theories of inevitable proletarian revolution were virtually unknown in Britain until after his death in 1883, but throughout the early 1880s in London there was a sense of impending revolutionary change. It was sparked by a series of violent events in England and elsewhere that became connected in the public mind. The assassination of the Czar and of President Garfield in 1881, the Phoenix Park murders in 1882, dynamite explosions in the London underground railway tunnels in 1883, and the bomb explosion in the House of Commons in January 1885, along with many other terrorist attacks, successful and unsuccessful, seemed to be part of an international wave of violence.

Through its reporting of the political changes, the various mass marches and strikes, and terrorist acts at home and abroad, the *Times* seemed to confirm suspicions amongst the prosperous middle classes that the well-heeled, well-oiled, stable world to which they had grown accustomed would soon be destroyed. As Joanne Shattock and Michael Wolff assert, "The press, in all its manifestations, became during the Victorian period the context within which people lived and worked and thought, and from which they derived their […] sense of the outside world" (xiv-xv). Newspapers, in other words, helped to construct social reality, and in the 1880s newspapers— especially the *Times*—were helping to create the fear of democracy by tying this political movement and foreign terrorists to more imminent threats of violence— from Irish nationalists, for example.

Two *Punch* cartoons of the 1880s demonstrate how the various threats were seen as connected: the octopus-like "Irish devil-fish," shown about to be stabbed by a fierce, bare-chested Gladstone in a *Punch* cartoon of 18 June 1881, has arms that are labeled Anarchy, Rebellion, Sedition, Terrorism, Lawlessness, Intimidation and Outrage. "Spirit of Anarchy," a cartoon from 1886, shows a ghoulish, skull-headed spirit welcoming the unemployed: "What! No work! Come and enlist with me,—I'll find work for you!!" Anarchy is associated in these cartoons both with Irish nationalism and with the unemployed; all were conspiring, it seemed, to overthrow the social order.[3] Terrorist attacks and the discontent of the unemployed became entangled with and fed the fear not only of the emerging democracy, but also of foreign anarchy, a fear that had its roots in class prejudice.

"As the picture is reality, so the novel is history"

It had been a commonplace of criticism and novel theory in the Victorian era to see the realistic novel as history, as a picture of the real world. Many had used the ploy

THE TEMPTER.

Spirit of Anarchy. "WHAT! NO WORK! COME AND ENLIST WITH ME,—I'LL FIND WORK FOR YOU!!"

Fig. 2.1 "Spirit of Anarchy" (*Punch*, 27 November 1886)

of pretending the story they were telling was true;[4] by so doing they were inviting and encouraging a willing suspension of disbelief. As I noted in my introduction, Dickens defended his inclusion of thieves and prostitutes in *Oliver Twist* by claiming he was telling the "truth" in his novel. He believed that, however unpalatable for some, its truthful reflection of reality made his novel morally efficacious. However, as we also saw, Dickens's version of the "truth" had been sentimentalized and watered down to suit the tastes of his middle-class readers. The reality reflected was one tailored for specific readers.

Not that the Victorian realistic novelists all had a simplistic and uncomplicated view of their realism. Two of the Victorian era's most popular novelists provide examples of this. Mid-career, Dickens had experimented with dual narrators in *Bleak House* (1853), thus taking some authority away from the omniscient narrator and giving it to a somewhat inconsequential young girl. These dueling narrators demonstrate a way in which fiction can attempt to reflect varying constructions of reality. Wilkie Collins took this concept a step further. In *The Woman in White* (1860) he deployed several narrators to contribute to Hartright's story, and much of the focus of *The Moonstone* (1868) is on perceptions and interpretations of reality narrated by various voices. Collins's novels certainly offer a more complex version of the novel as history.

In 1884, in "The Art of Fiction," Henry James had articulated his vision of the novelist as historian. "The only reason for the existence of a novel is that it does attempt to represent life," he says (46). But James does not infer merely a referential realism here; his own novels evidence this. Making an analogy between painting and novel writing, he asserts: "as the picture is reality, so the novel is history" (46). He claims that fiction "must speak with assurance, with the tone of a historian," and admonishes Trollope for admitting that he is only "making believe" (46). He equates the historian with the novelist, saying, "To represent and illustrate the past, the actions of men, is the task of either writer" (47). The only way in which the novelist differs from the historian is "in his having more difficulty collecting his evidence, which is so far from being purely literary" (47). The open admission of "making believe" is the "apparatus of narration" to which James objects. The problem is that "it implies that the novelist is less occupied in looking for the truth— than the historian" (46). While fiction is an art for James, not merely a mirror, looking for the "truth" with that art is what is important for him and what he equates with the telling of history. But "truth" was a concept that was no less slippery in 1884 when James made this claim for realist fiction than it had been in 1841 when Dickens had done so, and it seems to be their varying interpretations of this nebulous noun that cause Dickens and James to differ in their approach to realism. For one thing, in writing *Oliver*, Dickens feels he is writing the truth by representing the real world, while for James truth is the grail for which the novelist is searching. His imaginative transmutation of life into art may reveal something that could be labeled "truth," but it is not a matter simply of copying the world. As he had made clear in "The Art of Fiction," it is the "truth" about life that can be revealed in the *telling* of fiction that interests James. For him, fiction is about insight.

There has been some critical debate as to whether James was attempting accurately to reflect the historical context of London in the 1880s when he wrote his novel of terrorism and revolution. Lionel Trilling says, "The truth is that there is not a political event of *The Princess Casamassima*, not a detail of oath or a mystery or danger, which is not confirmed by multitudinous records" (64). By contrast John Lucas calls it a "superb bluff," claiming that "at the very point where we need precision we meet a baffling vagueness. The ignorance of the characters too often suggests the ignorance of their creator" (*Conservatism* 208). He goes on to complain that even when James is specific, he is in error: "To identify anarchism with the central threat to established order [...] is to misunderstand the nature of the threat. For as a revolutionary movement, anarchism was comparatively unimportant in England" (208-9). But both these arguments miss the point. It is the rhetoric of fear promulgated in the public discourse that James addresses, not the events themselves. And while James's 1886 novel, *The Princess Casamassima*, has been called his most political novel because it overtly concerns a political theme, it is not a political analysis or manifesto.

In *The Princess Casamassima*, James *appears* to be engaging with history itself, and yet it is the *Times* that James actually references. Wesley Tilley has convincingly identified the specific reports in the *Times* that James used as material for his novel. According to Tilley, James not only took the subject matter for *The Princess* from the pages of the *Times*, he based his characters on specific revolutionaries that he read about in the paper's pages.[5] But James's novel also takes issue with the *Times*'s construction of reality in its reporting, pointing up its anti-democracy fear-mongering, and even contesting the possibility of the objective narration of history.

James depicts a shadowy group of revolutionary foreigners, as the *Times* had done, in its reporting. But in contrast to the *Times*, James brings the revolution—and the problems of the working classes—to English shores. Furthermore, in *The Princess*, James is moving towards a center-of-consciousness technique and away from the authority of the narrator. In so doing, he is working against the all-knowing, middle-class, admonitory voice that was typical of the traditional Victorian novel and that the *Times* had used to report what it saw as class-based terrorist acts. If the class system is not the "natural" order of things and depends to a great extent on that authoritative voice, that is, on the discourse surrounding class, then by exposing the apparatus of narration in the *Times*, James also exposes the social class system as, in part, a rhetorical construction.

In this chapter I will first examine the reporting in the *Times* which illustrates the paper's anti-democratic fear-mongering. I will focus on its reporting of the assassination of the Czar in March 1881, the trial of some German anarchists in December 1884, and a discussion in the *Times* in April 1885 of a *Quarterly Review* article on democracy. The first two instances typify the in-depth reporting in the English press of violence occurring abroad in the mid-1880s. The trial of the German "dynamitards" is also relevant because of James's apparent choice of characters from this news story as models for his novel. The discussion of the article on democracy allows us to judge the extent to which the concept of democracy was being vilified by some in the press, and the way in which the *Times*, despite its claim to be objective and analytical, takes constant and direct aim at democracy. I will then go on to argue that James, by undermining the authority of the narrator in *The Princess Casamassima*, is not only going against the middle-class world-view and authoritative voice of the *Times*, but in so doing writes a fiction that embodies a more democratic world-view than previous realistic fiction writers. For despite the efforts of Dickens, Collins and others to complicate the narrative point of view, in the end a middle-class world-view, and therefore a middle-class value system, still presides.

"The avowed implacable enemy of Liberalism and Democracy"

In its reporting of terrorist activities at home and abroad, the *Times* plays on a combination of its readers' understandable fear of the all too real threats of Fenian bombings and its readers' vague fears of the growing power of the working classes at home and abroad. It characterizes the problems of the working classes and their demands for political reform—in other countries at least—as associated not only with the French Revolution, a frightening enough prospect in itself, but with anarchists, nihilists and socialists, all of whom were capable—in the *Times*'s view— of violent acts. We cannot have sympathy for these foreign working-class groups, the *Times* suggests, because they are violent. At the same time, the newspaper implies, English workers have no justification for demanding reform because the English are far more advanced in their civilization and not therefore mistreating workers. So while frightening its readers with lurid details of bloody assassinations and explosions, the *Times* placates them by suggesting that working-class revolt cannot happen in England, or perhaps more importantly, that it won't happen if those in power remain vigilant.

The *Times*'s reports, like James's novel, are full of shadowy, just perceptible presences and of the suggestion of violent anarchist or nihilist networks and conspiracies. For example, on 15 March 1881, the day after the assassination of Czar Alexander, the *Times* enhances its extensive reporting on the assassination with hints and suggestions of more: it speaks of "[t]he terrible event" which "seems shrouded in a great deal of mystery," mentioning "secret societies" and the "powers of evil" ("Assassination of the Emperor" 5). The *Times* reports on 17 March:

> The statement is repeated by an evening paper that the assassination of the Czar, though perpetrated by the Nihilists of Russia, *appears to have been instigated by an international society, having for its watchword the murder of Monarchs and the overthrow of Governments.* [...] the police and even the Czar himself shortly before his death received warnings both from Geneva and London, which, if heeded, might have averted the terrible catastrophe of Sunday. ("Late Emperor of Russia" 12, my emphasis)

As Lucy Brown points out in *Victorian News and Newspapers*, because it was difficult for foreign correspondents to gather news independently, "the great bulk of foreign news came not from independent investigation, but from sources in the capital city—or the city where the correspondent was stationed" (215). In the above account, the *Times*'s correspondent is repeating a report from a St. Petersburg paper. He notes: "At such a time of general excitement it is to be expected that all kinds of rumours and exaggerations will arise," and goes on to say: "All these [...] statements may possibly [...] be designed to throw the Russian police off scent" (12). But as we often see today, a respectable news organization can appear to avoid the charge of rumor-mongering by simply reporting the concrete and verifiable fact that other—less conscientious—news organizations are reporting rumors. Thus the *Times* can still lay claim to objective reporting, while promulgating the rumor of an indefinite and therefore seemingly more threatening international danger.

On 14 March, the day of the assassination, the *Times* ran two long, detailed articles that told—in narrative form—the life of Czar Alexander and the development of the revolutionary movement. The *Times*'s writer becomes the omniscient narrative voice making sense of the situation, putting it all in perspective. He discusses the repressive nature of the Czar's father—Nicholas—who became, according to one article, "the avowed implacable enemy of Liberalism and Democracy, not only in his own country but all over Europe" ("Alexander II" 10).

In contrast to his father—who apparently was disappointed in his son's kindly, non-military nature—Alexander had been reform-minded and the *Times* praises his liberation of the serfs: "All Europe will be thrilled with horror at the intelligence of this tragic termination of a career which was so full of promise at its commencement and which was marked in its earlier stages by great achievements" ("Desperate Revolutionists" 9). It goes on: "To those who were admitted to his intimacy he was a kind-hearted and courteous gentleman, desiring the welfare of his people, and labouring for it to the extent of his powers and his opportunities" (9). Note the qualification: "To the extent of his powers and his *opportunities*." It is in qualifications such as this that we see the disjunction between what has happened in Russia[6] and the version of events the *Times* wants to report, a version which ostensibly supports a reform-minded Czar while seeing his repressive government as necessary in light of excessive demands by the people. The report says:

> The late Czar, there can be little doubt, contemplated reforms much in excess of those which he was able to accomplish, and had intended the emancipation of the serfs to be only his first step in the direction of liberalism and of constitutional freedom. His people were not prepared to use with discretion the boons which he would have been ready to give, and he was forced by events to change his domestic policy for one of repression and reaction. ("Desperate Revolutionists" 9)

In this interpretation of events, it would seem to be the fault of the people that Alexander's regime turned out to be somewhat repressive even if it started as more benevolent than his father's. This serves as an admonition, perhaps, to those in England who encourage mass marches and other protests in support of reform. By their very protests, they prove themselves unworthy of such reforms.

The article on the Czar claims that although he "in great measure realized the reform aspirations of the educated classes," he "carefully guarded his autocratic rights and privileges and rigorously suppressed all attempts to push him further than he felt inclined to go" ("Alexander II" 10). This is, perhaps, another warning to those in England. It seems, according to the *Times,* as though one could not have expected more:

> Though the new institutions [created by the Czar as part of his reforms] have not proved as miraculously effective and beneficent as a sanguine, *inexperienced people expected,* there is no doubt that they have done much good. [...] It would be unfair [...] to compare these institutions with those of Western Europe, where the preparatory work has been going on slowly for many generations. (10, my emphasis)

Not only are his people expecting too much, but history itself is preventing the Czar from succeeding in a full program of reform. The *Times* points out that the Russians are not as "civilized" as the English:

> The [Russian] people labour under the disadvantage of having come late into the race of civilization [...]. The lower classes [...] are scarcely more advanced than the English peasantry of the Wars of the Roses [...]. A lad who in his native village has learnt little more than a superstitious belief in the saints of the Greek Church comes to Moscow or to St. Petersburg as a student or as an artisan, and finds the bookstalls loaded with [...] writings which promise unattainable benefits as the results of the adoption of political changes, and the fallacies which he is too ignorant to discover and too credulous to suspect. ("Desperate Revolutionists" 9)

Those in England who want to see radical reforms are hereby implicitly labeled by the *Times* as superstitious, ignorant and credulous like the Russian peasantry. In addition, proposed political changes will clearly not deliver what they promise. It is significant that the *Times* specifies students and artisans, for it was typically the artisan class and the intellectuals in England who supported radical reform.[7]

The Czar's assassin had been described as a "thick-set, short-necked, repulsive-looking, dark man" ("Assassination of the Emperor" 5), suggesting racial degeneration, which helps to separate the Russians from the English. But this image of seeming racial degeneration also evokes not only the racial othering of the working classes in England, but the simianization of the Irish that was common during the nineteenth century. This simianization was epitomized by the *Punch* cartoon that appeared on 20 May 1882, titled the "Irish Frankenstein," and depicted the Phoenix Park murders. It shows a cowering bewhiskered English gentleman facing an assailant twice his size—"the baneful and blood-stained Monster" says the caption—who is wielding a bloody knife and whose ape-like face and stubbly hair mark him as racially degenerate. Of course, the confusion of Dr. Frankenstein with his monster in the labeling here, and the well-known image from Mary Shelley's novel of the monster stabbing Frankenstein's young, beautiful and innocent bride as she lay on

THE IRISH FRANKENSTEIN.

"The baneful and blood-stained Monster * * * yet was it not my Master to the very extent that it was my Creature ? * * * Had I not breathed into it my own spirit ? " * * * (*Extract from the Works of* C. S. P-RN-LL, M.P.

Fig. 2.2 "Irish Frankenstein" (*Punch*, 20 May 1882)

the marriage bed, serves both to confuse the issue—who, after all, has created this monster?—and to heighten the racial tension by bringing to the fore all the echoes of sexual threat and promiscuity. L. Perry Curtis writes of the Irish in Victorian caricature:

> [T]he transformation of Paddy from a harmless or primitive peasant into a ferocious hybrid of man and ape became a way of not only justifying harsh measures against the agents of aggressive nationalism and agrarian outrage but of dismissing the political aspirations underlying those acts. (xi)

Racial degeneracy justifies harsh suppression in both Moscow and London. The narrative that the *Times*'s writer develops around the Czar's assassin is one that creates a "meaningful moral drama," or a class-based morality tale out of the frightening events occurring in the mid-1880s.[8]

"A fund of fanatical ardour"

In December 1884 the *Times* ran a report every day for a week, telegraphed in by its correspondent in Leipzig, on the trial of the Germans accused of an abortive attempt to blow up the Emperor of Germany, the King of Saxony and other dignitaries at the unveiling of a national monument. There are eight prisoners,[9] anarchists who belong, we are told, "without exception to the working class" ("Trial of German Dynamitards" 3). Among those on trial is Reinsdorf, the master-mind behind the group, and Rupsch, a young man who claims to have been unable, through want of courage, to carry out the assassination.

As Brown has indicated, communication being what it was, the *Times*'s London office could not exert much control over correspondents abroad, nor assess "what influences were being exerted" (Brown 211). For this reason the newspaper often used as correspondents those who had ties with the British embassy in the city in which they worked; they felt it was better that the correspondent be a mouthpiece for the British government than for a foreign one. However, in this case the *Times* correspondent (probably, at this time, Lowe who was based in Berlin) had been an eyewitness at the trial of the German dynamitards and was not merely parroting local sources. It seems the *Times*'s London staff had neither the time nor the inclination to edit reports from abroad in the days before 1891 when the paper's Foreign Department was created, so telegraphed reports from foreign correspondents and from the Reuters news service were printed verbatim (Brown 234), as were the reports, apparently, from the eyewitness reporter at the trial of the German dynamitards. He began his reporting on the trial by showing a great deal of sympathy for the prisoners. He notes that "All show a degree of education and intelligence above the average of their class, and each expresses himself with clearness and fluency" ("German Dynamitards" 18 Dec. 3). Rupsch, the young man designated to carry out the assassination, is described as "a mere boy with a rather pleasant face" (3). And of Reinsdorf the correspondent writes: "His language was wonderfully well chosen [...] with classical and literary allusions," and he "omitted no opportunity of cross-examining witnesses, detecting with great adroitness any small flaws in their testimony" (3). He goes on to say,

> Reinsdorf [...] has the courage of his opinions, and tries rather to shield than to incriminate his accomplices. He is said to have been noted for his kindheartedness to his fellow-workmen, and to have been remarkably gentle to women and children. (3)

The correspondent notes that the main object of the group's activities was "to show the deep-rooted discontent of the masses by organized demonstrations" (3). On 23 December he telegraphed the news of the sentences that have been handed down, including death for both Reinsdorf and Rupsch. He then summed up the trial, saying,

> And now that the sentence on the accused has been pronounced, I may be permitted to make a few general remarks about this remarkable case. The whole course of the trial has made me feel very vividly what a huge amount of festering discontent there is below the surface of German society. [...] The constant espionage of the German police [...] seems to exercise a degrading effect upon the lower classes [...]. Reinsdorf [...] made a great impression [...]. He is a true idealist possessed by an idea [...]. ("German Dynamitards" 3)

He explains further:

> Under the term "anarchy" he does not seem to understand a State absolutely without government, but one in which the central government is abolished and its place taken by a government "by the people for the people." (3)[10]

He ends with a tribute to Reinsdorf: "[H]is unselfishness in trying to take all the blame and screen his accomplices was one of the more pleasing features of the trial, and one cannot help sympathizing with him up to a certain point" (3).

Interestingly, the *Times* ran an article on the same day in which, in its usual authoritative narrative voice, it seems to refute much of what has been expressed by its eyewitness correspondent in Leipzig. In contrast to the correspondent's sympathetic attitude towards Reinsdorf, it emphasizes his initial description of Reinsdorf's appearance, saying, "he is described by our Correspondent as 'tall, thin, and haggard, with keen and deep-set eyes, and the lean and hungry look that is popularly supposed to mark the conspirator.' [...] He is eloquent, very influential among his companions and 'believed to be possessed of a dangerous power of moulding others to his will'" ("Trial of the German Dynamite Conspirators" 7). The leader writer sums up Reinsdorf thus: "His conduct during the trial showed him to be endowed with great acuteness of mind and with a fund of fanatical ardour which mark him out as emphatically a dangerous man" (7). Of course, this is not at all the impression we are left with from the correspondent who witnessed the trial. The article goes on to say, "Reinsdorf is an extremist no doubt and he is guilty of an overt act which no State can tolerate or pardon" (7). The reader is not allowed any feelings of sympathy for a man fighting for what appears to be democracy of a sort. In the slippage between the correspondent's reporting and the *Times*'s leading article, we are aware of the "spin" the editors are putting on events. The *History of the Times* points out that the young editor at this time, George Earle Buckle, saw it as the purpose of the paper to "obtain authentic information of political, social and economic affairs and to comment upon them without regard to private ambitions or interests" (*History* 3:13). Later the *History* claims "the paper was resolutely impersonal just as the staff was absolutely anonymous" (3: 16). Despite these good intentions claimed later, the *Times*'s leader writer wants to leave his readers with a specific impression of the German dynamitards: they do not deserve sympathy.

"Towards Democracy, as towards Death"

The *Times*'s lack of objectivity is shown on 15 April 1885, when the paper reports on and quotes liberally from an article which had been run in the *Quarterly Review*, under the title "Age of Progress," one of a series in which, according to the *Times*, "the 'Nature of Democracy' and the ideas connected therewith are subjected to a searching analysis" ("New Number of the *Quarterly Review*" 9).[11] The *Quarterly Review* article asks, "What is the origin of this zeal for political movement which is gradually identifying itself with a taste for Democracy, and what is its justification? [...] The natural condition of mankind [...] is not the progressive condition [...]. The immobility of society is the rule" (qtd. in "New number" 9).[12] The *Times*'s writer interjects here that "the historical truth of these propositions cannot be disputed," and adds that "if we examine man [...] we find him intensely conservative in his habits and his manners; while women almost universally are steadfast opponents of change"(9). So conservative, indeed, is the natural and non-political man that he still retains a good deal of the savage: "Like the savage, the Englishman, Frenchman, or American makes war; like the savage, he hunts," and so on. "Like the savage, he is a man of party, with a newspaper for totem." As to the voice of the people: "In reality," says the *Quarterly Review* as quoted in the *Times*, "the devotee of Democracy is much in the same position as the Greeks with their oracles. All agreed that the voice of an oracle was the voice of a god; but everybody allowed that when he spoke he was not as intelligible as might be desired" (9). The *Quarterly Review* goes on to suggest "a general belief that, in these matters, we are propelled by an irresistible force on a definite path towards an unavoidable end—towards Democracy, as towards Death" (9).

The *Times*'s writer characterizes the article as "brilliant" and, after judiciously and politely complaining about one small aspect of the writer's style, notes, "But we are less concerned with the character of the writer's opinions, or with his mode of giving expression to them, than with the amount of truth and instruction they convey" ("New number" 9). And he notes that the article "offers much food for reflection" (9). The *Times* is clearly sympathetic to what turns out to be a blatant condemnation of democracy and far from the "searching analysis" the *Times* claimed.

It was under Buckle's editorship in the 1880s that the *Times* began to be seen, and indeed to see itself, as an institution. Buckle saw his task as not only reporting the news objectively, but maintaining the paper as the "best" (as well as the biggest) paper that the "educated Englishman" could read, a sentiment which kept him in line with the Chief Proprietor. For "[f]rom the beginning of his career, [John] Walter was, for him, a Chief Proprietor to be served" (*History* 3:9). Furthermore, says the *History of the Times*, two generations before, under the controversial editorship of Barnes, the paper was read "throughout the country and reached every class," whereas in the 1880s under Buckle, "[t]he audience for which the paper was produced had gradually defined itself and had begun even [...] to exercise an influence upon the conductors of the paper it chose to read" (15). That the writers of the *History of the Times* (written in the 1940s) see no tension here between Buckle's belief in objective reporting, his serving the Chief Proprietor and his being influenced by his audience—not now of every class—seems to be symptomatic of the attitude of the paper itself during the last years of the nineteenth century. In its ongoing reporting during the early 1880s under the editorship of Buckle, on issues such as democracy, anarchy and terrorism, there is a constant questioning of political reform. The *Times*'s voice and attitude express the old world-view, one which saw the social class system as not only fixed, but absolutely natural. Though some of its correspondents were influenced, it would seem, by a world outside of Printing House Square.[13]

"Some sinister anarchic underworld, heaving in its pain"

In the 1880s, anarchy and revolution, dynamite and guns became the topic of fiction, probably in part due to the wide coverage of terrorist attacks in the press.[14] A new genre appeared which has been labeled by Barbara Arnett Melchiori as the "dynamite novels" (2).[15] While they have plots based in terrorism or revolution, according to Melchiori, they are not revolutionary novels:

> [H]owever up-to-date in content, their tone and message belong to the past. [...] Dynamite found its way into fiction but did little to disrupt either the form of the novel or the social *mores* with which it was dealing. [...] Security may be tottering, but money, social position and a "good" wife are the status symbols awarded to those who stand firm against the attacks on society, while the dynamitard, as often as not, is hoist with this own petard. (222)

While Melchiori sees *The Princess Casamassima* as indistinct from the other novels of revolution she studies, I view James's approach as far more revolutionary. Though one has to admit that Hyacinth, James's terrorist hero, could be said to have been "hoist[ed] with his own petard," as I have said, in *The Princess* James uses a narrative technique that is less authoritative than the narrative voice of the traditional realistic novel, and refuses to offer a comprehensible explanation of the situation. And as Marcia Jacobson observes in *Henry James and the Mass Market*, James rejects the sentimental solutions to the problems of the working classes commonly seen in popular novels published around the same time such as Walter Besant's *All Sorts and Conditions of Men* (1882) and *Children of Gibeon* (1886). In the process, James helps to disrupt the middle-class stance that had held sway in much of realist fiction.

In his 1909 New York Edition Preface to *The Princess Casamassima*, James writes,

> My scheme called for the suggested nearness (to all our apparently ordered life) of some sinister anarchic underworld, heaving in its pain, its power and its hate; a presentation not of sharp particulars, but of loose appearances, vague motions and sounds and symptoms, just perceptible presences and general looming possibilities. (47)

Although one cannot read the preface necessarily as evidence of James's original intention at the time of writing, it does describe well what he managed to accomplish. He evokes the same sinister anarchic underworld which often seems present, as I have said, in suggestion rather than in fact, in the *Times*. But the only truly revolutionary moment in James's plot is avoided because Hyacinth, like Rupsch, the real-life revolutionary reported on in the *Times*, is unable to act. Revolution is not so much a physical threat in this novel as it is a perceptible part of the atmosphere felt by Hyacinth:

> [T]he forces secretly arrayed against the present social order were pervasive and universal, in the air one breathed, in the ground one trod, in the hand of an acquaintance that one might touch, or the eye of a stranger that might rest a moment on one's own. They were above, below, within, without, in every contact and combination of life. (486)

So just as the *Times* had created a sense of impending but somewhat indistinct crisis through its reporting on terrorist acts abroad and on the growing threat of democracy at home, so James impregnated the atmosphere of his novel with the same blurry sense of coming turmoil.

"The old ferocious selfishnesses *must* come down"

The Princess Casamassima was serialized in the *Atlantic* from September 1885 through October 1886, and then published in London in book form in 1886. Published in the same year as James's all-American novel *The Bostonians* (1886), *The Princess Casamassima* and his subsequent novels, *The Tragic Muse* (1890) and *What Maisie*

Knew (1896), are notable for their lack of American characters. They are novels that demonstrate James's concern with the current state of affairs in England, his adopted home. That state of affairs as far as the working classes were concerned was grim, and so the topic of working-class unrest and brewing revolution that James makes use of in *The Princess* was a startlingly timely one.

James's version of revolution and terrorism comes with a cast of sympathetic characters and what appears to be a worthwhile cause from what little we know of it. Indeed, James's characters more closely resemble the German dynamitards described by the *Times*'s Leipzig correspondent. Hyacinth Robinson is intended to be an appealing character despite the fact that he has pledged to carry out some order handed down by the international revolutionary organization, an order that we feel fairly sure will involve the assassination of someone important. Hyacinth is the son of a certain Lord Frederick and a poor French seamstress. Having impregnated the French woman, Lord Frederick had abandoned her and left her with nothing but Hyacinth, whose existence, therefore, is the very concrete result of class exploitation. Before the novel opens, the seamstress is imprisoned for having taken revenge by stabbing the unscrupulous Lord to death. Hyacinth had been adopted by a poor woman and brought up among working people. He characterizes himself as "the bastard of a murderess, spawned in a gutter, out of which he had been picked up by a sewing-girl" (445).[16] He grows up to be an artistic binder of books who aspires to write and to whom everyone in the novel is drawn. He is a sympathetic assassin and is not a product of racial degeneracy.

As for the Princess Casamassima, she appears to be sincere in her radical beliefs, even though, for Hyacinth when he is staying at the grand country estate the Princess has rented, "it added much to the way life practised on his sense of the tragic-comical to think of the Princess's having retired to that magnificent residence in order to concentrate her mind upon the London slums" (309). The Princess has left her husband and come to England to become part of a revolutionary cause, and she eventually gives up her aristocratic way of life and goes to live in a small house with ugly things in order to show her commitment to socialist principles. She disdains the idea of class division, saying, "I have very little respect for distinctions of class—the sort of thing they make so much of in this country" (247). In this she echoes the radical upper-class ladies in Russia about whom the *Pall Mall Gazette* ran an article on 9 May 1882: "High-born and wealthy ladies betook themselves to the factory, worked fifteen and sixteen hours a day at the machine, slept in dog-holes with peasants, went barefoot as our working women go, bringing water for the house" (4). They apparently wanted to bring about government reform that was not based merely on theory. The *PMG* praised these efforts, describing them as "an enthusiasm which outside Russia seems almost to have perished from the world!"(4) Whether James had read the article in the *Pall Mall Gazette* is not clear, but his American princess seems to have been suggested at least to some extent by these events in Russia.

The Princess is a character that James recycled from *Roderick Hudson*, written ten years before. In that novel she is Christina Light, a character born, apparently illegitimately, of an American mother and an Italian father, neither of whom were aristocratic. She had been attracted to Roderick Hudson, a sculptor of some talent, who killed himself when she married the Prince Casamassima. There is clearly some parallel here; perhaps the handsome, young, artistic bookbinder reminds Christina, in her reincarnation as the Princess, of her former love—perhaps even more so when he, too, kills himself partly in the belief that she is the lover of someone else.

Hyacinth's first view of the Princess significantly enough takes place at the theater:

> [T]here was an extraordinary *light* nobleness in the way she held her head. That head [...] suggested to Hyacinth something antique and celebrated, which he had admired of old [...] and Hyacinth [...] wondered whether she were not altogether of some different substance from the humanity he had hitherto known. She might be divine [...]. (191-2, my emphasis)

John Lucas writes that "in Hyacinth's initial vision of the Princess we have also an embodiment of the old, civilized values" ("Conservatism" 196). He goes on to say, "I see no point in trying to argue that the passage is ironic, that Hyacinth is too ignorant to realize that the Princess is no high-born lady but Christina Light. For James has totally altered her from the girl who appeared in *Roderick Hudson*" (196). Yet how is it possible not to argue some irony? Why would James reuse this character from a novel he wrote ten years before—a technique rare enough in James—if he had not intended to allude to her past? One concludes, then, that her past *is* important. Ignoring the word *light* in the beginning of this passage, Lucas misses the point, which is that she can be totally altered from the girl who appeared in the previous novel and yet still be the same person. This is why it is significant that Hyacinth first sees her in a theater; she is performing her role, in much the same way that we are told of Hyacinth that "he was to go through life in a mask, in a borrowed, mantle; he was to be, every day and every hour an actor" (109).[17]

The two most important characters in this novel—Hyacinth and the Princess—are both class "passers." The Princess is in some sense passing, since she started out as Christina Light, an illegitimate child, like Hyacinth, with origins of questionable class status, but is now married to a wealthy Neapolitan prince. Hyacinth also passes in two ways: he keeps his aristocratic forebears a secret on the one hand, but when he visits the Princess, ostensibly as her official bookbinder, she treats him as a guest in her palatial country home and so in this situation he is passing as upper-class. The Princess has him pass as upper-class with some of her neighbours—the Marchants—and is delighted when they do not discern the truth about his working-class status. All of this suggests that beneath the ordered surface of class distinctions there is, in this novel, less distinction than one might expect, for much of the perceived distinction depends on the performance of class.

Also fairly sympathetic is James's socialist leader, Paul Muniment, a chemist's assistant from Lancashire. Hero-worshipped by Hyacinth, who sees him as a possible future prime minister—note his appropriate initials—Muniment is also adored by all the women in his life. Even his bed-ridden sister, Rosie, idolizes him, though she greatly admires the aristocracy and opposes her brother's socialist ideas. Lady Aurora and the Princess—two women clearly above his own class—both appear to be in love with Muniment, and both share his political views. Though Paul does not attempt to pass as higher in social class than he is, he seems to transcend class, especially for the women who love him. In writing about Muniment, Melchiori is willing to admit that he "is given in this novel [...] the characteristics not of a fanatic but a single-minded and extremely competent man [...]. James put across Muniment's arguments with considerable fairness" (34). But she goes on to argue:

> [B]y the simple fact of making him an industrial chemist, and by drawing attention to the stains on his hands, [James] contrives to throw suspicion on his activities in the eyes of the contemporary reader and to invite the chemist-dynamiter connection which, inevitably, discredits the ideas of a man who might otherwise appear to attack the established order all too convincingly, and even to have a workable alternative to offer. (34)

But, in my view, the opposite is true. Muniment's ability to transcend class marks him as someone whom James's readers cannot despise as a "thick-set, short-necked, repulsive-looking, dark man," as was the Czar's assassin in the *Times*'s reports. Though working-class, Muniment can command the respect not only of the other characters in the book, but of the reader, contemporary or otherwise.

James expands his depiction of sympathetic revolutionary characters even to Poupin, Hyacinth's work-mate, who is a Frenchman unable to go back to France because of his radical views. Poupin and his wife are warm, friendly people who love Hyacinth and who want to stop him killing the Duke because they know this act will put his own life in danger. As Margaret Scanlan remarks, "For James, as for Karl Marx, the French were the exemplary revolutionary nation, and no general meditation on revolutionary principles could ignore them" (384). It is, of course, Jacobinism that is feared, with the increasing of the franchise and a coming democracy in England, so it is particularly significant that James should make this French couple so completely non-threatening.

While Lady Aurora is not overtly a revolutionary, she is at least a rather radical aristocrat. She visits and helps the poor, including Paul's bed-ridden sister. She spends much of her time explaining to Hyacinth why she prefers the poor to the rich, whom she denigrates: "she knew a great deal about the poor [...] she was often struck with their great talents, with their quick wit, with their conversation being really much more entertaining, to her at least, than what one usually heard in drawing-rooms. She often found them immensely clever" (218). Middle-class readers would have enjoyed the slighting here of the aristocracy, while at the same time appreciating the gentle irony aimed at poor Lady Aurora, who is so taken with Muniment and so intent on being sympathetic to the poor that she can find them quick of wit and entertaining, characteristics not often found in literary depictions of the poor.

James, then, makes his little band of revolutionaries sympathetic, a move which must have gone against the grain for Londoners who were experiencing Fenian terrorist attacks fairly frequently, and who were reading the bloody details in the *Times*. Whereas the Fenians depicted in *Punch* and anarchists depicted in the *Times* are robbed of their dignity and therefore their right to a political voice, James gives revolution a dignified, sympathetic face—at least as far as Hyacinth and Paul are concerned. And while—except for Paul—his revolutionaries are mostly foreign, in keeping with the *Times*'s reports of foreign terrorist organizations, James makes it clear that the cause they are fighting for is a decidedly English one. We hear of "the deep perpetual groan of London misery" (283); it is a "huge tragic city where unmeasured misery lurked beneath the dirty night" (293). We are told that "about half a million people in London [...] didn't know where [...] the morrow's meal was to come from" (291). The Princess, who has visited the slums, says, "in the depths of this huge, luxurious, wanton, wasteful city we have seen sights of unspeakable misery and horror" (464), and she asks Hyacinth, "what do you propose for the thousands and thousands for whom no work on the overcrowded earth, under the pitiless heaven—is to be found? [...] The old ferocious selfishnesses *must* come down. They won't come down gracefully, so they must be smashed" (573). While it could be argued that the beauty of the language James uses to describe the misery of the city serves to aestheticize the problem rather than to solve it, still James does not attempt to ameliorate the problem by offering a facile solution.

"Omniscient authority is held up to scrutiny and indicted"

Because of the circumstances of his birth, Hyacinth is the embodiment of the struggle between the radical left and the aristocratic right, and a sort of psychomachia between these two factions takes place within him. For while Hyacinth wants to preserve the culture he has come to know through the Princess, a culture associated with the aristocracy, he is not bent on saving the aristocracy for its own sake, but on saving art and beauty. As one critic points out, Hyacinth "anticipates Walter Benjamin's argument that there is 'no document of civilization which is not at the same time a document of barbarism.'"[18]   So that while James in this novel is indeed concerned with inequality and social unrest, he tries to bring this debate into a new arena; he tries to define the debate in terms of art.

Perhaps for that reason, for much of the twentieth century James was seen by critics as a non-political novelist: "[a] technical and formalist emphasis has dominated Jamesian criticism, and problems of social reference have characteristically been converted into problems of textual self-reference" (Seltzer 14). And the more overt intersection in *The Princess Casamassima* between politics and fiction prompted a critical debate, as has been noted, over the accuracy of James's portrayal of the threat of terrorism in 1880s London. The accuracy debate has recently been, to some extent, supplanted by a discussion of ways in which this novel is revolutionary, a debate which seeks to combine the Jamesian aesthetic with the subtly political. Margaret Scanlan, for example, aligns Hyacinth's revolutionary project with James's own revolutionary bid to create an art novel. She sees *The Princess* as "an exploration of a terror shared alike by novelist and revolutionary that, no matter how they plot, they will never change the world" (382). Mark Seltzer's Foucauldian reading finds ways in which Panoptical surveillance can be said to represent both the form and function of the novel. And what earlier critics see as an ignorance on the part of the narrator in this text, Seltzer sees as a displacement of authority. [19] As Seltzer notes, James seems to have given over to Hoffendahl, the leader of this international revolutionary group, the omniscient role that had traditionally been reserved for the narrator. Hoffendahl, we are told by the narrator, "had in his hand innumerable [...] threads. Hyacinth knew nothing of these, and didn't much want to know" (334). Hoffendahl is described as a great musician: "he treated all things, persons, institutions, ideas, as so many notes in his great symphonic revolt" (334). Hoffendahl not only knows everything, but appears to be orchestrating the plot. And by using the analogy of the musician, James assigns Hoffendahl a role similar to that of a Jamesian-style novelist, one who turns life into art.

In this novel, James turns away from the omniscient authority of the narrative voice used in the *Times* and in many Victorian novels, a voice that explained and interpreted all events through middle-class values, thereby helping to shore up the sense of that world-view as dominant. James is thus writing a fiction that represents a more democratic world-view. In contrast to the all-knowing, omniscient narrator of old, the narrator of *The Princess* often seems to be in the dark, and therefore so is the reader, while Hoffendahl and his "party" are said to know all: "They know everything—everything" (559). Even though Hyacinth is the point-of-view character for much of the novel, the narrator does not follow him to Hoffendahl's inner sanctum. We do not know about the oath Hyacinth has taken until he later reveals it to the Princess. And when Schinkel is delegated by the Party to pass on to Hyacinth the letter containing the order to kill the Duke, he does not do so immediately even though Hyacinth—and indeed the reader—have anticipated this order through half the novel. Hyacinth must walk home through the streets of London with Schinkel, who has the letter in his pocket, in an agonizingly long and drawn-out scene. Schinkel gradually reveals through a narrative how he came to have the letter. Schinkel usurps some of the narrator's authority by demonstrating in his narration that he, too, has the power to withhold or reveal knowledge. When Hyacinth finally opens the letter, the contents are not revealed to the reader because, it would seem, the narrator cannot read over Hyacinth's shoulder. The economy of this novel is one based on knowledge, and the perception of who has power through that knowledge. And in contrast to the traditional Victorian novel, James manages cleverly to intimate that it is seldom the narrator.

The extent of the knowledge held by various characters is sometimes thrown into question. Schinkel suggests to Hyacinth that because Paul did not receive the letter containing Hyacinth's orders, it must mean that, at headquarters, Paul is not trusted with such knowledge. Paul then tells Christina that *she* is not trusted at headquarters.

But she tells Hyacinth, "I know you won't be called [...]. Mr. Muniment tells me so [...]. We have information. My dear fellow [...] you are so much out of it now that if I were to tell you, you wouldn't understand" (573). What is ironic and somewhat pathetic about Christina's bid to be an all-knowing and powerful party member is that she claims to "have information" *after* Hyacinth has received his order to kill the Duke—one of the rare moments in the book in which the reader knows more than a character. And finally, at the end of the book, no one knows what has happened to Hyacinth, until Christina and Schinkel find him laid out on his bed. For I must disagree with Seltzer's conclusion: though Hoffendahl appears to have all the knowledge and therefore all the power, he fails to fulfill the same function as the omniscient narrator. We never meet him and do not hear his voice, a voice that, as omniscient narrator, would presumably have helped us to interpret, understand, and digest these events.

"Revolution was ripe at last"

It is an interesting point that, as in Gissing's *The Nether World*, we do not meet the middle classes in the pages of this book. James does present us with upper-class characters, however, and so in his novel we see a contrast between social extremes: the proletariat and the aristocracy. Hyacinth, of course, embodies the struggle between these two groups. The aristocracy is, on the whole, certainly not shown as sympathetic: the Prince, husband of the Princess Casamassima, is seen as impotent, wanting to control his wife and caring more for his old family name than for her. The Princess describes Captain Sholto as "one of those strange beings produced by old societies that have run to seed, corrupt, exhausted civilisations. He was a cumberer of the earth, and purely selfish" (352). And Paul Muniment says of what he calls the "pampered classes": "their bloated luxury begets evil [...] they are capable of doing harm for the sake of harm" (207). It is not a sentiment that is strongly gainsaid by the ethos of this book.

But what of the bourgeoisie? By excluding them, James contravenes the conventions of the so-called social problem novels published earlier in the century, which had largely been written by and for the middle classes. These took place largely in a middle-class world, and their resolutions usually were designed to bring comfort to the middle-class reader. Generally, violent protesters were seen as aberrant, while generous middle-class characters helped the "deserving" working-class characters, who were "deserving" in that they willingly participated not only in the existing order of the social classes, but in middle-class values, too.[20]

In Elizabeth Gaskell's *North and South* (1855), for example, a novel that also deals with proletarian unrest, the protesting strikers are made to seem like animals. In the chapter entitled "A Blow and Its Consequences," the striking workers of Milton finally take to the streets and converge on John Thornton's mill. While the crowd of strikers tries to break down the gates, the narrator begins to describe them in terms of wild beasts. Their anger is unleashed when they hear Thornton's voice:

it "seemed to have been like the taste of blood to the infuriated multitude outside." And the narrator tells us, "[H]earing [Thornton] speak inside, they set up a fierce unearthly groan" (174). The strikers are described as emitting sounds rather than speech: they were "sending forth their awful threatening roar" (175), and a "fierce growl ... that had a ferocious murmur of satisfaction" (176), or a noise "inarticulate as that of a troop of animals" (177). They "set up a yell,—to call it not human is nothing—it was as the demoniac desire of some terrible wild beast for the food that is withheld from his ravening" (176). To the reader, then, the strikers become wild beasts just as the Irish who were portrayed in *Punch* cartoons. As with the simianization of the Irish, this serves not only to eliminate our sympathy and any possibility that we would see the strikers as having a legitimate cause for which to fight, but justifies harsh measures such as the summoning of the soldiers in order to break up the mob. In *North and South*, it is Nicholas Higgins who is deserving of the middle-class sympathy he receives from the Hale family, not the violent strikers. Nicholas is a union man, but he is not a supporter of the riot. He is willing to protest bad pay, but not willing to resort to violent measures. He feels he is fighting "for justice and fair play" (133); it is not just a matter of personal greed with him. Nicholas clearly understands middle-class values; when he goes to tea with Mr. Hale after the death of his daughter, he says, "I should m'appen ha'cleaned mysel', first?" (223). The need for cleanliness is a point that is always important in novels with a middle-class world-view, and a value the deserving poor must share.

In Gaskell's riot scene, not only the middle classes but more specifically middle-class women are under attack, since the scene is narrated from the point of view of Margaret Hale and Mrs. Thornton, who view the riot from the drawing room in the Thornton house next to the mill. This narrative choice on Gaskell's part makes the rioters seem even more threatening, because it puts the reader firmly on the side of the threatened women and against the striking workers. When James describes a scene in *The Princess* similar to the riot scene in *North and South*, there are no middle-class people in direct danger from physical attack, allowing the reader to be far more open to the cause of the workers, and to such statements as that by Poupin that "in the east of London, that night, there were forty thousand men out of work" (284).

In James's scene, a group of workers gathers for a meeting in the back room of the Sun and Moon tavern where, we are told, "it was brought home to our hero on more than one occasion that revolution was ripe at last" (284). Some critics have found James's description of the socialist meetings at the Sun and Moon derogatory; Derek Brewer, for example, in his introduction to the novel writes, "The discontented starving working men who met in the dirty smoky club-room of the 'Sun and Moon' speak foolishly and repetitively" (11). And the main characters are not necessarily complimentary about their fellow socialists: Hyacinth, once he has met Hoffendahl, sees the activity at the Sun and Moon as "a hopeless sham" (328), because he has, in all seriousness, pledged his life for the cause. Yet we have Paul Muniment who says of them: "The low tone of our fellow-mortals is a result of bad conditions; it is the conditions I want to alter. When those that have no start to speak of have a good one, it is but fair to infer that they will go further. I want to try them, you know" (444). Hyacinth's view of those with whom he is fighting for revolution is often one that appears less than sympathetic:

> [H]e was absorbed with the struggles and sufferings of the millions whose life flowed in the same current as his, and who, though they constantly excited his disgust, and made him shrink and turn away, had the power to chain his sympathy, to make it glow to a kind of ecstasy, to convince him, for the time at least, that real success in the world would be to do something with them and for them. (160)

And later:

> [H]e thought the people in his own class generally very stupid—what he should call third-rate minds. He wished it were not so, for heaven knew that he felt kindly to them and only asked to cast his lot with theirs; but he was obliged to confess that centuries of poverty, of ill-paid toil, of bad, insufficient food and wretched homes had not a favourable effect upon the higher faculties. (217)

One has to admit that this passage is confusing, for James appears to be blaming the environment for the poor thinking capacity of the working classes. Yet where does Hyacinth fit into this scheme? He was brought up by Pinnie and has been obliged to work for his living; yet he is artistic, has the ability to speak French easily, and his bearing prompts the Princess to say of him, "He's a tremendous aristocrat" (463). The only reason we have to explain all this is his blood, his aristocratic father. As Hyacinth himself says, "I have blood in my veins that is not the blood of the people" (219). James, then, seems to be skirting the issue here, having it both ways. Does he believe, like Gissing, in the effects of environmental conditions, or does he believe in "race," that blurry term used in the nineteenth century to describe inherited traits?

One thing is certain, the discussion at the Sun and Moon is what inspires Hyacinth to take his oath: "there was genuine emotion, to-night, in the rear of the 'Sun and Moon', and he felt the contagion of excited purpose" even though "[t]he loud, contradictory, vain, unpractical babble went on about him" (291). But all the same, "[h]e was in a state of inward exaltation [...] a breath of popular passion had passed over him, and he seemed to see, immensely magnified, the monstrosity of the great ulcers and sores of London—sick, eternal misery crying, in the darkness, in vain" (291). Despite his ability to see the workers around him without sentimentality, Hyacinth is ready to act for and with them:

> If he had a definite wish while he stood there it was that that exalted, deluded company should pour itself forth, with Muniment at its head, and surge through the sleeping city, gathering the myriad miserable out of their slums and burrows, and roll into the selfish squares, and lift a tremendous hungry voice, and waken the gorged indifferent to a terror that would bring them down. (293)

But characteristically, the revolutionaries at the Sun and Moon disperse jovially, again accomplishing nothing. James has not only avoided making his protesters threatening to the middle classes; ultimately they seem to pose no threat at all.

In Gaskell's *North and South* the union of the factions that have been at loggerheads is symbolized at the end by the marriage of John Thornton and Margaret Hale. But this very merger serves to underscore the class assumptions of the narrator. The teleology of Gaskell's novel works towards a utopic vision of a society in which the classes can live in harmony by getting to know each other and being more understanding, one in which all "recognize that 'we have all of us one human heart'" (422). But this utopia does not include the elimination of the social class system, nor a true crossing of boundaries. It sees the social class system as fixed; the solution to the problem of class exploitation lies in each class taking responsibility for its position in that system and being willing at the same time to have sympathy for those on other levels, whether higher or lower. It is, in the end, a utopia from the middle-class point of view *only*.

Earlier novelists such as Gaskell had tried to find ways to render class inequality acceptable and to diffuse tense class situations by proposing idealistic, sentimentalized solutions. James did not present a solution to the problems he depicted. He was not trying to mitigate the problems of the poor and give succor and comfort to the middle-class reader who felt threatened by the current situation in England. But neither did he see revolution as the answer to the problems he points to; the very fact that Hyacinth is unable to carry out his mission and must commit suicide is proof of this. In the end James's novel is about the problem of discourse surrounding class-based problems, not a solution to the problems themselves.

"Mr. Robinson has shot himself through the heart"

While James does not seek to appease the middle class, and even though he clearly acknowledges the problems that exist for the working classes in London, this book is not James's support of, or plea for, a socialist or an anarchist revolution. For although James may write as an American and therefore an outsider to the English social class system, still one cannot dispute the fact that James himself derived advantages from his own and his family's social standing. With the ending of *The Princess Casamassima*, then, James leaves everything unresolved, except for the fate of the bookbinder. Hyacinth's suicide leaves him lying in a scene resembling that of the death of Chatterton, as painted by Henry Wallis in 1856. This allusion to Wallis's painting suggests we are to see Hyacinth ultimately as a poet rather than a political activist.[21] The status of Paul Muniment has been left in some doubt by his exclusion from circumstances concerning Hyacinth's orders from the party, and the Princess's status has been questioned by Muniment, who suspects her of running back to her husband as soon as the Prince cuts off her allowance. And, as has been noted, the brave souls at the Sun and Moon have accomplished little towards their revolution.

But there *is* something subtly revolutionary going on here.

The words James saves for the end of the novel are revolutionary. The scene is the discovery of Hyacinth dead on his bed:

> [Schinkel] had determined to remain calm, so that [...] he was able to say, very quietly and gravely, "Mr. Robinson has shot himself through the heart," [...] and then Schinkel perceived the small revolver lying just under the bed. He picked it up and carefully placed it on the mantel-shelf, keeping, equally carefully, to himself the reflection that it would certainly have served much better for the Duke. (590-91)

This leaves us with a revolutionary ending in more than one sense. Because these words are given the place of importance as the novel's last words, they leave a question as to whether perhaps James is indeed supporting the idea of revolutionary assassination. However, since it is a Duke who is threatened, a member of an aristocracy that has already been condemned in this novel, the revolutionary threat is somewhat muted. But as I have been arguing, James's novel embodies a more democratic world-view than had been possible earlier in the century. For James's character, Schinkel, is suggesting an alternate ending to the novel; in so doing he is rebelling against the plot devised by the narrator/author, and in democratic fashion, the narrator is allowing him to do so.

This chapter started with two men—one of them Lord Frederick Cavendish— stabbed to death and lying dead on tables in a room whose luxury contrasted dramatically with their butchered bodies. It ends with a young man lying dead on a bed in a room that was far more modest. Intriguingly, Hyacinth is the son of a certain Lord Frederick who also had been stabbed to death. James's "little bookbinder" is a writer *manqué*; rather than binding books, he wants to *write* them,[22] thus the Chatterton-like death scene is pregnant with poetic echoes.

Thomas Chatterton (1752-70), with whom Hyacinth seems to be identified here, was a young poet who had been inspirational to some of the young Romantics early in the nineteenth century. He killed himself at the age of seventeen because his poetic genius had gone unappreciated and he was close to starvation. James's own identification with Hyacinth Robinson has often been remarked by critics. That he should then suggest an identification between Hyacinth and Chatterton may point to the fact that James in some ways identifies with Chatterton, too. For like the young poet's, James's work, despite his genius, was not nearly as remunerative as he would have liked. It is surely the idea of the writer as a victim, perhaps martyr of an uncaring, unappreciative society that the Pre-Raphaelite Wallis emphasizes in his painting and that appeals to James. By sacrificing Hyacinth, in a way similar to the martyrdom of Chatterton, James suggests the incompatibility of poetry and hunger, of low wages and high art.[23] But inasmuch as Hyacinth has been a symbolic character throughout the novel, so his death is symbolic, too. It symbolizes what James sees as the tragic yet insoluble problem of social class. As we saw in "The

Fig. 2.3 Henry Wallis, *Chatterton*, 1856. Oil on canvas (© Tate, London 2005)

Art of Fiction," for James, it is the "truth" revealed in a work of art that matters. For him, this is not simply the truthful depiction of the world in naturalist narrative— even though *The Princess* was seen by James as his most naturalistic work. In this revolutionary novel, he seeks to express a truth about social class that has been distorted by the middle-class narratorial authority of traditional Victorian novels and by the *Times*. By allowing the authority of the narrator to be undermined in his novel, James can at least let his readers envisage the problem without enclosing it in a comfortable, comforting solution.

Notes

[1] The Representation of the People Act 1884 and the Redistribution of Seats Act 1885.

[2] Letter to T.S. Perry, 26 Sept., 1884. Virginia Harlow. *Thomas Sergeant Perry: A Biography* (1950).

[3] See Melchiori for a more complete discussion of the merging of these groups in the press. Melchiori also argues that English novelists continued this blurring of political factions because, unlike Irish novelists, they were unwilling to bring Fenian motives to the forefront for fear of inciting sympathy for the Fenians.

[4] Even Thomas More in his *Utopia* (1516) had used this artifice, telling of a traveler named Raphael Hythloday whom the author encounters and who regales the author with tales of his journey to Utopia. Henry Fielding had, of course, entitled his great work *The History of Tom Jones, a Foundling* (1749), and begins his second chapter by describing Squire Allworthy: "In that Part of the western Division of this Kingdom, which is commonly called Somersetshire, there lately lived (and perhaps lives still) a Gentleman whose Name was Allworthy" (27).

[5] Wesley H. Tilley, *The Background of* The Princess Casamassima. Gainesville: U of Florida P, 1961.

[6] As Hugh Seton-Watson explains, there were various movements by nobles in Russia during Alexander's reign, most notably in Tver province, to achieve reforms and more representative institutions. The Czar ordered a public rebuke for those who signed addresses asking not only for reforms, but, more radically, for an elected authority to ensure against bureaucratic abuse. In 1862, when the Tver nobles resolved to be guided by "the people's wishes" instead of the government, the Czar had them locked up. Seton-Watson writes that the Czar's refusal to entertain any notion of a more representative government "and the repressive action taken against those who proposed such action, mark a turning-point in Russian history. This was the moment, if ever there was one, when the foundations of a Russian parliamentary democracy might have been laid" (48).

[7] Charles Booth writes: "Class E contains those whose lot to-day is most aggravated by a raised ideal. [...] Here, rather than in the ruffianism of Class A, or the starvation of Class B, or the wasted energy of Class C, or the bitter anxieties of Class D, do we find the springs of Socialism and Revolution" (1: 597). In his classification, Class E is the group immediately above the so-called "line of poverty" described as having "Regular standard earnings" and therefore most likely of the artisan class.

[8] Judith Walkowitz has argued that "Narratives of the 'real' such as [...] news reporting, impose a formal coherence on events: they 'narrativize' data into a coherent [...] tale," thus providing a "meaningful moral drama" out of what would otherwise appear to be chaotic experience (*City* 83).

[9] This is one of the groups on which James is believed to have modeled his revolutionaries.

[10] These are, of course, words taken from President Lincoln's *The Gettysburg Address* (19 November 1863).

[11] "The Age of Progress." *Quarterly Review* 159 (1885): 267-98.

[12] Since the focus here is on the *Times*'s reporting, all page references, even for quotations from the article in the *Quarterly Review*, refer to the pages of the *Times*.

[13] Home of the *Times*.

[14] Dynamite was invented by Nobel in 1863, and the fulminate of mercury detonating process in 1867.

[15] Examples are Grant Allen's *For Maimie's Sake: A Tale of Love and Dynamite* (1886), Eliza Lynn Linton's *The Autobiography of Christopher Kirkland* (1885), George Gissing's *Demos* (1886), W.H. Mallock's *The Old Order Changes* (1886), and the humorous collection of stories by Robert Louis Stevenson and his wife, Fanny Van de Grift, *More New Arabian Nights: The Dynamiter* (1885).

[16] The Penguin edition of James's novel has been used here because it reproduces the first edition of 1886, except, of course, for the Preface. Even though the New York Edition of 1909 obviously represents James's later refinement of the novel, it seems more appropriate to use the version produced in the 1880s, because I examine the text in the context of that time.

[17] It is significant that James uses the metaphor of the *mantle* here because it is the same metaphor that Lord Randolph Churchill had used in his famous *Fortnightly Review* article, "Elijah's Mantle" (1883), on the unveiling of a statue of Lord Beaconsfield. Churchill bemoans on this occasion the lost power of the Tories and hopes that his version of democracy, what he calls Tory Democracy, will rally the support of the working classes for whoever will step into Disraeli's shoes, "whoever he may be, upon whom the mantle of Elijah has descended" (621). Appropriately, Churchill's is a version of democracy which echoes the vision of Young England, a vision which, in James's novel, is depicted as blatantly untenable.

[18] Margaret Scanlan

[19] John Lucas, for example.

[20] For more on this see the introduction to this book and P.J. Keating, *The Working Classes in Victorian Fiction*.

[21] "Hyacinth lay there as if he were asleep [...]. His arm hung limp beside him, downwards, off the narrow couch; his face was white and his eyes were closed" (590).

[22] In her excellent article on *The Princess Casamassima*, Margaret Scanlan notes that by 1885 bookbinding as an occupation was an anachronism (385).

[23] The fact that Chatterton passed off his own poetry as having been written by a fifteenth-century monk named Thomas Rowley adds a suggestive layer of complication. Chatterton's "Rowley" poems are often called forgeries, but in fact they are original to Chatterton, only enhanced with a medieval pseudonym, archaic language and fake antique manuscript paper.

Chapter 3

"A cloud of moral hobgoblins": Gender, Morality and Class in Hardy's *Tess of the d'Urbervilles*

> [T]he patrons of literature [...] acting under the censorship of prudery, rigorously exclude from the pages they regulate subjects that have been made [...] the bases of the finest imaginative compositions since literature rose to the dignity of an art.
> (Hardy, "Candour" 128-9)

Thomas Hardy's complaints in "Candour in English Fiction" (1890) about the stultifying effects of the moral code as applied to English fiction via the lending libraries and magazines were a reaction to the problems he had experienced with publishing *Tess of the d'Urbervilles*. *Tess* had been chopped up into parts in order to make it palatable for publishing in periodicals.[1] It wasn't until the 1891 edition—published after "Candour"—that Hardy could finally "piece the trunk and limbs of the novel together and print it complete, as originally written" (*Tess* ix).

Hardy's experience with *Tess* is not surprising in view of the moralizing atmosphere of the late nineteenth century in England when the social purity movement was influential. This movement was driven by groups of reformers, drawn mainly from the middle classes, who banded together to politicize matters of morality.[2] The movement coalesced around the fight to pass the Criminal Law Amendment Bill, a bill that called—amongst other things—for the raising of the age of consent from 13 to 16. (It had been raised from 12 to 13 in 1875.[3]) Those opposing passage of the age-of-consent legislation saw the possibility of young men being trapped by morally reprehensible, underage, working-class women who would seduce them, then try to profit by taking legal action against them. This view equates moral purity with social status, making middle- and upper-class young men more vulnerable as sexual prey.

By contrast, those defending the age-of-consent legislation blamed male aristocrats for "ruining" young working-class girls, turning them to prostitution with the lure of easy money. In reality, evidence seems to show that a large number of prostitutes were patronized by men of their own class, and therefore had more say in their own sexual practices than was being recognized by those wishing to help them (Walkowitz, *Prostitution* 249). Unfortunately, the Criminal Law Amendment

Act (1885) afforded the police great latitude in arresting and physically examining poor women suspected of prostitution, thus victimizing the very group it intended to help (Walkowitz, *City* 83). It seems that inevitably the lower classes, and especially lower-class wom,en, were viewed as morally inferior.

Debate over the Criminal Law Amendment Bill came to a climax with W.T. Stead's sensational campaign in the *Pall Mall Gazette* headlined "The Maiden Tribute to Modern Babylon."[4] By 1885 the fight for passage of the Criminal Law Amendment Bill had been waging for some years; it had passed the House of Lords more than once, but had always been defeated in the Commons. In April, another version of the bill passed in the Lords, but again faced probable defeat in the Commons. Benjamin Scott, chairman of the London Committee for the Exposure and Suppression of the Traffic in English Girls for the Purposes of Continental Prostitution, turned to Stead, who was editor of the *Pall Mall Gazette*, asking him to wage a publicity campaign. In order to investigate the so-called "white slave trade," Stead purchased a fourteen-year-old girl for five pounds and took her over to France, ostensibly with her mother's consent. However, the mother came forward later and reported her daughter missing, at which point Stead was arrested and sentenced to three months in prison for abduction.

In his *PMG* stories Stead described his adventures both in purchasing the girl and in being imprisoned. His reporting represents a confluence of the discourses of social purity and class which were commonly associated during this period, portraying upper-class males as the source of the immorality. He gives the example of "Mr. — [a] wealthy man whose whole life is dedicated to the gratification of lust [. . .] a striking illustration of the extent to which it is possible for a wealthy man to ruin not merely hundreds, but thousands of poor women. It is actually Mr. —'s boast that he has ruined 2,000 women in his time" (qtd. in Schults 139-40). But even Stead, the would-be protector of the virtue of poor young women, at the height of his campaign drew an analogy between the hunting of birds and fish and the hunting of girls. Under the heading "A Close Time[5] for Girls," he wrote:

> Why not let us have a close time for bipeds in petticoats as well as for bipeds with feathers? [. . .] Fish out of season are not fit to be eaten. Girls who have not reached the age of puberty are unfit even to be seduced [. . .]. It is also a scientific fact that such children are far more likely to transmit disease than full grown women.[6] Scientifically, therefore, the close time should be extended until the woman has at least completed sixteen years of life. (qtd. in Schults 139)

However good his intentions may have been towards these young women, Stead's hunting metaphor in this passage suggests he sees the seduction of young women as a sport, and his introduction of disease suggests that he, too, saw some underlying evil lurking in these girls instead of innocence.

Even after passage of the Criminal Law Amendment Act, and after the excitement over the "Maiden Tribute" campaign had died down, Stead continued ostensibly to promote social purity by emphasizing sexual crimes in his paper. Hardy complains in "Candour in English Fiction" about this tendency in newspaper reporting: "A sincere and comprehensive sequence of the ruling passions, however moral in its ultimate bearings, must not be put on paper as the foundation of imaginative works, [. . .] though it is extensively welcomed in the form of newspaper reports. […]," he writes (Hardy, "Candour" 128-9). For, of course, under the guise of the fight for social purity, this sensational reporting boosted sales of the *PMG*. And Stead "tried to highlight sex exploitation as class exploitation, to expose the iniquity of wicked baronets who preyed on schoolgirls" (Walkowitz, *City* 125).

Issues of morality, it seems, were inextricably linked with class issues, and sexual morality was always a gendered concept. In his poem "The Ruined Maid," Hardy brings together these three strands: gender, class and morality.[7] When Amelia, the ruined maid in the poem, meets a country girl she used to know when she too was an innocent country maid, the girl is most surprised, apparently, to see how far Amelia has risen in the world, and says so:

"O 'Melia, my dear, this does everything crown!
Who could have supposed I should meet you in Town?
And whence such fair garments, such prosperi-ty?"— (1-3)

Amelia gives a straightforward explanation: "'O didn't you know I'd been ruined?' said she" (4).

The country girl examines all the impressive accoutrements of Amelia's new social status: she admires her jewelry and feathers; she notices that both her hands and her speech have become refined; and she also remarks on her friend's high spirits. All are indications of Amelia's present position in life, which is the more impressive when compared to her previous poverty-stricken state, entailing cold, hunger and depression. Of course, Amelia puts it all down, with equanimity, to the fact that she has been "ruined." The old friend is envious: "—'I wish I had feathers, a fine sweeping gown, /And a delicate face, and could strut about Town!'—"(21-2). But Amelia stands on her new-found dignity: "'My dear—a raw country girl, such as you be, /Cannot quite expect that. You ain't ruined,' said she" (23-4).

The girls' conversation contradicts our expectations inasmuch as we expect a "ruined" woman to be ashamed of her condition. Thus the reader gains a sense of satisfaction from having a larger knowledge of the world and of the moral code than these two characters. In middle-class parlance, a "ruined" woman has "fallen." Once "fallen," she has lost her good character and reputation and, in the spirit of Victorian middle-class morality, gives up her claim to respectability. She has therefore fallen in class status as well as in the biblical sense. But in the eyes of the country girl in the poem, Amelia has risen in social status, for now she does not have work-worn hands, nor hunger written on her face; she not only has shoes and socks, but nice clothes and even jewelry.[8] In the end, the irony works against the middle-class reader who is enjoying a feeling of superiority over the naïve characters. These country girls cannot afford middle-class morality. Sir George Clausen's painting *Winter Work* (1883-4), completed a few years before Hardy started work on *Tess*, depicts the poor conditions Hardy implies the girls in his poem have suffered. Rather than idealizing the country life as many painters did, Clausen shows a woman whose face seems marked by cold and hunger, whose hands are red and swollen and whose feet are wrapped in rags.[9] Tess undergoes similarly hard conditions when she is working at Flintcombe Ash and because of these conditions is, for a moment, tempted to give in to Alec's pressure to give herself to the life of a "ruined maid" in order to escape the hardships.

Inasmuch as a class-based moral stance is essential to the irony of "The Ruined Maid," this poem makes a point about class, for it is class here that in a great degree determines morality. But it also makes a point about gender, because this is a morality that is specific to women. While a "ruined" man may fall in social status because he has lost his money, sexual or moral issues are not necessarily involved. Hardy illustrates this point in his story "On the Western Circuit" (1891), in which one "Charles Bradford Raye, Esquire—stuff-gownsman, educated at Wintoncester, called to the Bar at Lincoln's Inn, now going the Western Circuit"—deceitfully lies to a poor country girl and seduces her, making her pregnant. This situation could have ended in her losing her job as a domestic and probably turning to prostitution from lack of any other method of earning a living to support herself and her baby. But Raye bemoans his own fate because he is tricked into marrying this illiterate country girl. He knows such a wife will be bad for his career and so he whines, "You have deceived me—ruined me!" (1932), unmindful of the fact that these are accusations the girl could have leveled at him, and with far more justification, if he had not married her. Hardy reuses what he calls a "well-known catastrophe," a scenario exploited by Stead and many fiction writers. But in this case the seducer receives a suitable punishment for abusing his class power.[10]

While making the point that the middle classes sought to impose their own moral standards on other classes regardless of economic situation, Hardy's poem and story also suggest a shoring up of middle-class privilege through the ideologies of gender and morality.[11] By judging the "lower" classes as morally lacking, the middle classes could, of course, exonerate themselves from responsibility for the inequalities in society, the inequalities that had been made apparent by investigators such as Booth, and fiction writers such as Gissing and even James. Hardy uses this same association of class with gender and morality in *Tess of the d'Urbervilles*, but instead of using this association to reinforce and strengthen the middle-class identity, as many novelists had, seeing class as a natural and fixed system, Hardy brings them together to question the system. In his 1892 Preface Hardy claims that "a novel is an impression, not an argument" (xi). Even so, in this novel he exposes this deployment of gendered morality to enforce class identities, not only in fiction, but in the social purity movement generally.

Fig. 3.1 Sir George Clausen, *Winter Work*, 1883-4. Oil on canvas (© Tate, London 2005. Reproduced with permission of Jane K. Smith)

"Little Thomas Hardy"

Hardy himself had suffered from class prejudice. Like Gissing, Hardy (1840-1928) was not born of the privileged, well-educated, financially independent class that traditionally had produced the writers of mainstream Victorian novels. Ironically, after visiting Hardy in 1895, Gissing snidely remarked of Hardy that "he had a great deal of coarseness in his nature," probably due to his "humble origins" (qtd. in Seymour-Smith 391). As with the other writers I examine, Hardy's origins are relevant inasmuch as they enable him to look at issues of social class differently from those middle-class writers who had come before.[12] But it is important not to become hampered in reading Hardy's work by the image of "little Thomas Hardy" created by Henry James. In other words, Hardy's class origins should not color one's view of his intellectual achievement. Many past readers have seen Hardy as the self-taught country boy who was at his best depicting his home milieu of Dorset as its timeless rustic ways came under attack from city influences causing it to suffer from "the ache of modernism" (*Tess* 98). The image that has been created of what Peter Widdowson calls "the Ur-Hardy of Higher Bockhampton" (130) is a false one. Hardy was, of course, a sophisticated and critical observer both of country life and of the city life of his educated, middle-class readers.

The concept of the "author" has been discussed at length by Roland Barthes, Michel Foucault and others.[13] As Foucault points out, "The author's name is not [. . .] just a proper name like the rest" ("Author" 345), because it represents what he calls the "author-function"—that is, the persona by which we, the readers, know the writer of the work:

> [The] aspects of an individual which we designate as making him an author are only a projection, in more or less psychologizing terms, of the operations that we force texts to undergo, the connections that we make, the traits that we establish as pertinent, the continuities that we recognize, or the exclusions that we practice. All these operations vary according to periods and types of discourse. (347)

Foucault argues that those who exercise power over Culture, and therefore texts, can do so through their construction of the author, and Hardy is a case in point. In mythologizing "Thomas Hardy the country boy," critics have often condescended to the empirical Hardy. Philip Collins, for example, in his essay on Hardy and education, explains that "Hardy bridled when a commentator, writing in French, described him as 'ce Saxon autodidacte'" (51). And he comments parenthetically—though rather pompously—"we dons who write about Hardy must beware of patronizing him, for [he] lack[ed] the advantages which we have enjoyed" (51). But Collins goes on to say that he agrees with Michael Millgate,[14] one of Hardy's biographers, who writes, "The mark of the autodidact is perhaps to be found not so much in what he knows as in how he regards the world of knowledge" (qtd. in Collins 51). Such critics prove Foucault's point about power: for while they are ostensibly being careful not to patronize Hardy, the very idea that they are in a position to do so constructs "Hardy the author" as a self-educated—and consequently a poorly educated—rustic, equating him with someone like his own creation Jude.

This old view of "Hardy the author" loses sight of his engagement with important issues of his day. The *Norton Anthology of English Literature*, for example, assures students that Hardy's novels are set "[a]gainst a background of immemorial agricultural labor," and that while the "characteristic Victorian novelist—e.g., Dickens or Thackeray—was concerned with the behavior and problems of people in a given social milieu [. . .] Hardy preferred to go directly for the elemental in human behavior with a minimum of contemporary social detail" (1692).[15] It is true that Hardy refrains from indulging in the heavily detailed realism that Virginia Woolf refers to as the "Edwardian tool" (207), or what Roland Barthes refers to as an "*effet de réel*" (140), the piling on of description, "a kind of narrative *luxury*, profligate to the extent of throwing up 'useless' details and increasing the cost of narrative information" (140). But Hardy does engage with the specific social milieu about which he is writing, and he engages particularly with contemporary class issues. No wonder, then, that the class prejudice of these critics came into play, for Hardy's work is not simply an expression of his own class anxiety, but a critique of the class system itself. Earlier writers such as George Eliot and Elizabeth Gaskell who had used the same scenario—upper-class man seduces lower-class woman—in their novels to examine class problems treated social class as though it were a fixed system to which characters must adapt. The question Hardy investigates is a far more fundamental one: in what does the power of social class consist? Is it moral superiority? Is it in money, education, and manners? Or are there essential qualities transmitted in the blood? In other words, Hardy does not blindly accept the system as it exists.

"My dear, you mustn't say 'gentlemen' nowadays"

Hardy examines the question of what constitutes social superiority and the possibility of transition from one social class to another in several of his novels. In *A Pair of Blue Eyes* (1873), his irony is directed at the triviality of what constitutes class difference. The "lower-class" character, Stephen Smith, is an educated young man, an architect with good prospects. But although initially he is greatly liked and encouraged by the father of the woman he loves, once that gentleman finds out that Stephen is the son of local villagers, he turns the young man out of the house. Elfride is rather surprised at her father's change of heart: "but he is the same man, papa; the same in every particular; and how can he be less fit for me than he was before?" (133).

There is something about Stephen, however, that separates him from those born into privilege. Although Stephen has not been to the university, his acquaintance Mr. Knight has been kind enough to provide some classical education via correspondence. While education was becoming more accessible to all classes of English people towards century's end—Stephen had attended a dame school and a national school—the educational system itself was organized in such a way as to separate the classes. The sons of the upper middle class, for example, were taught the classics and other subjects that assumed their future held a life of contemplation of the higher things, not the making of money. Despite his smattering of upper-class education, however, Stephen does not have the refinements that would have come naturally to him—as they come naturally to Knight—if he had grown up in a well-to-do family. Elfride sums up the situation once she finds out his true parentage: "How plain everything about you seems after this explanation! Your peculiarities in chess-playing, the pronunciation papa noticed in your Latin, your odd mixture of book-knowledge with ignorance of ordinary social accomplishments, are accounted for in a moment" (124).

That these nuances separating the laboring classes from the well-to-do are nothing more than an ability to perform in a certain manner is suggested by the words Hardy puts into the mouth of Mr. Swancourt, even while that worthy gentleman intends to deny exactly this point: "anybody can be what you call graceful," he says to his daughter when discussing Stephen, "if he lives a little time in a city, and keeps his eyes open. And he might have picked up his gentlemanliness by going to the galleries of theatres, and watching stage drawing-room manners" (134). That Hardy should bring in the performance of manners on the stage tells us that he wants to draw a comparison between a theater performance and the performance of class. We saw James make the same connection: when Hyacinth sees the Princess Casamassima for the first time, he is at the theater, suggesting that Christina Light is merely performing her royal role.

Even the enviable label *gentleman*, the label Dickens dissects in *Great Expectations* when Pip spends his youth pursuing it, is thrown into question in Hardy's novel. Elfride's new stepmother, higher in class and more fashionable than Elfride or her father, tells her when they are in London, "My dear, you mustn't say 'gentlemen' nowadays [. . .]. We have handed over 'gentlemen' to the lower middle class, where the word is still to be heard at tradesmen's balls and provincial tea-parties, I believe. It is done with here" (193). While the supercilious tone of Mrs. Swancourt's utterance suggests that what is at stake is a matter of being *au fait* with the language fashion of the time, Hardy's novels suggest that there is more to it. The very concept of the gentleman is an affectation devoid of content or value.

Conventional gentlemanly traits are not often manifested by those of the gentlemanly class in Hardy's novels. Mr. Knight, despite his name and his class, does not behave in a knightly fashion towards Elfride and is ready to abandon her at, what seems to the reader, the slightest provocation. The fact that he has refrained from kissing a woman until Elfride, even though he is in his thirties, suggests a moral niceness that reveals Hardy's ironic stance towards this character, and therefore towards the "knightly" class of men. This is a Victorian novel, and so moral decorum can be expected to be important, and we know that Hardy felt its constraints; he expresses his frustration in "Candour in English Fiction." Even so, Victorian novel conventions notwithstanding, that Knight should back out of the engagement on the strength of one past kiss bestowed by Elfride on a previous beau suggests a defect of character in this "gentleman." And Hardy makes fun of the unkissed, un-knightly Mr. Knight: when he is hanging off the Cliff with No Name and must be rescued by Elfride's underwear (which she takes off and ties together to make a rope), he suffers an indignity indeed.

In *The Woodlanders* (1887), the higher-class, more refined character, Fitzpiers, behaves in a less moral manner than the lower-class Winterborne. Fitzpiers has an affair with a village girl before he is married to Grace, and then with Mrs. Charmond after he is married, whereas Giles Winterborne is nothing if not faithful and noble, even though he knows his love for Grace is hopeless. When Grace runs away from home and comes to him for help after learning about Fitzpiers' affair, Giles does not want to compromise her and so sleeps outside, in spite of his illness, killing himself in the process. The humble yet noble Winterborne is willing to die to protect the reputation of the woman he loves and Hardy shows no irony with regard to poor Giles.

Hardy's critique of the upper classes and sympathy with the working classes is far more subtle in *Tess*, and he makes us aware of the overriding importance of class issues from the very beginning. When the novel opens, we find a man tottering along drunkenly towards the Wessex village of Marlott. Though he is addressed by the parson whom he meets as "Sir John," we immediately recognize him as a working man. "Sir John" carries an empty egg-basket, and of his hat we are told "a patch [had been] quite worn away at its brim where his thumb came in taking it off" (1). The rustic who is addressed as Sir John by parson Tringham is, of course, "plain Jack Durbeyfield the haggler" (1), but as the parson informs him, he is "the lineal representative of the ancient and knightly family of the d'Urbervilles, who derive their descent from Sir Pagan d'Urberville, that renowned knight who came from Normandy with William the Conqueror" (1). Jack Durbeyfield is not only surprised, but illogically rather put out that he has been, as he says, "knocking about year after year from pillar to post as if I was no more than the commonest feller in the parish" (2). Through this bit of stage business, Hardy sets up the question of what constitutes social class in the first pages of *Tess*, and Jack Durbeyfield's association with the old Norman family of d'Urbervilles has ramifications that reverberate throughout the novel.

The ancient d'Urbervilles seem to dog Tess's footsteps almost as surely as Alec, usurper of the old name.[16] When she goes to work at Talbothay's dairy, Kingsbere, the ancient seat of her ancestors, is close by, and when she marries Angel, their wedding night is spent at Wellbridge, in a house that used to be a d'Urberville mansion and where the faces of Tess's d'Urberville forebears look down on her disapprovingly from the walls. When Tess's father dies and the Durbeyfields are turned out of their Marlott cottage, they end up spending the night in the d'Urberville vault at Kingsbere. Angel, at one point, blames Tess's ancestors for all his woes: "He was embittered by the conviction that all this desolation had been brought about by the accident of her being a d'Urberville" (204). But this is just one symptom of the underlying problem of class exploitation.

One might argue that degeneration, a topic that was prominent during the 1880s and 1890s, had some influence on Hardy, causing him to make Tess's forebears a constant focus of this novel. Certainly Angel seems to subscribe to the theory of degeneration. Dairyman Crick says of Angel, "if there's one thing that he do hate more than another 'tis the notion of what's called a' old family. He says that it stands to reason that old families have done their spurt of work in past days, and can't have anything left in 'em now" (100). But while Hardy shows us that Tess resembles her ancient ancestors shown in the portraits at Wellbridge ("her fine features were unquestionably traceable in these exaggerated forms" [170]), still she claims that her beauty has been handed down to her from her mother, who was nothing more than a dairymaid. And her education comes from the board school that she attends. While she is noticeably superior to the other dairymaids, Hardy does not seem to claim that this is some vestige of her aristocratic blood—and her passivity, and inability to fend off Alec and his immorality therefore a result of degenerated morals—for her beauty and education have nothing to do with her aristocratic antecedents.

Some critics have argued that the fall of the d'Urbervilles is the tragic fall of this novel: "It is assumed that [Tess's] tragedy consists in her family's loss of its ancestral inheritance; that her being a real d'Urberville and Alec a fake one symbolizes the ruin and betrayal of the old aristocracy by a new urban class bent on exploiting the land" (Merryn Williams 170). But the novel does not idealize the old aristocracy, the ancient d'Urberville line. Tess's ancestors were degenerate centuries ago. In the famous passage that substitutes for a description of the rape/seduction of Tess, the narrator says, "Doubtless some of Tess d'Urberville's mailed ancestors rollicking home from a fray had dealt the same measure even more ruthlessly towards peasant girls of their time" (57). In other words, when their bloodlines were young, the d'Urbervilles had brutally taken advantage of the gender and class power differential, just as Alec, the merchant's son, is doing now. And, when Tess's family is turned out of their Marlott cottage, we are told,

> Thus the Durbeyfields, once d'Urbervilles, saw descending upon them the destiny which, no doubt, when they were among the Olympians of the county, they had caused to descend many a time, and severely enough, upon the heads of such landless ones as they themselves were now. (277)

Hardy is not only depicting ignoble behavior among the upper classes, but suggesting that class is an unstable category that does not depend on one's bloodlines.[17]

Mariage de Convenance

As I noted in Chapter 1, Gissing suggests that traditional Victorian novelistic paradigms are dangerous because of the class myths they underwrite. Hardy, too, attacks the fictional representation of class in *The Hand of Ethelberta* (1876), long considered by critics one of his less successful novels.[18] The relationship between the destructiveness of the class system and the fiction of class embodied in the performance of class is the complicated subject both of the novel itself and of Ethelberta's storytelling. The eponymous heroine of the novel, born into a poor country family, marries a man above her station against his parents' wishes. Her husband dies and she is left with nothing but a five-year occupancy of a house in London, a house she can hardly afford to keep up. Hoping again to marry well and thereby give her younger siblings a better chance in the world, Ethelberta brings her mother and her siblings to live in her house as her servants. Meanwhile, she earns money by telling stories on the stage professionally. One of the apparent fictions she tells publicly is the story of living a fiction with regard to class. Thus, while Ethelberta's life is a fiction, her stage fictions tell her life.

Fig. 3.2 Sir William Quiller Orchardson, *Mariage de Convenance*, 1883. Oil on canvas (Reproduced with permission of the Glasgow Museums: Art Gallery and Museum, Kelvingrove)

Ethelberta claims to be keeping up her appearance of being higher-class in order to give the children a better chance in the world. While we know that Hardy does not idealize country life—note, for example, Tess's hard life working in the fields, and the Durbeyfields' precarious housing situation—Ethelberta's siblings seemed much happier when they were living their lives simply in the country. When her family is working in Ethleberta's London house, there is a sense of the destructiveness of this self-conscious class situation. They can never be themselves; ironically, they pretend *not* to be related to the lady of the house, denying their higher social contacts. They must always, therefore, be hiding and dissembling, and there is something profoundly disturbing and very pointed about the way in which Ethelberta exploits her family, but all apparently for their own good.

Ethelberta does finally secure her class position, not only by becoming the wife of Lord Mountclere, but by seemingly ruling over him: she runs his finances and he, it is said, looks to her for approval before offering his opinion on any subject. She even receives grudging respect from his servants, who at first had looked down on her. Still, one feels that she has paid too high a price. It is a marriage that could have been the model for Sir William Quiller Orchardson's painting *Mariage de Convenance* (1883), in which a husband and wife sit at opposite ends of a table laden with wines and good food surrounded by a richly appointed décor. The only movement in the scene is the butler who quietly, unobtrusively, pours the wine, emphasizing the blanket of silence that hangs over the scene. The attractive wife, clearly much younger than her elderly, bewhiskered husband, has pushed her chair back from the table and cupped her chin in her hand. She is thoroughly bored with the situation and trying to disengage herself from it. She has not touched her meal. The husband, while he also looks somewhat tired of the relationship, looks possessively, perhaps accusingly at his wife. Orchardson's sequel (*Mariage de Convenance—After*, 1886) shows the disillusioned old codger sitting alone by his cold hearth, intimating that here is a lesson to be learned.

The difference, one can assume, between Ethelberta's marriage and the *mariage de convenance* depicted in the painting is that Ethelberta's aristocrat is *not* bored, and it is this crucial difference that allows her to wield power over him. Like the "ruined maid" in Hardy's poem, Ethelberta is exchanging sex for both money and class status. In both the poem and the novel, Hardy points up one of the great contradictions of Victorian middle-class morality, just as Orchardson had done in his painting: the behavior of a woman such as Amelia, while condemned morally, is rewarded materially, and prostitution, while condemned by society, is encouraged when it involves a marriage license.[19] In fact, marriage for money had become a middle-class institution.

Marriage for money—or, as a last resort, giving oneself without the benefit of marriage—is one of the options offered to Tess, working-class woman that she is, as a solution to her family's financial problems. Tess Durbeyfield's mother accepts with equanimity the idea of Tess using her good looks to earn herself a living through marriage to someone of a higher class. She discusses with her husband Tess's chances of winning Alec d'Urberville:

> "Well, as one of the genuine stock, she ought to make her way with 'en, if she plays her trump card aright. And if he don't marry her afore he will after [. . .]"
> "What's her trump card? Her d'Urberville blood, you mean?" [says her husband]
> "No, stupid; her face—as 'twas mine." (38)

When Tess returns home after the seduction/rape, her mother scolds her for not profiting from the situation: "'Why didn't ye think of doing some good for your family instead o' thinking only of yourself?'" (64). Joan possesses a pragmatic turn of mind that would have met the "ruined maid" with admiration. Tess is distressed by this:

> "O mother, my mother! [. . .] How could I be expected to know? I was a child when I left this house four months ago. Why didn't you tell me there was danger in men-folk? [. . .] Ladies know what to fend hands against, because they read novels that tell them of these tricks; but I never had the chance." (64)

Hardy is tongue-in-cheek here, for well-brought up young ladies were protected from "men-folk" mostly by lack of opportunity, and novels were often condemned for imparting to such protected females knowledge that would lead them astray. Tess is making the point that Anne Brontë tried to make earlier in the century in *The Tenant of Wildfell Hall* (1848): women cannot be expected to guard against evils they know nothing about. But we see from the above passage that, while Tess's mother knows the game and wants Tess to play it, Tess's views are far different; she is not willing to sell herself in this way.[20]

The "ruin" of a poor girl by an upper-class man, the scenario that was exploited by Stead in the "Maiden Tribute," had been used successfully in *Adam Bede* (1859) and *Ruth* (1853). Eliot and Gaskell told the stories of Hetty and Ruth from a decidedly middle-class viewpoint, investigating the question of how to deal with those who, as in the case of Arthur Donnithorne in *Adam Bede*, and Henry Bellingham in *Ruth*, had abused their class status. This scenario is reworked by Hardy in *Tess* not merely to place blame, but to question the exploitative nature of the class system. One of the ways he does this is to tell Tess's story in a way that often allows us to see the situation through her working-class, female eyes.[21] In *Adam Bede* and *Ruth*, the power provided to the male seducer by the class system is abused; by giving us Tess's viewpoint, Hardy questions why that power exists at all.

"Hetty's dreams were all of luxuries"

For those unfortunate working-class literary heroines, like Tess, whose name is linked with that of a man higher in social status without the benefit of marriage, the consequences are dire. Such a woman who has broken the middle-class moral code loses her place in society, whether or not that place had been a middle-class one. Many middle-class women at the time had sympathy for their fallen sisters, as did George Eliot when she created Hetty Sorrel in *Adam Bede*. But Eliot still works within the traditional paradigm of the fallen woman: that is, Hetty cannot be reintegrated into the society of Hayslope after what has happened. Hardy in *Tess*, by contrast, is trying to undercut this middle-class notion of the fallen woman. He attempts to make clear, as he does in "The Ruined Maid," that when everyday survival is at stake, morality takes on a different shape.

Hetty Sorrel and Tess Durbeyfield have often been compared by critics, and there are several similarities in their stories suggesting an intentional allusion to Eliot's *Adam Bede* by Hardy in *Tess*: both girls are dairymaids, both seducers have the initials A.D., and both sexual incidents occur in a place called the Chase, an appropriate location it would seem for the bagging of a young virgin. But most importantly, both pretty young country girls are seduced (some think in Tess's case raped) by the rich, young heir of the family for whom they work. They are both in this sense the victims of a power differential created by the social class system. The difference between the two novels (aside from the fact that praise was heaped upon Eliot's novel, while Hardy's caused an eruption of vitriol from some critics) lies in how their creators viewed that system.

In particular, the coming-of-age feast for Arthur Donnithorne, the squire's grandson, in *Adam Bede* suggests Eliot's support of the class system as it stands at mid-century. The narrator makes it clear that the local people, all tenants of the Donnithornes, are to be placed at the birthday dinner according to class protocol. Since the novel takes place in 1799, one might argue that Eliot's focus on class has no relevance to the class situation in which her 1859 readers found themselves before the Second Reform Bill. But the historicization of the class system is one of several devices she uses to make class division seem "natural." By presenting the class system as an age-old system passed down from the "golden-age" of English rural life, Eliot makes it seem acceptable, even desirable, to her mid-Victorian readers. And what better scene symbolically to showcase this system than the traditional coming-of-age feast, a feast that by definition celebrates the inheritance of power, wealth and class privilege, a scene where the minutest class distinctions are made apparent and where all ranks happily validate the superior position of the landed gentry.

Even nature herself appears to be in tune with Arthur Donnithorne's birthday celebrations, making the whole day—including the social organization graphically embodied therein—appear blessed by nature: "the weather was perfect for that time of year [. . .]. Perfect weather for an outdoor July merrymaking" (292). To add to nature's blessing, "The air had been merry with the ringing of church bells very early this morning" (293). And once the invitees begin to head towards their destination, we hear that "[t]he church bells had struck up again now—a last tune, before the ringers came down the hill to have their share of the festival" (298). It is as though even God looks down happily and nods his approval of this day of celebration. The constant references to the historical continuation of the community help validate its organization, too. Mr. Irwine in his speech refers to the babies he has christened who are now grown men and women—the class organization, in other words, stretches back into the eighteenth century. And Arthur invites the local children to the celebration because he knows they will grow up to be his tenants and look back fondly on his beneficence. This system, then, will continue into the nineteenth century.

When the tenants of larger farms arrive at the feast, there is some dispute as to who should sit at the head of the table. Should it be the oldest tenant, the largest tenant (according to how much land he farms) or, as is finally decided upon, the largest tenant according to girth? (While choosing according to girth might suggest a certain levity in viewing the decision, in other words, a diminishment of the importance of the class protocol—and it does cause some mirth among the farmers— one would suppose that a man of some girth [in 1799] might be considered not only well-fed, but less engaged in manual labor also, indicating therefore a comfortable economic situation.) The tables of the large tenants have been placed in the upstairs gallery overlooking the cottagers; they are above their social inferiors. The cottagers are seated in the cloisters of the old abbey attached to the Donnithorne home, helping to make them aware that the position the Donnithorne family holds has been sanctioned by God. To refine this graphic illustration of social organization, the women and children are separated from the men, both above and below.

The ranking of those present is so accepted by all as the natural arrangement of their world that there is a little eyebrow raising when Adam Bede, at the special request of Arthur Donnithorne, goes to sit upstairs, a special honor because of his new position as manager of the Donnithorne woods. Mr. Casson, once butler at the house and now the landlord of the Donnithorne Arms, cannot resist a comment on Adam's speedy social climb: " 'Well, Mr. Bede,'" he says, "'you're one o'them as mounts hup'ards apace'" (306).

Emphasis is given in this scene not only to the organization of the classes but to the distance this organization creates between Hetty and her lover. When Hetty first arrives with her family she looks up at the Donnithorne house and imagines Arthur, oblivious to her presence, taken up with people of his own class. And when she does see him after dinner, she feels even more distant from him:

> Arthur did not venture to stop near Hetty, but merely bowed to her as he passed [. . .]. Arthur, who had seemed so near to her only a few hours before, was separated from her, as the hero of a great procession is separated from a small outsider in the crowd. (316)

This final thought seems to be Hetty's and it is typical of her. (This is somewhat ironic on the part of the narrator since Arthur's nature is essentially unheroic. His only seemingly heroic act in this novel is his final gesture which saves Hetty from death but condemns her to transportation—a dubious redemption. Of course, even this seemingly heroic act is a sham in view of the fact that it is his own self-indulgence and exploitation of his power that has landed Hetty in so much trouble in the first place.) If this image of the "hero" and the "small outsider" springs, indeed, from Hetty's imagination, then we see how much power and influence Arthur has over Hetty in her own mind.

An arrangement for an assignation between Arthur and Hetty three days hence is made at the birthday dance, and it is probably at that meeting that the seduction occurs. The juxtaposition of the party and the seduction seems to emphasize for the reader just what it is that is being disrupted by the sexual congress between these two people from different spheres. As we have seen, it is a time-honored, God-given, nature-blessed, intricate social organization that is being attacked by this act. Adam, who is aligned with the moral heart of this novel, is quick to understand and condemn all the wrong implicit in this situation, though he doesn't know the extent of the damage. He sees the two lovers kissing and he says to Arthur: "You know, as well as I do, what it's to lead to, when a gentleman like you kisses and makes love to a young woman like Hetty" (344). And later, "things don't lie level between Hetty and you" (353). Adam's condemnation is of Arthur's aberrant behavior, not of the system itself that not only keeps lovers apart, but allows a vain youth such as Arthur to have power over other people's lives simply because they are lower in class.

Importantly, Arthur himself clearly understands the problem with what he is doing. He shows this when he writes to Hetty:

> I know you can never be happy except by marrying a man in your own station; and if I were to marry you now, I should only be adding to any wrong I have done, besides offending against my duty in the other relations of life. You know nothing [. . .] of the world in which I must always live. (378)

The fact that Arthur *does* understand the gulf between himself and Hetty —for how could he not?—makes his behavior towards her the more wrong.

But Hetty is not merely an innocent victim in this novel. Eliot depicts Hetty as a vain, frivolous young woman more concerned with her own adornment—albeit in the secrecy of her own room—than with her family duties or the attentions given her by such a serious-minded and deserving fellow as Adam Bede. Earlier in the century, Elizabeth Gaskell seems to protect *her* fallen woman, Ruth, in her book of the same name, by trying to make her seem innocent of everything except loving her upper-class seducer and not having parents or friends to advise her. During the period of her gradual seduction, she is portrayed as innocent, wanting to please, dependent on others and almost unaware of the implications of the fact that she has been living openly with a man who is not her husband. By contrast, in *Adam Bede*, Hetty Sorrel is likened to kittens and canaries, emphasizing the lightweight nature of her character, and the unflattering comparison with her non-frivolous and morally upright cousin Dinah also paints Hetty as lacking moral fiber. We are to understand that it is not the power structure in Hayslope that gets Hetty into trouble, but Hetty's nature. The narrator tells us that "Hetty's dreams were all of luxuries"

(144). We see her in her room trying on her earrings and looking at herself in the mirror:

> Some day she will be able to wear any earring she likes, and already she lives in an invisible world of brilliant costumes, shimmering gauze, soft satin, and velvet, such as the lady's-maid at the Chase has shown her in Miss Lydia's wardrobe: she feels the bracelets on her arms, and treads on a soft carpet in front of a tall mirror. (296)

Eliot appears to be having it both ways here. For while she blames Hetty's own nature for her misfortune, it is clear from this passage that it is precisely the inequalities of the social class system that cause Hetty to feel the need to imagine herself as higher in class. It is precisely Hetty's desire for the clothes, the luxuries, the admiration, the power that the gentry have that gives Arthur influence over the poor girl. Hetty is not so much in love with Arthur as with the possibility of social elevation that he represents. Arthur symbolizes everything the gentry have and she doesn't. Adam Bede climbs up the social ladder just a little when, through hard work and upright living, he is given his new job at the Chase. But there is a very definite limit to the number of steps he can take on that ladder (not to mention, of course, the fact that it is problematic to consider the social class system as a meritocracy—what, after all, has Arthur done to deserve his privileged position?). But for Hetty to marry Arthur would not be for her to climb up the social ladder, it would magically change her from a dairymaid into a lady. Such a magical transformation is the stuff of fairy tale, the story of Cinderella come true, and as such it is clear to everyone except Hetty that it is also an impossibility.[22]

Eliot positions Hetty in the traditional role of the fallen woman who disrupts the social order and must therefore be cast out; transportation to Australia is the perfect answer. Arthur Donnithorne, while condemned for his aberrant behaviour in fraternizing with the "lower" classes and required to do penance, still retains his position, and more importantly his power, in society, a fact which is emphasized at the end of *Adam Bede* when he rides in like a knight in shining armor to rescue the fair maiden from death. As a frivolous fallen woman Hetty is not worthy of the drama death by hanging would have afforded her story, nor the sympathy it would have earned her from the reader. By hanging her, Eliot would have created a symbol of injustice—as Hardy did with Tess later in the century; by transporting her, Eliot makes her fade away into nothingness, leaving Hayslope unbesmirched and the class system intact.

Eliot has sympathy for Hetty's woes, as did the many Victorian juries who refused to convict mothers for infanticide. "Juries consistently acquitted mothers who were accused of killing their infants and young children," Virginia Morris explains in *Double Jeopardy: Women Who Kill in Victorian Fiction* (77). "Since the majority of infanticide defendants were [. . .] single, working-class women who had been abandoned by men, juries saw them as victims rather than criminals" (77). But despite her sympathy for Hetty, Eliot clearly blames the girl. And at the same time that she abhors Arthur's misuse of his power, she *accepts* that power as part of the social organization, an organization that is showcased at the coming-of-age feast and in many ways packaged to appear to be in tune with nature, God, and the "golden age" of English history.

Tess of the d'Urbervilles: A Pure Woman

While apparently alluding to Eliot's earlier, very popular work in *Tess*, Hardy changes the parameters of that story. Not only does he make the fallen woman the eponymous heroine of his novel and have Tess kill her tormentor instead of her innocent baby, but he also subjoins the phrase "A Pure Woman" to his novel's title in the first three-volume edition in 1891. By labeling Tess in this way, despite all that happens in the novel, Hardy directly confronts the social purity advocates and questions the basis of their use of the word *pure*.

As Hardy well knew, at the end of the nineteenth century in England the word *pure* carried some specific connotations. This was the word applied by social purity movement reformers to describe the standards of sexual morality they intended to set. But, as we have seen, setting these standards involved judging others through class-based constructions of their sexual behavior. Hardy claims his use of the word *pure* to be different from what he describes in his 1892 preface as "the artificial and derivative meaning which has resulted to it from the ordinances of civilization" (x). He wants "the meaning of the word in Nature" to be read into his use of it (x). This is somewhat disingenuous, however, since Hardy obviously knew the strong connotations that would be brought to his sub-title by his readers. He was surely invoking this ideal of moral purity even while protesting against it. He writes in the preface to the 1912 edition that the sub-title "was appended at the last moment [...] as being the estimate left in a candid mind of the heroine's character" (xii). This comes closer to the point, for it suggests that despite Tess's situation, sympathy is due her because of her lack of options as a female member of the laboring class. By questioning the conventional middle-class morality that condemns Tess despite her lack of power, he indicts a society that accepts such a fate for a powerless woman because she is a woman, and because she is working-class and questions one of the foundation stones upon which middle-class power is built—the intertwining of a gendered sexuality morality with class.

"See how you've mastered me!"

Tess's lack of power is underlined for us through Alec d'Urberville's power over her. It is, of course, Alec, that scion of the bourgeoisie, who has all the power in this novel, and his power comes not from his lineage—which is a solidly middle-class one—but simply from his money, which allowed his father to buy the name d'Urberville. Old Simon Stoke had made money in the north and then settled in the south, "annexing" to his own name one that he had found when "[c]onning for an hour in the British Museum the pages of works devoted to extinct, half-extinct, obscured, and ruined families appertaining to the quarter of England in which he proposed to settle" (27). In the world of this novel, class inequality has more to do with the wielding of power, the mastery of others one gains through money or education or gender, than through the divinely appointed rank given to one at birth—that is, through a bloodline.

Someone like Alec gains power through his birth because his father is wealthy and he will inherit money, but it is not his rank at birth that affords him this, it is money and all that it buys him. Alec represents wealthy, middle-class, masculine power. He is constantly smoking a cigar, which in this case is not *just a cigar*; Hardy uses it to symbolize—fairly obviously—Alec's gender power, but also his class mastery over Tess. After the seduction/rape of Tess, when she is trying to escape from the Slopes, Alec catches up with Tess and persuades her to accept his offer to drive her home. She says pathetically: "'I didn't understand your meaning till it was too late'" (60). Smoking his cigar, and comfortable with his own powerful gender and class position Alec answers, "'That's what every woman says'" (60). He freely admits his culpability: "'I did wrong—I admit it,'" he says. Alec's position allows him moral leniency because in his society blame will be automatically transferred to the lower-class woman. But while he admits he has done wrong, he is unrepentant and wants to compound the wrong. He says to Tess, "'I am ready to pay to the uttermost farthing. You know you need not work in the fields or dairies again. You know you may clothe yourself with the best, instead of in the bald plain way you have lately affected, as if you couldn't get a ribbon more than you earned'" (60).

This idea of mastery brings with it both gender and class issues suggesting the ancient feudal system in existence in the time of Tess's ancestors, a system still—during the late nineteenth century—to some extent the model around which country life is formed. Like Eliot, Hardy harks back to the olden days, but does so to expose them as brutal rather than golden. The word *master* is often used to describe relations between Tess and Alec: for example, when the narrator tells us that "d'Urberville gave her the kiss of mastery" (40), and it comes back later when Alec is at Flintcombe Ash trying to persuade Tess to marry him. He says, "'I was your master once; I will be your master again'" (261). Alec makes his way in the world, as Tess's ancestors had done, by abusing the power that he wields because of the inequality of the social class system. As Tess herself says, "'You, and those like you, take your fill of pleasure on earth by making the life of such as me bitter and black with sorrow'" (242).

Alec wants Tess to become like the ruined maid of Hardy's poem, but in Tess, Hardy has created a different kind of character. For while she is a victim of her class position, her sense of herself, her subjectivity is not constituted by it. Although her circumstances are dire, Tess does not see her situation in terms of possibilities for advantage. Her affection for Angel never has a hint of social climbing attached to it. Like the maid in the poem, she could improve the material conditions of her life—

her class status, even—and that of her family because Alec wants her to profit from the attentions he has forced upon her, and there is no doubt that his argument is persuasive. He has already given her father a new horse to replace Prince, the one Tess feels responsible for killing, and he has given the Durbeyfield children some toys. But he does not reckon with Tess's self-respect. "'I have said I will not take anything more from you, and I will not—I cannot! I *should* be your creature to go on doing that; and I won't!'" she says with some vehemence. But when he lets her out of the vehicle she passively allows him to kiss her, saying, "'See how you've mastered me!'" (60). While she fights against her powerless position by refusing Alec, Tess cannot but recognize his power.

Tess does recant her refusal to become "his creature" towards the end of the book, after she has continued to refuse Alec through many hardships and indignities. Some critics appear to blame Tess for submitting finally to Alec, thus bringing her troubles down on herself. [23] It is almost as though she succumbs to her sexuality and then has to pay for it. This is, of course, a decidedly Victorian middle-class way of thinking. In other words, the woman's fallen nature is blamed for her fate, or, in twenty-first-century language, the victim is blamed. Tess accepts Alec's offer in order to benefit her family, not herself. Unlike the maid of the poem, Tess does not take joy in the apparent rise in social status gained through submission to Alec. Even so, she is momentarily tempted by frustration at her own powerlessness at Flintcombe Ash to think about how she could benefit if she had been free to marry Alec: "It would have lifted her completely out of subjection, not only to her present oppressive employer, but to a whole world who seemed to despise her" (250). That even Tess, who clearly despises Alec, should be tempted in this way suggests the depth of frustration felt by those subjected to the inequalities of the social class system, and their degradation—not in the sense of sexual morals, but in the sense of abandoning one's integrity and beliefs.

As I have said, even though readers of "The Ruined Maid" feel sure that the two country girls are naïve in thinking that genuine social status is to be gained from being "ruined," social status, in a very real sense, *has* been gained in this case. No more real rise in social status could be accomplished than not being cold or hungry or having to work endlessly at manual labor. And this is what Tess has gained, not only for herself but, more importantly, for her family when, towards the end of the novel, Angel finds her living in Sandbourne as Alec's wife. When he first arrives in Sandbourne, a "fashionable watering-place" (296), a "pleasure-city" (296), Angel ponders the strangeness of it: "Where could Tess possibly be, a cottage girl, his young wife, amidst all this wealth and fashion?" (296). But when she emerges from her "stylish lodging-house" (297), she is "fully dressed [. . .] in the walking-costume of a well-to-do lady" (301). She is not flaunting it like the maid in the poem, but Tess has become just like her. Although the most obvious signs of change are her good clothes, the real change is in the fact that she is no longer working in the fields and her family is, presumably, no longer homeless. She has succumbed to a system which has rewarded her materially for what it condemns morally. In "The

Ruined Maid," Hardy subtly undercuts the reader's middle-class stance with irony. But in Tess he portrays a woman who commands the reader's sympathy when she fights against the system but loses.

"A cloud of moral hobgoblins"

Just as George Eliot in *Adam Bede* describes a party being held immediately before the "fall" of Hetty Sorrel, so Hardy describes a dance before Tess's fall. But whereas Eliot celebrates the social ordering of society according to class in her elaborate description of the event, Hardy shows a discomfort in the ordering of society's various strata. His party scene concerns "workfolk" exclusively. These workfolk are so immersed in their dance, shrouded as they are in the dust of the barn in which it is held, that Hardy describes them thus:

> Through this floating fusty *débris* of peat and hay, mixed with the perspirations and warmth of the dancers, and forming together a sort of vegeto-human pollen, the muted fiddles feebly pushed their notes [. . .]. They coughed as they danced, and laughed as they coughed [. . .] a multiplicity of Pans whirling a multiplicity of Syrinxes. (48)

Falling on top of one another as they dance, these villagers do not represent a well-ordered society such as Eliot describes. In fact, the Trantridge villagers are not the type of laborers who would appeal to Hardy's middle-class readers. "Every village has its idiosyncrasy [. . .]," the narrator tells us, "often its own code of morality. Trantridge [. . .] had also a more abiding defect; it drank hard" (46).[24]

The differences between Eliot's party and Hardy's suggest more than the fact that Hardy refuses to idealize rural England. The only representative of the middle-classes present in the dance scene is Alec who appears on the margins: "A loud laugh from behind Tess's back in the shade of the garden united with the titter within the room. She looked round, and saw the red coal of a cigar: Alec d'Urberville was standing there alone. He beckoned to her, and she reluctantly retreated towards him" (49-50). With the inevitable cigar to mark his power, Alec is not integrated into this celebration but stalks the periphery on the lookout for his prey. Once the Trantridge people recognize Alec lurking on the edges of their dance, they prepare to leave; his presence dampens their fun. But it is not because he will disapprove; far from representing traditional middle-class morality and the strict ordering of society, of course, Alec is here to corrupt. Tess, however, refuses his offer of a ride and so Alec lights yet another cigar before he takes himself off, making clear that his lust still burns strongly and that there has been no diminution of his power.

Whereas Eliot's description of the ordering of the local worthies at Arthur Donnithorne's coming-of-age, placed where it is in the novel—that is, immediately before the seduction of Hetty—points to the extent of the social disruption that

Hetty's and Arthur's behavior causes, Hardy's dance invokes just the opposite. As these dust-covered "demigods" make their weary way home, "wandering in their gait" from having "partaken too freely"" (50), they quarrel with Tess because they know her to be Alec's favorite. And it is Alec who rescues her. Unlike a knight in shining armor, however, Alec "had ridden creepingly forward" in order to spy on the group (52). For, in fact, this is far from a rescue. And while the drunken "workfolk" are surprised to see their quarry escape their grasp so easily, and with Alec, they are in no way shocked at this young couple's being alone late at night in the woods. "'Out of the frying-pan into the fire!'" laughs Car's mother. These "children of the open air" laugh knowingly at her fate. For, in the world of Hardy's novel, Tess's refusal to submit willingly to Alec is an abnormality. These workfolk do not subscribe to, and are not upholders of, middle-class Christian morality. And by comparing these villagers to Pans, satyrs and Sileni, Hardy emphasizes their paganism.

Surprisingly, while Hardy wants to controvert the middle-class ideology, there is very little middle-class morality on display in this novel except in the form of Angel Clare—which is ironic in view of Angel's iconoclastic democratic views. Of Angel we are told, "he began to evince considerable indifference to social forms and observances. The material distinctions of rank and wealth he increasingly despised" (91). And of Tess he tells his parents, "'she is not what in common parlance is called a lady [. . .] for she is a cottager's daughter, as I am proud to say. But she *is* a lady, nevertheless—in feeling and nature'" (128). This is a sentiment which echoes Tess's view of herself when she says, "'I am only a peasant by position, not by nature'" (182). So that while Angel appears to espouse a more democratic social order, his reaction to Tess's confession reeks of hypocritical self-righteousness, especially in view of his own admissions. Angel, it appears, has not thrown off his own family's values as much as he would like to think. But Angel's family cannot really be said to represent the weight of middle-class morality. Angel feels that "single-minded and self-sacrificing as his parents were, there existed certain latent prejudices of theirs, as middle-class people, which it would require some tact to overcome" (129). Yet Hardy does not allow Angel's parents to meet Tess nor have the chance to demonstrate their prejudices or even their kindness towards her. They never find out about her "immorality" or her troubles.

Tess does feel a sense of shame, however, at her situation. She has had enough education to realize that the educated, middle-class world looks with disapproval on a girl in her state. The weight of moral opinion is, then, as we are told by the narrator, "generated by [Tess's] conventional aspect" (71) and the "cloud of moral hobgoblins" within Tess herself (67). When she goes into the woods and contemplates nature, the narrator tells us that "she looked upon herself as a figure of Guilt intruding into the haunts of Innocence. But all the while she was making a distinction where there was no difference. [. . .] She had been made to break an accepted social law, but no law known to the environment in which she fancied herself such an anomaly" (67). Despite her unwed state, Tess is not rejected by the workfolk in her agricultural community. She is able to go on working in the fields near the village and her sister brings the baby at lunch-time for her to feed. The narrator goes on to explain that "[s]he might have seen that what had bowed her head so profoundly—the thought of the world's concern at her situation—was founded on an illusion" (71). The rural world is an environment readers would associate with the "natural" and would probably idealize because of the tendency of other writers and, indeed, painters to romanticize the rural life. And yet the bourgeois system of morality and sexual purity does not apply in Hardy's countryside. As Hardy indicates in his preface, the word *pure* has a different meaning here. In contrast to Eliot's *Adam Bede*, Hardy's *Tess* reveals morality along with class and gender inequality to be cultural rather than "natural" phenomena. By making Tess's fears self-inflicted, Hardy suggests that the moral code that would label Tess as a fallen woman or a ruined maid is somehow conjured up out of thin air; she fears a hobgoblin, something that does not have foundation in anything real.

"A little more than persuading"

At the very heart of *Tess* is the sexual encounter that takes place between Alec d'Urberville and Tess Durbeyfield. Although this is the pivotal point of the novel, it is one that is, strangely, present only through its absence. But while omitted from the narrative, this encounter symbolizes the coming together of the gender, morality and class issues that Hardy addresses. The incident has, of course, been discussed at great length by critics who are often concerned about the fact that we are not told whether Tess is raped or seduced. Keeping in mind this critical dialogue, I have, throughout this chapter, referred to the sexual encounter as a rape/seduction, even though my own response as a reader is to acknowledge it as a rape.

Critics have analyzed the legal issues surrounding the difference between seduction and rape. Hardy was a practicing justice of the peace during the time of the composition of *Tess*, and therefore should have been knowledgeable about the law's definition of rape. For example, the law specifically sees sexual intercourse with a sleeping woman as rape, and one of the few details we know about Tess's rape/seduction is that she is sleeping when Alec finds her.[25]

What strikes me as interesting about this rape or seduction debate, however, is that the arguments for or against rape take on a tenor that would be appropriate if one or the other had actually happened to Tess in the Chase. Surprisingly, what seems to get lost in this debate over definition and the law is the simple fact that there was neither a seduction nor a rape; there are only Hardy's words.

To support their positions for or against the charge of rape, several critics bring into play Hardy's changes to the text over a period of years to show how he was reinforcing—or not—the idea of rape. (Hardy's changes to the text of *Tess* were so substantial and frequent that J.T. Laird felt the need to publish a book on it: *The Shaping of* Tess of the d'Urbervilles). The text of Hardy's 1912 Wessex Edition (as represented in the current Norton Critical Edition) is deliberately ambiguous about whether the incident in the Chase is a rape or a seduction. In blurring the line between them, Hardy points to the unfairness of the stigma created by middle-class morality, the fact that, in the nineteenth century, women were treated as tainted whether they were raped or seduced. Of course, as with sexual harassment cases today, the important point is that if a man has a power advantage over a woman when he seduces her (in addition to the gender advantage society bestows on him), then one might easily consider that seduction the equivalent of rape.[26] Alec definitely has a power advantage: he is not only the male representative of the great d'Urberville family—so Tess believes—but he is older than she. He is about twenty-three, while she could be considered still a child even though she has the body of a woman. Tess seems to be about sixteen or seventeen when the novel begins, so she has reached the age of consent.[27] But the narrator assures us that "for all her bouncing handsome womanliness, you could sometimes see her twelfth year in her cheeks, or her ninth sparkling from her eyes; and even her fifth would flit over the curves of her mouth now and then" (8). Hardy wants us to see Tess, in other words, as still a child to some degree. Tess's passivity stems from her perception that this man has power over her in many ways, not the least of which is his class position. His most important means of manipulation, and the one he has recourse to frequently, is the fact that he has wealth and she is poor. Her family has lost Prince, due to Tess's carelessness, and is consequently depending upon her to ingratiate herself with the d'Urbervilles to make money enough for them to live.

While we have seen much of the story from Tess's point of view, her viewpoint is suppressed, as far as the reader is concerned, in the non-narration of the sexual incident itself and we are not privy to the telling of it either in the letter to Angel or in the confession to Angel on their wedding night. But the argument that Tess is silenced by Hardy and unable to tell her story is surely beside the point. While in many ways Hardy enables the reader to become a voyeur in that the narrator often dwells on Tess's physical appearance, at the same time, we see much of Tess's story very much from her point of view. Indeed, in many ways it is society that silences Tess because she is of the laboring class and because she is a woman. Beyond the world of the text, it is the middle-class reader who, for moral purity's sake, wants to sweep her story under the rug, which is, of course, what happens to it literally in the novel. In "Candour in English Fiction,"[28] Hardy describes the proscription of the contents of novels caused by circulating libraries and periodicals trying to suit themselves to "household reading," and the rape/seduction scene in *Tess* was initially removed completely when the work was serialized in the *Graphic*.

Just as the irony in "The Ruined Maid" depends on the moral, middle-class stance of the reader, the ambiguity of the rape/seduction in Tess also depends to a great extent on the reader's stance. Those who see Tess's passivity as her crime, those who use the argument that she did not remove herself from the situation or avoid contact with Alec d'Urberville, also ignore Tess's lack of power, or more precisely Alec's power over her. Tess needs Alec's goodwill in order that her family might survive; it's as simple as that. In view of Alec's power, to see Tess as blameworthy is to assume a moral laxity in her because she is lower in class status, a fairly common view in late nineteenth-century middle-class reformers. It has been argued that the rape/seduction dichotomy depends to a great extent on what it *means* to the woman.[29] Since Hardy never gives us her version of the sexual encounter; we don't know what the incident means to her. But we can surmise that to such a woman as Tess, her sexual surrender to Alec would not be a submission to which she would freely give her consent. For in the end, Tess is different from the ruined maid. She may have been forced to barter her body, but she will not give up her sense of herself, a self that is constituted outside of the social class system and the morality code engendered thereof.

"Have they come for me?"

Some critics have seen Hardy's ending as similar to Eliot's in *Adam Bede*. Nina Auerbach, for example, calls the hanging of Tess "Hardy's final conformity to Victorian conventions" (170). But I would argue that Tess's dramatic death at society's hand is a critique of late-Victorian moral values. Unlike Hetty Sorrel's transportation, Tess's hanging within sight of the "broad Cathedral tower [. . .] the spire of St. Thomas's, the pinnacled tower of the College" stands as a potent rebuke in the face of these symbols of Christian middle-class values (313).

In the last pages of the novel, Angel and Tess, husband and wife, are outcasts from society. They stand outside the moral code because of what Tess has done. They spend their short time together in an empty mansion as interlopers, suggestive of their outlaw status. Tess has decided to submit no more to her tormentor. Using a knife, a masculine method of murder, Tess has struck a blow for Hetty and Ruth and all the fallen women that came before her. She will enjoy her time with Angel and their mutual love no matter what the consequences or the future.

But the consequences of her action are inevitable. Once more Tess sleeps at a crucial moment in her story. The image of Tess asleep on the altar at Stonehenge is a multivalent one. This "heathen temple," "[o]lder than the centuries, older than the d'Urbervilles" (310) and therefore older than the present class system and its code of morality, is certainly a more suitable resting place for Tess than the spired town of Wintoncester—the very town where Charles Bradford Raye of "On the Western Circuit" was educated. And while Tess may appear to be on a sacrificial alter, she is taken from there by the representatives of society's laws. The real sacrifice takes place within the walls of "that fine old city." But it is while she is lying in the "heathen" place that Tess asks Angel to marry her sister Liza-Lu. "She is so good, and simple, and *pure*," she tells Angel (311, my emphasis), deploying that very tricky word that Hardy here seems to fling at Tess's detractors dare they even think of criticizing Clare for marrying his sister-in-law. While Tess's d'Urberville ancestors sleep in their tombs—irrelevant to the new order Tess has created by killing Alec and by the symbolism of her own death—her pure sister sets off with Angel walking away from Wintoncester and all it represents, all it holds. They walk hand in hand like Adam and Eve, but this is the sister of Eve walking, one might say, with an angel in a world created anew.

While Hardy may conjure up the "President of the Immortals" in the last paragraph of his novel, he also holds up "Justice." Since clearly his use of "justice" here is an irony (his use of quotation marks suggests this, as well as his obvious sympathy for her who has been hanged), I would argue that his reference to the immortals is ironic also. For what Hardy has exposed in this novel, the force that he sees as having "sported" with Tess, is the cold reality of the economic forces and social structures that hold this poor girl in their grasp. The fault does not lie with what God has created, but with what man has created—the class system itself.

Notes

[1] See J.T Laird's *The Shaping of* Tess of the d'Urbervilles for a detailed account of this process.

[2] Groups involved included the National Vigilance Association, the Social Purity Alliance, and the White Cross League (*Victorian Britain* 656), and one of their purposes was to call for chaste behavior in both men and women.

[3] In America, under common law, the age had been 10, but had changed during the nineteenth century under state statutes which variously set it between 13 and 18.

[4] As editor of the *Gazette* from 1883 to 1889, Stead oversaw the advent of what was to become known as the "new journalism," a technique which he used to promote an assortment of causes such as social purity, the Salvation Army, universal military service (for both men and women) and antivivisection (Mitchell, "Stead" 756-7).

[5] "Close time" is the phrase used to denote a season during which killing of game is prohibited.

[6] Gorham describes a nineteenth-century superstition that venereal disease could be cured by having intercourse with a virgin (370). Stead may have had this in mind in this passage, but even if he did, his approach is, at the very best, clumsy and in extremely poor taste.

[7] Written in 1866; published in 1901. The controversial Contagious Diseases Acts (enabling the police to compel women to undergo a physical examination if suspected of prostitution) were passed in 1864 and amended in 1866.

[8] In her article, "The Love of Finery: Fashion and the Fallen Woman in Nineteenth-Century Social Discourse" Mariana Valverde claims that one of the ways in which working-class women were stigmatized is by their being blamed for wasting their money on "showy" clothes. It was also thought that many a poor girl had been lured into prostitution by the desire for "finery." She examines medical and political discourse to show how this desire for "finery" was seen as a primary cause of prostitution. Even though this contextualization helps illuminate Hardy's poem, I would argue that Hardy is working to undercut this view rather than support it. And the fact that Tess is dressed in lady's clothes when Angel finally finds her living with Alec seems to me to emphasize the total mastery Alec has over her rather than to suggest that Tess has herself been seduced by a desire for fine clothes.

[9] In the 1880s, after seeing the paintings of French artist Jules Bastien-Lepage (1848–84), Clausen himself worked on realistic rural scenes, going against the tendency of Royal Academicians to idealize country life. In *Winter Work* he shows the hard work of topping and tailing swedes in the cold. It was painted at Chilwick Green near St. Albans.

[10] While this well-used scenario of sexual exploitation is almost always one in which the female is the victim, Peter Casagrande sees Jude as the male counterpart to Tess in that he is "sexually ruined" by Arabella Donn (see "'Something More to be Said': Hardy's Creative Process and the Case of *Tess* and *Jude*," in *New Perspectives on Thomas Hardy*).

[11] This idea that the joint ideologies of gender and morality were used to shore up middle-class identity has been much examined by feminist critics in recent years. The trope of fallenness has been seen by Mary Poovey, for example, as representing a repressed female sexuality unacceptable in conjunction with the idealized, sexless female image. Amanda Anderson suggests that this trope in fact represented far more in the way of cultural anxiety. For just as "feminine virtue could symbolize or help promote normative models of inherent, autonomous, or self-regulating identity, fallenness represented manifold challenges to those models" (14).

[12] As I have emphasized in my introduction, the lower-middle-class background of Hardy, Gissing and Wells is only one of the factors enabling this new fictional depiction of the social class system. But it is a factor. Hardy makes this point in "The Dorsetshire Labourer," when he discusses the view the upper classes have of the agricultural laboring class, and how a caricature—such as "Hodge"—"begins to be taken as truth" when the lower class is viewed from a distance (168). "Moreover," says Hardy, "the original is held to be an actual unit of the multitude signified. He ceases to be an abstract figure and becomes a sample" (168).

[13] See, for example, Barthes' essay "The Death of the Author" (1968), and Foucault's "What Is an Author?" (1969).

[14] *Thomas Hardy, a Biography* (Oxford: Oxford UP, 1982).

[15] *Norton Anthology of English Literature*, 7th edition, Volume 2, Ed. by M. H. Abrams (1999).

[16] Oddly enough, little attention has been paid by critics to the class issues in this novel (except by Raymond and Merryn Williams), nor have critics explained adequately why Hardy gave so much emphasis to Tess's ancestors.

[17] As many critics have noted, Hardy himself claimed that his family was of an ancient lineage, though his father had been a mason, and the idea of the once aristocratic family now debased was fairly common in Dorset where Hardy grew up. As Angel Clare remarks, "it is surprising how many of the present tillers of the soil were once owners of it" (148).

[18] My reading of this novel is illuminated by the work of Peter Widdowson in *Hardy in History: A Study in Literary Sociology* (1989). Widdowson sees Hardy as "a writer obsessed by class to such a degree that he has to recast his life as a written fiction" (154), and it is in *The Life* that Widdowson sees this fiction occurring. Hardy, of course, wrote most of what is referred to here as *The Life* himself, though it was published under the name of his second wife, Florence Emily Hardy. It consisted of two books: *The Early Life of Thomas Hardy 1840-1891*, and *The Later Years of Thomas Hardy 1892-1928*. It is Hardy's own subterfuges in *The Life*, his way of rewriting his own relationship to the problem of social class, and even disavowing his own hand in that subterfuge, that Widdowson sees replicated in Ethelberta's telling of her own life in fiction.

[19] Although this Victorian marital prostitution is most noticed by historians and cultural critics today as it involved women, there were some men, of course, who married simply for financial security. Hardy shows us one such man in Parson Swancourt, father of Elfride in *A Pair of Blue Eyes*, who marries a wealthy widow.

[20] Hardy links marriage with social status—an idea that had been worked by novelists since the days when it was "a truth universally acknowledged, that a single man in possession of a good fortune, must be in want of a wife." Many of Hardy's novels explore the problem of women marrying either above or below their class status. In *Under the Greenwood Tree* (1872), *A Pair of Blue Eyes* (1873), *Far From the Madding Crowd* (1874), *The Hand of Ethelberta*

(1876) and *The Woodlanders* (1887), for example, the plot revolves around a woman having to choose between men of different classes. In most cases—except for Fancy and Bathsheba—the woman ends up married to the higher-class man, but not with good results, indicating that, contrary to conventional wisdom, marrying a prince does not guarantee a fairy-tale ending.

[21] Charles P. C. Petit explores this in detail in "Hardy's Vision of the Individual in *Tess of the d'Urbervilles,*" in *New Perspectives on Thomas Hardy.* He argues that through Hardy's narrator, "we [the readers] modulate unostentatiously from the eyes of one character to those of another character" (177). But it is the constant recourse to Tess's viewpoint that is important to my argument. Petit writes: "This technique, of sliding into and out of Tess's consciousness and vision, is used again and again, and plays a significant part in creating that intimacy between Tess and the reader which is such a remarkable feature of the novel, for it is Tess's eyes which predominate" (179).

[22] The story of Cinderella had been included in *German Popular Stories*, the English translation of the Grimm brothers' fairy-tales which first appeared in England in 1823. Of course, versions of the story had been around for centuries.

[23] See Morris (130).

[24] The episode of the dance in Chaseborough was not included in any published edition of the novel until the Wessex Edition in 1912, even though it had been part of the original manuscript (*Tess* 47).

[25] William A. Davis, in "The Rape of Tess: Hardy, English Law, and the Case for Sexual Assault," details this legal approach to the problem.

[26] Some feminist critics claim that a binary does not exist between rape and seduction. In their view, either scenario denies the woman's agency, especially as regards her own sexual desire. See Ellen Rooney in " 'A Little More than Persuading': Tess and the Subject of Sexual Violence," for example.

[27] We know Tess's age when the novel begins because we are told "[t]here was an interval of four years and more between Tess and the next of the family" (15). The next to her is the twelve-and-a-half-year-old Liza-Lu.

[28] Contribution to a symposium in the *New Review*, January 1890, pp. 15-21.

[29] See Rooney.

Chapter 4

"The splintering frame": Wells's
Tono-Bungay and Edwardian Class

"We grovel before fat Edward," Henry James was to write to Oliver Wendell Holmes when Queen Victoria died early in 1901 and the fifty-nine-year-old Prince of Wales finally became King Edward VII (qtd. in Edel, *The Master* 91). "The Prince of Wales is an arch-vulgarian," James writes to another correspondent. He goes on, "the Queen's magnificent duration had held things magnificently—beneficently— together and prevented all sorts of accidents. Her death, in short, will let loose incalculable forces for possible ill. I am very pessimistic" (88). James here, with his usual sharp perception, characterizes the shift that was about to take place. For the new king's reign, which coincided with the advent of the new century, ushered in an era very different from that presided over by Victoria. Edward was king during the swift decline of the British aristocracy, yet lived a lavish lifestyle himself. He was charming, but decidedly non-intellectual; self-indulgent, yet portrayed as caring about the lower classes.[1] He was an inveterate philanderer, yet kept up the pretence of a happy family life. He was labeled bourgeois, yet insisted on royal prerogative. In short, the elderly playboy king appeared to embody many of the contradictions and new attitudes of the short Edwardian era (1901-10).

Certainly important changes occurred in the years between the death of Victoria and the First World War that had great significance for the social class system. As we have seen in the previous chapters, the late nineteenth century brought the country slowly towards democracy, and both fiction writers and society at large began to focus on issues of class. But what would happen in the new century with a very different monarch on the throne?

One observer, C.F.G. Masterman, in looking at the issue of class in his book *The Condition of England* (1909), sees the nation as "a civilisation containing many of the elements of human welfare and enjoying a widespread happiness and personal comfort." He goes on, however, to point out that it is still a nation divided by class:

> A main body of adequately rewarded and generally satisfied workers are set between the unnaturally wealthy on the one side, on the other the unnaturally poor. The superficial appearance is of a "plutocracy" with riches extravagantly accumulated and extravagantly expended; a middle class industrious and a little bewildered; a

labouring population industrious, and in times of prosperity contented; below, a life which cries almost unheeded from a condition of perpetual privation. (277)

In this passage, Masterman notes the persistence of inequality in English society including the problem of perpetual privation for the segment of the population that had been the subject of concern to Booth, Gissing and others. But he also astutely notes that there is something "superficial" about the extravagance of the wealthy segment of the population and that the middle classes seem "bewildered," suggesting an anxiety about their class position. In the same chapter he claims that there is an *"illusion* of security" (my emphasis) at the time of his writing. And as historian David Cannadine chronicles in his recent account of this period, *The Decline and Fall of the British Aristocracy*, vast eruptions were taking place in the class ordering of British society, especially with regard to the upper echelons.

Cannadine points out the gross inequality that existed in land ownership during the Victorian era; a small segment of the population possessed vast wealth. Earlier in the century enclosure laws had helped consolidate and strengthen the position of the already wealthy, and by the 1870s just over seven hundred individuals owned one-quarter of the land of England and Wales. Nearly three-quarters of the British Isles was in the hands of less than five thousand people, and it was claimed that twelve men between them possessed more than four million acres (55). But by the time Edward took the throne, the economic and political climates were bringing ill winds for these wealthy families. Estate rentals began to drop due to the world-wide collapse in agriculture prices, resulting in falling land values. Simultaneously, business and industry were producing plutocrats with vast fortunes that far exceeded those of the some of the largest land owners. Then, in 1909, Lloyd George as Chancellor of the Exchequer, deployed his People's Budget, a budget that was aimed at undermining the position of the landed rich, a position already weakened (48). The People's Budget imposed heavy death duties and land taxes, and included a shilling in the pound duty on mining royalties, inflicting pain on even those less affected by the world-wide crop price slump. The great British country house system, relic of feudal times, which both represented and constituted the power and wealth of the ruling elite, was about to collapse. The third Reform Act in 1884-5 had again changed the balance of power in government by expanding the franchise even further, and so during Edward's reign the landed elite were under siege in Parliament as well as at home in the country. Democracy was becoming more of a reality; the working classes were finally having a say in government. The class system itself was under pressure in these changing times.

It was anxiety caused by this state of affairs, this pressure on the class system, that engendered its depiction in novels of the era as had been the case back in the 1840s when Elizabeth Gaskell and Benjamin Disraeli were publishing their condition-of-England novels. In his 1910 novel, *Howards End*, E.M. Forster worries about the changing face of England. However, the narrator claims, perhaps ironically, perhaps not, "We are not concerned with the very poor. They are unthinkable, and only to be approached by the statistician or the poet. This story deals with gentlefolk, or with those who are obliged to pretend that they are gentlefolk" (38). Setting aside the poor, and clearly sympathizing with the lower-middle-class Edward Bast, who is yearning to be more than he is, to take advantage of the supposedly more fluid class system, Forster's real concern is with the changes taking place in the elite world of the Schlegel sisters and their difficulties in dealing with the new world order. Class friction not only exists between rich and poor; the inheritors of old money and old culture are seen in these novels to be a different sort from those who have made money through industry. Like Margaret Hale in Gaskell's *North and South*, the Schlegels have trouble integrating a rich industrialist into their world. But just like Margaret Hale, the Schlegels must learn to appreciate the strength and energy of the new industrialist class. Published in the year of King Edward's death, *Howards End* mourns the disappearing world of elite culture that had been supported by the leisure classes—those whom Lloyd George had sarcastically labeled "the unemployed" (Cannadine 49). But like Gaskell more than fifty years before him, Forster promotes personal relationships as the necessary cornerstone of a harmonious society, a society that will meld old money and new and that, in fact, will bring new energy and wealth to old leisure-class families. Hence, whether they were from the old cultured classes or the newly wealthy class growing in power, readers of both Gaskell and Forster could feel satisfied that in the novel's vision, at least, their sort would be valued.

Wells's 1909 novel *Tono-Bungay*, like Forster's, depicts the frictions caused by the changing face of England at the beginning of the twentieth century, but even though both novels paint a picture of the class system at the time, they do so from diverging viewpoints. Forster is uneasy in *Howards End* about the changing face of the British class system, and so his novel not only connects the old world and the new in its characters, but in its form; Forster's fiction is an amalgam of Victorian realism and modernism. *Tono-Bungay* alludes to the Victorian novel in order to critique the old realism, implying that traditional Victorian novels had been complicit in sustaining class inequalities.

Tono-Bungay, in both content and form, contradicts the idea that Edwardian "democracy" has brought with it a collapse of the class system. While the other writers I have studied in this volume have exposed this system as a fiction, a social construction, Wells suggests that the fiction is still at work even when the country house system—the outward symbol of the old class power—to all intents and purposes is now powerless. Changes are taking place in England in the last decades of the nineteenth century and the first years of the new one, but though England may have a different monarch and a whole new look during the Edwardian era, the class system is still embedded there, suggests Wells, and its strength now comes from the *nouveau riche* who fight to sustain the fiction of class for their own ends.

"An almost unavoidable freshness of approach"

During the Victorian period there had, of course, been a clear division between the mainstream novel and such cheap productions as the "penny dreadfuls."[2] However, mainstream middle-class novelists such as Dickens, Thackeray and Eliot were both well-respected and very popular and they were therefore able to earn a substantial living through their writing. By the end of the century a split had occurred: popular fiction had become synonymous with mass culture, and serious fiction, *Literature*, was fiction that was not intended to appeal to the so-called masses and was therefore not commercially successful. It was a cultural divide in which writers had a personal stake: their need to earn a living ran contrary to their desire to see themselves as literary and non-commercial and therefore (by definition under the new rules) not popular. The literary debates in the 1880s and 90s over the status of the novel and the novelist (the most famous contribution to which was James's "The Art of Fiction" in *Longman's Magazine* in 1884, which he wrote in response to a lecture by Walter Besant), were not only a result of the personal threat felt by some writers—that is, the bind in which they found themselves caught—but a reflection of wider class tensions.[3]

The class-based division between high culture and popular culture at the end of the century was caused to a great extent by the speeding up of commercialism and mass-production especially in the field of publishing. While some observers saw great promise for the coming century in the increased power afforded the newly urbanized and industrialized working class through widespread literacy and the increased commercialization of publishing, others saw the growing influence of capitalism in the publishing world as the exploitation of the working class by those already in power through what Patrick Brantlinger calls "bread and circuses"[4] (give the masses a handout and some sensational [print] entertainment and they won't revolt). Yet others saw the commercialization and democratization of the print media—in other words, the beginnings of mass culture[5]—as the end of civilization as they knew it. These different viewpoints were debated by novelists, for while many were sympathetic to democratic ideals, some found that their intellectual bent could not sympathize with its incarnation in the form of mass culture. Gissing, who had had a classical education at Owens College in Manchester[6] even though he was lower-middle-class, saw education and the ability to read as the road to salvation for the lower classes, while at the same time despising the wider reading public as not properly educated, and therefore not truly capable of reading.[7] Walter Besant welcomed the expanded availability of printed materials and the collapse of the power of the circulating libraries because this meant new financial opportunities for authors, and a widening of the pool of writers, with more of them coming from the lower middle class.

H.G. Wells (1866-1946) was one of those lower-middle-class writers who benefited from the more democratic education system, and also from the expansion of opportunities for lower-middle-class writers in the publishing world. As with Gissing, James and Hardy, Wells's fictional representation of the class system also comes to some extent from a position outside of the traditional English middle-class view prevalent in Victorian novels. Wells identifies his class status as "petty bourgeois" (69),[8] and he writes, in *Experiment in Autobiography* (1934), "my exceptional origins and training gave me an almost unavoidable freshness of approach" (428). Wells's life had many outward similarities to that of Gissing. His family was lower-middle-class and his father, like Gissing's, had kept a shop. But while Gissing's father had been a reasonably successful shopkeeping chemist, Wells's father had been a ne'er-do-well who started out in life following in his own father's footsteps working as a gardener on a country house estate. When he married Wells's mother, a maid in a country house, they had fallen into shopkeeping in order to be together and keep their family. The family—more because of the mother's efforts Wells suggests—had clung lovingly to their lower-middle-class status and the young H.G. Wells had been sent to a small private school to receive his education while being taught by his mother to eschew those children in town who were beneath him. But the china shop had never been a successful venture, and when, due to an injury, Wells's father could no longer supplement their income by playing professional cricket and tutoring boys in cricket, they had fallen on hard times and money was scarce. Wells's mother had had to go back into service—the only other way she knew of earning a living—at Up Park, the country house where she had previously been a maid and which was to become the model for Bladesover in *Tono-Bungay*. Luckily she managed to hold down a job as housekeeper for thirteen years—despite, according to Wells, her inability to do the job even adequately well.

Wells stayed with his mother at Up Park on several occasions, in particular for a period of convalescence of four months in 1887-88 after sustaining a football injury. Consequently, while his own experience of the class system growing up in the 1860s and 1870s was as a hard-up, lower-middle-class boy, he was able to have an intimate acquaintance with life at a country house when he was a young man, albeit an acquaintance based on the view from the housekeeper's room and servants' hall, a view from the bottom as it were.

"Of Art, of Literature, Of Mr. Henry James"

Wells's class position is important because it not only influenced his own view of class as manifested in his novels, but it also biased the way his work was viewed. Just as James's label for Hardy seemed to permeate critics' view of that author's work for much of the twentieth century, so James's view of Wells would influence critics, too, making Wells into a parvenu who, while brilliant, was not sufficiently refined. The famous quarrel between James and Wells is an example of how their differing views of the novel were class-based, and how subsequent reporting on the quarrel was itself inflected by class attitudes. The Wells/James quarrel can be seen as more than simply a matter of personal resentments. What turned into a permanent split between these very different writers was symptomatic of the larger divide that was taking place in the turn-of-the-century culture in England, the split between mass-produced, commercial, popular culture and the culture of the Schlegel sisters, a cultural capital that had been handed down from generation to generation along with titles and land.

Wells's relationship with Henry James formed part of the background context for Wells's writing of *Tono-Bungay* because this book has been seen as Wells's attempt to formulate his own version of the novel, a version that differed from that of James. Wells struggled against the concept of the aesthetic novel that James so fervently believed in, and against the elitism it represented. James's work and his ideas about the novel as a genre struck Wells as part of an elitist culture and therefore as a symbol of class inequality.

The nature of the relationship between James and Wells is fairly well known. James—over twenty years Wells's senior—took the role that he loved to play of wise adviser to a younger writer. As Wells writes, "he [James] was plainly sorry that 'Cher Maître' was not an English expression" (*Autobiography* 411). Wells always sent James a copy of his latest book, and they came fast and furious during these years; he published twenty-five books between 1900 and 1913. James always had advice and sometimes praise for his younger colleague. The written record of their friendship is lopsided: many of the letters to Wells from James have been preserved (and are published in Leon Edel and Gordon N. Ray's 1958 volume, *Henry James and H.G. Wells: A Record of their Friendship, their Debate on the Art of Fiction, and their Quarrel*), while most letters from Wells to James have not. However, there is a record of Wells's side of the relationship; he gives his version of events in his *Experiment in Autobiography*. The problem is that this was written in 1934 by the older Wells reflecting on those earlier days, and as Wells points out through his narrator in *Tono-Bungay*, one's memory is an "inconsecutive and irrational thing" (26).

In many of the letters James wrote in response to new work from Wells's pen he is simultaneously effusive and elusive, coy and annoying, endearing and domineering; in short, he is Henry James. For example, he writes of *Love and Mr. Lewisham* on 17 June 1900:

> I now *have* read it, and can speak with assurance. I have found in it a great charm and a great deal of the real thing—that is of the note of life, if not *all* of it (as distinguished from the said great deal.) Why I haven't found "all" I will some day try and tell you: it may be more feasible viva voce. Meanwhile be assured of my appreciation of your humour and your pathos—your homely truth and your unquenchable fancy. I am not quite sure that I see your *idea*—I mean your Subject, so to speak, as determined or constituted: but in short the thing is a bloody little chunk of life, of not small substance, and I wish it a great and continuous fortune. (Edel and Ray 67)

One can imagine that Wells would have been somewhat confused by this sort of critique. At first glance it appears positive, but on reading a second time one discovers all of the qualifications and niggling negatives. It is, in Jamesian fashion, indirect: James brings up a problem and then defers elucidation until he can see Wells in person, but uses the insistently erudite Latin term *viva voce* to indicate this. James uses such a foreign term with ease and aplomb, unlike Edward Ponderevo in *Tono-Bungay*. Can one believe that James *really* admires Wells's "*homely* truth and unquenchable *fancy*" (my italics)? Neither of these terms seem descriptive of James's version of *Art*. He describes the book as "a bloody little chunk of life," a phrase that is ambiguous, it could be positive or negative, but it certainly keeps Wells's work at ground-level, as it were. In offering a statement that is actually positive—he describes the book as "of not small substance"—he uses indirection and twisted syntax, giving an impression that is decidedly negative. As one can see, it is not easy to interpret James—even in his letters to his friends.

James could be overwhelmingly positive, however. After reading *A Modern Utopia* and *Kipps* (1905), James writes, "I am lost in amazement at the diversity of your genius" (Edel and Ray 103). He goes on in the same vein:

> Let me tell you, however, simply, that they have left me prostrate with admiration, and that you are, for me more than ever, the most interesting "literary man" of your generation—in fact, the only interesting one. (105)

It must have been difficult after this kind of private praise from the revered American author—however convoluted and indirect and even if often tempered by criticism—for Wells to accept the *public* criticism James offered in his article for the *Times Literary Supplement* 19 March and 2 April 1914 entitled "The Younger Generation." James smothers the "cluster of interesting juniors" with his voluptuous prose, at one point explaining their style as the squeezing out "to the utmost the plump and more or less juicy orange" (182-3). It is not easy to disinter James's point in this essay with regard to Wells. He tells us that Wells "affects us as taking all knowledge for his province and as inspiring in us to the very highest degree the confidence enjoyed by himself" (189). But again James's effusiveness is doused by qualifications. While he clearly admires Wells's mind, he feels that this younger writer simply turns "out his mind and its contents upon us by any free familiar gesture as from a high window forever open" (190). He refers to this turning out of Wells's mind as "leakage" and accuses Wells of "offhandedness," even though evidence now shows that Wells was a careful craftsman who took great pains with his work. Yes, he's a smart young whippersnapper, James seems to be saying in his own ponderous way, but he has no idea of how to put that smartness to work in writing a *real* novel, a book that could be considered *Art*. In other words, James can see Wells's brilliance, but he is also making a distinction between Wells's creations and his own; his own are definitely *Art*.

What had caused James to publish this negative assessment of Wells, someone who considered him a friend? Perhaps James was resentful because Wells, among others, while not perhaps considered a great literary figure, was selling far more books than James and becoming very well known. James notes in a letter to Wells dated 14 October 1903: "My book [*The Ambassadors*] has been out upwards of a month and, not emulating your 4,000, has sold, I believe, to the extent of 4 copies. In America it is doing better—promises to reach 400" (Edel and Ray 88). Again here we see the double-edged James; while he seems to be envious of Wells's sales, he could be underscoring Wells's popularity against his own distinction as a *Artist*. He is pitting high culture against popular culture.

Whatever the reason for James's public criticism of Wells, it seems to have sparked a need for response in the younger author. In *Boon* (1915), a book which purported to be the unpublished papers of a dead author, Wells wrote a chapter entitled "Of Art, of Literature, Of Mr. Henry James." The chapter contains an amusing fictional dialogue between Henry James and George Moore that parodies Jamesian prose style well. But the conversation about James between some of the characters becomes rather sniping. "The elaborate, copious emptiness of the whole Henry James exploit," says one, "is only redeemed and made endurable by the elaborate, copious wit" (248). And later James's style is described as "a magnificent but painful hippopotamus resolved at any cost, even at the cost of its dignity, upon picking up a pea which has got into a corner of its den" (249). Wells, then, is sticking a pin in what he sees as the inflated bladder of James's self-conscious but empty aestheticism.

As Edel and Ray contend, perhaps James's "'The Younger Generation' was not really the act of treachery that Wells implied" (34), but clearly Wells's attack on James in *Boon*, though funny, was wholehearted and unmistakable. According to his custom, however, Wells sent James a copy of his book—whether he thought James would be amused or whether he simply wanted to make sure his point was made is not clear. James was, predictably, not amused. But he does try earnestly to explain his position on literature in a letter to Wells, and it is at this point in their correspondence that he makes his now famous declaration in defense of aesthetics: "It is art that *makes* life, makes interest, makes importance [...] and I know of no substitute whatever for the force and beauty of its process" (267). But the damage was done and the two men did not renew their friendship.

A year later James died, and, in his autobiography, Wells tried to describe the American:

> James was a strange unnatural human being, a sensitive man lost in an immensely abundant brain, which had had neither a scientific nor a philosophical training, but which was by education and natural aptitude alike, formal, formally aesthetic, conscientiously fastidious and delicate. (451)

This point about scientific training is an important one for Wells. He had trained as a scientist at the Normal School of Science (now part of the Imperial College of Science, Technology and Medicine) under T.H. Huxley, whom he admired greatly. Wells's education engenders what he sees as a crucial difference between his work and James's. He writes, "James never scuffled with Fact; he treated her as a perfect and unchallengeable lady" (452). While the above quotation is Wells's description of Henry James the person, it could clearly be a description of James's prose and it emphasizes that refinement, what one might call elitism, that marked James's work.

When they discuss this breakup between James and Wells in their book's introduction, Edel and Ray come to the facile conclusion that because Wells was a lower-middle-class person and James was quite clearly of a higher class, Wells must be resentful and therefore at fault in this series of events. "Wells, who never lost the cockney impudence of his youth, was grateful for this friendship, but could not accept it without some underlying resentment," they write (17). This tone continues:

> James had an easy acceptance of himself and the world; Wells was working hard to make the world accept him. James knew his place and had always known it: he was reconciled to the man-made hierarchies and wielded his pen as if it were a sceptre. Wells carried on his shoulder the invisible chip of inferior social rank in a society where such matters still deeply counted. One suspects that he experienced the American novelist as he experienced the British upper classes: there remained always an underedge of hostility. When he could experience his friendship with James on a footing of equality he was fairly comfortable; but when James criticized his work, there was a certain inner squirming, not because of the criticism *per se*, but because the raw surfaces of old inferiorities and "below-stairs" insecurities were being touched unwittingly by the older artist. (18)

The language in this passage indicts Wells and exonerates James simply because James is of a higher social class. James's presumed class-consciousness is turned into the image of "the master" wielding his pen like a scepter—a gesture that sounds graceful and dignified, not to mention regal and loaded with power, while Wells's supposed class consciousness becomes an "invisible chip of inferior social rank" or "raw surfaces of old inferiorities and 'below-stairs' insecurities." While there is much evidence in his letters that James, though clearly an affectionate and interested friend, was at the same time pontificating and somewhat arrogant, there is little evidence that I have found in Wells's writing of his supposed shoulder-borne "invisible chip." Wells, in fact, sometimes denigrated himself in his letters to James. After James criticizes *Marriage*, Wells writes to him: "the next book is 'scandalously' bad in form, mixed pickles and I know it. [...] thereafter I will seek earnestly to make my pen lead a decent life" (169). And he writes to James of *Passionate Friends*, "[t]hat book is *gawky*. It's legs and arms and misfitting clothes. It has spots like an ill grown young man. Its manners are sly and clumsy," and later in the same letter, "[m]y art is abortion"(176). One can see in Wells's self-disparagement, however, a great deal of irony, perhaps even an attempt at caricaturing his class position with the domestic imagery and the comment about clumsy manners. Later he writes in his autobiography that "Occasionally I make inelegant gestures of self-effacement but they deceive nobody, and they do not suit me. I am a typical Cockney without either reverence or a sincere conviction of inferiority to any fellow creature" (7). He certainly evinces no reverence for the elitist aestheticism James professed.

The disagreement between these two writers has, I believe, been inaccurately characterized by Edel and Ray as one in which the upstart Wells was resentful of the socially superior James. Instead of noting Wells's view of what the novel should be as a valid opinion—even if it differs from that of James—they refer to "the mischievous small boy in Wells," while referring to James's "mandarin politeness," and claim that *Experiment in Autobiography* "is written somewhat in the spirit of these spurts of naughtiness" (22). There is a definite tendency here to apportion dignity and nobility to James, and to infantilize Wells just as James had done to Hardy in calling him "little Thomas Hardy." It appears to me that the judgment of Edel and Ray is greatly affected by their *own* class prejudice, a class prejudice of which they are unaware, and is typical of the kind of critical class prejudice that has followed Wells through the twentieth century, as it did Hardy. Wells, in fact, wrote "I'm just a journalist [...] I refuse to play the 'artist'" and critics have taken him quite literally at his word (*Autobiography* 531). Wells's claim to being a journalist rather than an artist can be read as a reaction to the elite position James claims for himself and to Wells's wanting to distance himself from that *haute* literary establishment as represented by the American. As Wells describes it, from James's point of view, "there were not so much 'novels' as The Novel, and it was a very high and important achievement. He thought of it as an Art Form and of novelists as artists of a very special and exalted type. He was concerned about their greatness and repute" (*Autobiography* 411). Wells goes on, "One could not be in a room with him [James] for ten minutes without realizing the importance he attached to the dignity of this art of his" (411).

Although the problem between Wells and James *was* class-based, it was not in the way Edel and Ray would have us believe. For while it was a fight about the novel as a form, it was also a fight about the class system itself and is crucial to a reading of *Tono-Bungay*. Raymond Williams describes a parting of the ways between novel styles at this time as the difference between "what separated out as 'individual' or 'psychological' fiction on the one hand and 'social' or 'sociological' fiction on the other" (*The English Novel* 119). But it is a far more class-inflected issue than Williams's division suggests. *Tono-Bungay* represents an approach to the novel that opposes elitism in both form and content, at the same time, depicting changes in the class system from a world-view very different from Forster's in his so-called condition-of-England novel, *Howards End*. And while James's attempts at innovation in such novels as *What Maisie Knew*[9] and *The Princess Casamassima* represent more engagement with current social issues in England than many critics—including H.G. Wells—have recognized, at the beginning of the new century, he had been writing in that highly refined, insistently aesthetic and somewhat difficult style that is now associated with his "Later Phase."[10] The novels of this phase would have been readily recognized by Wells as "The Novel," that "high and important achievement" for which, in the end, James stood, and which Wells seems to have recognized as a symbol of elitism.

"The stupid little tragedies of these clipped and limited lives!"

But Wells's resistance was not *only* a reaction to his American friend's view of the art of fiction. It was also a rebellion against the novel as it had developed throughout the nineteenth century. As we have seen, the new king's reign saw not only the decline of the aristocracy and the rise of the plutocracy, but the decline of the traditional Victorian realistic novel as well, a literary form that stemmed from and helped to sustain the nineteenth-century class system. Wells describes it thus:

> Throughout the broad smooth flow of nineteenth century life in Great Britain, the art of fiction floated in this [. . .] assumption of social fixity. The Novel in English was produced in an atmosphere of security for the entertainment of secure people who liked to feel established and safe for good. Its standards were established within that apparently permanent frame and the criticism of it began to be irritated and perplexed when, through a new instability, the splintering frame began to get into the picture. (*Autobiography* 416)

The Victorian novel seemed to represent reality, to depict an ordered world that made sense, a solid structure. But, of course, that social fixity and feeling of security had been merely a construction made up of literary conventions and fiction. Once writers started to pick away at that frame in their fiction, the frame began to splinter. Similarly, suggests Wells in *Tono-Bungay*, while the class system appeared to be a reality, bound up as it was in very real land ownership and those very solid country houses, it had been in a sense a fictional structure, a fictional frame. By this I mean that, while money and land clearly meant power in a very real sense, the respect and authority the working classes themselves gave to those whom they saw as naturally above them—not only in degree, but in kind—their willing acceptance of their so-called place in the world, was in many ways far more potent, and was only real while it was believed to be so by the participants.

Despite the ways in which class had been exposed as a socially constructed fiction by other writers, and despite the changes in England at the turn of the century because of the beginnings of democracy, the advent of the new monarch and the commercial boom bringing with it the rise of the plutocracy, the class system was still very powerful according to H.G. Wells. Wells implicated the novel itself as a tool and supporter of that class system, especially "The Novel" as written by Henry James. As Robert L. Caserio notes, while much of Wells's work has remained unappreciated by literary scholars, his "distrust of value judgements and of the ritualized literary canon" should earn him a reassessment since this skepticism is in line with current critical trends. He writes, "Wells's idea that 'art' is a bourgeois invention that masks political and economic realities we cannot afford to leave covered up complements the latest analysis of 'literature' as a history-bound, class-bound ideological artifact" (88).

Wells worked in various ways against traditional Victorian novel conventions and James's notion of the aesthetic novel. He did this not only by avoiding the genre altogether when he decided to write futuristic romances, but by writing realistic fiction with a difference. Wells delivered a paper to the Times Book Club in 1912 that laid out how he saw the scope of the novel changing. "We (novelists)," he writes, "are going to deal with political questions and religious questions and social questions" (*Autobiography* 416). This, for Wells, was the splintering frame getting into the picture. Beginning in 1896, Wells published a series of books that were a decided departure from the scientific romances that had recently made him both popular and well off. *The Wheels of Chance* (1896), *Love and Mr. Lewisham* (1900), *Kipps* (1905), *Tono-Bungay* (1909) and *The History of Mr. Polly* (1910) are realistic novels, and the most obvious way in which these books depart from the Victorian realistic tradition is in their use of lower-middle-class men as their protagonists.

Raymond Williams reminds us that there is far more to this shift in the class of a novel's main character than meets the eye; this is not just a matter of window dressing, for it represents a different world-view. The middle-class consciousness that had dominated the Victorian novel had been one forged in the power center of society. As Williams explains, "in the schools, the colleges, the clubs, the country-houses—nobody supposed himself in the presence of a sector, a sect; he was now at the centre, the centre of the world" (*English Novel* 123). So that to explore the class system from the point of view of a group that has been marginalized, in society and in literature, gives one not only a completely new view of it, but a view filtered through a completely different form of consciousness. In fact, I am struck here by the ways in which Williams's description of this notion of the consciousness-forming center could be applied today to post-colonial issues, bringing out an important similarity between post-colonial studies and the study of class. For to have one's world-view formed in the knowledge of one's inferior status to another group, to grow up seeing one's self as other, or in this case "lower," through the eyes of that central group, is to be robbed of one's view of one's self. Without the sense of group identity the working classes were forming through trade unions, mass demonstrations and strike actions, and a real cognizance of being exploited by the capitalist system, the lower-middle classes were aware only of not being part of the central power-wielding group, while yet not wanting to be identified with the working classes. They retained, then, a sort of negative identity that was certainly not helped by literature. Previous fictional representatives of the lower middle classes had always been somewhat foolish, and even if likeable, never well-developed—Dickens's Wemmick being perhaps a debatable exception—for they are a group impenetrable by the middle-class consciousness except as stereotypes. Wells's protagonists not only have their own world-view, they have an inner life, something which had always been denied lower-middle-class characters in literature.[11]

Williams accuses Wells of having failed to poke holes in the middle-class consciousness in any serious way through his fiction, instead "he emigrated," writes Williams, "to World Government as clearly as Lawrence to Mexico" (128). The great Marxist critic is referring here, of course, to the fact that Wells not only moved away from realist fiction and worked on science fiction—an escape from the possibility of asking the difficult questions in any real way—but also wrote non-fictional works about the condition of the world and the importance of a world government. Further, according to Williams, Wells's lower-middle-class characters such as Mr. Polly and Kipps present what he calls "the appealing side, the nice side, of the petit bourgeois; with the emphasis on the small man, the little human peninsula, trying to forget what the high bourgeois mainland is like" (129). I would argue that Wells, writing when he did and assigning a world-view and an inner life to lower-middle-class protagonists, achieved more than Williams gives him credit for—especially in *Tono-Bungay*. As I have pointed out with regard to some critics' prejudicial treatment of Wells due to his lower-middle-class status, the fiction of lower-middle-class writers has been underestimated, even by Williams.[12]

There is no doubt, however, that Mr. Polly and Kipps, those two memorable eponymous characters, while they are well-developed in their own way, are in the end both types, comedic characters who—at least in their fictional worlds—represent no serious threat to the status quo, though in my view their very existence in the popular fiction of the day, written by a well-known and popular novelist, constitutes in itself such a threat.

Wells describes Kipps in the sub-title of his book as "a Simple Soul." What is exquisitely sad about this comic character is his constant yearning. This yearning is, suggests Wells, symptomatic of the lower middle class; it is certainly common to the lower-middle-class protagonists in Wells's social novels. Kipps wants more out of life than his lower-middle-class status is able to give him. He wants to partake of the world glimpsed at in his haphazard education: "He perceived great bogs of ignorance about him, fumbling traps, where other people, it was alleged, *real* gentlemen and ladies, for example, and the clergy, had knowledge and assurance, bogs which it was sometimes difficult to elude" (42). He buys some books to try to educate himself:

> He battled with Shakespeare all one Sunday afternoon, and found the "English Literature", with which Mr. Woodrow [at the local academy] had equipped him, had vanished down some crack in his mind. He had no doubt it was very splendid stuff, but he couldn't quite make out what it was all about. There was an occult meaning, he knew, in literature, and he had forgotten it. (42)

He signs up for a woodcarving class in the evenings in the hopes of enlarging his mind. But unfortunately it serves only to expand his knowledge of his own inferiority because his teacher, Miss Walshingham, is a beautiful woman from a middle-class family who is visited by others from that exalted sphere of life:

> All these personages impressed Kipps with a sense of inferiority that in the case of Miss Walshingham became positively abysmal. The ideas and knowledge they appeared to have, their personal capacity and freedom, opened a new world to his imagination. These people came and went with a sense of absolute assurance, against an overwhelming background of plaster casts, diagrams and tables, benches and

blackboard, a background that seemed to him to be saturated with recondite knowledge and the occult and jealously guarded tips and secrets that constitute Art and the Higher Life. They went home, he imagined, to homes where the piano was played with distinction and freedom, and books littered the tables and foreign languages were habitually used. They had complicated meals no doubt. They "knew etiquette", and how to avoid all the errors for which Kipps bought penny manuals – –*What to Avoid, Common Errors in Speaking*, and the like. He knew nothing about it all, nothing whatever; he was a creature of the outer darkness blinking in an unsuspected light. (45-6)

Kipps soon gets it into his head that one of the ways of bridging the gap between the social classes was to become a writer: "And at the next woodcarving class he let it be drawn from him that his real choice in life was to be a Nawther" (53). It is, of course, a "nawther," a lower-middle-class author, who is poking fun at poor Kipps, and his pathetic ambitions. But this is not the shallow, idiotic stereotype of a lower-middle-class character that had popped up in Victorian novels, this is a man with whom we can have infinite sympathy in his plight because his author cares for him deeply and treats him tenderly: "figure him a small respectably attired person going slowly through a sometimes immensely difficult and always immense world," the narrator tells us (212). And later: "His soul looked out upon life in general as a very small nestling might peep out of its nest" (213).

Emphasizing the difficulties supposedly facing lower-middle-class people hoping to climb the social ladder are the scenes after Kipps inherits a large house and twelve thousand pounds a year and struggles to become "a *real* gentleman." He tries to learn the ways of that "upper" world through Coote, the teacher of style and class who is ever patient and, we suspect, ever aware of the advantage to be gained from ingratiating himself with a man of Kipps's means. Kipps's humiliation at the Royal Grand Hotel in London epitomizes the discomfort he feels as a class misfit, for it is a hotel that represents that strata of society to which Kipps feels he will never have an *entrée*. However, much of what he experiences at the hotel is a result of his own sense of inferiority rather than an overt expression of superiority on the part of the customers and employees. "He felt that every one was watching him and making fun of him, and the injustice of this angered him. After all, they had had every advantage he hadn't" (217). It is, then, the internalized class system that defeats Kipps, his sense that he can't become a part of that grand group, even if he has suddenly inherited the income necessary to become a gentleman. The narrator tells us that "Kipps endured splendour at the Royal Grand Hotel for three nights and days, and then he retreated in disorder. The Royal Grand defeated and overcame and routed Kipps not of intention, but by sheer royal grandeur, grandeur combined with an organization for his comfort carried to excess" (215).

While Kipps may be a laughable figure trying to fit in at the Royal Grand, we cannot despise him and his limitations for the narrator defends him, does not blame him. When Kipps becomes upset with Ann, his wife, an erstwhile maid, because when visited by some ladies from the town and they mistake her for the maid, the humiliation is too much for poor old Kipps who is just enough of a snob to really care, and the two go to bed angry with each other. It is a moment that brings out the anger in the paternalistic narrator who claims Kipps and his wife as "my Kippses." He blames the social class system for ruining lives: "The stupid little tragedies of these clipped and limited lives!" he exclaims.

> As I think of them lying unhappily there in the darkness, my vision pierces the night. See what I can see! Above them, brooding over them, I tell you there is a monster, a lumpish monster, like some great clumsy griffin thing, [...] like some fat, proud flunkey, like pride, like indolence, like all that is darkening and heavy and obstructive in life. It is matter and darkness, it is the anti-soul, it is the ruling power of this land, Stupidity. My Kippses live in its shadow. [...] But for that monster [...] the glowing promise of childhood and youth might have had a happier fruition; thought might have awakened in them to meet the thought of the world, the quickening sunshine of literature pierced to the substance of their souls; their lives might not have been divorced, as now they are divorced, from the apprehension of beauty that we favoured ones are given,—the vision of the Grail that makes life fine for ever. I have laughed, and I laugh at these two people; I have sought to make you laugh. . . .
>
> But I see through the darkness the souls of my Kippses as they are, as little pink strips of quivering living stuff, as things like the bodies of little, ill-nourished, ailing, ignorant children—children who feel pain, who are naughty and muddled and suffer, and do not understand why. And the claw of this Beast rests upon them! (279)

The narrator claims that he laughs at the Kippses, but his tone here and in the subsequent paragraph that describes them as "children who feel pain" suggests that, in fact, he feels sympathy with them and sees them as victims. Indeed, while this passage claims that the Beast is Stupidity, surely that stupidity is the stupidity of a belief in social class. For Kipps, while naïve and easily led, is not damned by his own stupidity, but by his squirming sense of social inferiority. Kipps ends up running a book shop, gainsaying any suggestion that he is stupid. And Kipps has, after all, shown a great deal of common sense and some courage when he realizes finally his true love for Sid's sister Ann and claims her for his wife instead of the haughty, self-serving Helen Walshingham.

Wells's putting forward a lower-middle-class protagonist who is not only funny but with whom we can sympathize and for whose "clipped and limited" life we can feel sorry is indeed an innovation in the novel. But he goes even further. The self-reflexive moment at the end of *Kipps* brings this novel into perspective. Not only does Wells attempt to blur fiction and fact by claiming that the bookshop Kipps ends up owning is a real book shop on Hythe High Street, but he then claims that the very book one is reading can be bought from Kipps himself:

> The bookshop of Kipps is on the left-hand side of the Hythe High Street coming from Folkestone, between the yard of the livery-stable and the shop window full of old silver and suchlike things—it is quite easy to find—and there you may see him

for yourself and speak to him and buy this book of him if you like. He has it in stock I know. Very delicately I've seen to that. His name is not Kipps, of course, you must understand that; but everything else is exactly as I have told you. (300)

Placing Kipps in his final days significantly wedged between horse manure and symbols of old, inherited wealth, and urging the reader not to tell the bookseller that he "*is* 'Kipps'," or that he has "put him in *this book*," the narrator leaves us with a cozy picture of himself as "an old and trusted customer" of that same bookseller (301, my emphasis). The narrator creates a frame for the novel that purports to be fact not fiction, but, in so doing, suggests that the story of Kipps is, therefore, fact and not fiction. If the book is already for sale in Kipps's bookshop even as the narrator is telling us so, then not only is there an attempt at the blurring of fact and fiction, the world of the novel with the "real" world, but there is a also a conflating of past, present and future. This seemingly innocuous moment at the end of this novel is, when one thinks about it, a very important and, indeed, rather complex one. Not only are there two Kippses—one in the novel's main plot and one in the novel's frame, but there are two readers: one who is a fictional reader interpellated by the fictional character of the narrator in the novel's frame, and one who—in the real world—is reading Wells's novel. Thus the reader—past or present—is brought into closer proximity with Kipps than she at first suspects, and is therefore implicated more in the world of this novel than she had originally realized.

While this strange ending appears to blur fact and fiction, the dividing line holds fast—the frame holds the fiction enclosed. The only part of this complicated puzzle that cannot be contained solely within either the fictional or the real world is the book itself. For as soon as the narrator refers to Kipps selling "this book," he brings the book he is writing, the book the reader is holding, into the novel's world. Significantly, it is the book itself that splinters the frame and enters the picture. It is Wells's book that brings, then, a new kind of reality into fiction.

Mr. Polly is another comical, eponymous character, and his history, like that of Kipps, is the history of a non-hero, a decidedly unromanticized, lower-middle-class nobody. This is made evident on the very first page when we find out that he is "suffering acutely from indigestion" (5). The name Wells has chosen for his protagonist labels him as feminized and non-serious. Mr. Polly, like Kipps, has a yearning for a life better than the one to which he has been consigned. Reading literature helps both to satisfy and to increase this yearning. "Mr. Polly had been drinking at the poisoned fountains of English literature, fountains so unsuited to the needs of a decent clerk or shopman, fountains charged with the dangerous suggestion that it becomes a man of gaiety and spirit to make love gallantly and rather carelessly" (80). Literature, of course, does him no good at all; it simply feeds his romantic notions and he ends up making a fool of himself by imagining he is a knight in shining armor talking to his cloistered lady, when actually he is a rather pathetic little man talking to a schoolgirl over the school wall. In looking to literature to satisfy his yearning, Mr.

Polly is similar to Leonard Bast in *Howards End*, published the same year. Leonard, who goes to concerts and reads Ruskin in his spare time, but ekes out a meager living as a clerk, is a project for the Schlegel sisters. They want to prove how liberal they are by taking an interest in him. But as I have said, despite Forster's sympathy for Leonard, his main concern is with the Schlegel sisters. Even though Helen is impulsive enough to become impregnated by him, she cannot live with Mr. Bast nor make him part of her world in any way but through the child. The child she bears is incorporated into their life at Howards End, a life that suggests an uneasy class harmony. Leonard is killed off by a book case falling on him; his yearning for a better life has been his death.

Whereas poor Leonard cannot be Forster's protagonist, Mr. Polly is elevated to that status by Wells. While Polly himself may be amusing, the narrator's description of his life as a shopkeeper, married to a woman who combines "earnestness of spirit with great practical incapacity" (127) is not funny:

> Suddenly, one day it came to him—forgetful of those books and all he had lived and seen through them—that he had been in his shop for exactly fifteen years, that he would soon be forty, and that his life during that time had not been worth living, that it had been in apathetic and feebly hostile and critical company, ugly in detail and mean in scope, and that it had brought him at last to an outlook utterly hopeless and grey [not to mention, of course, the chronic indigestion!]. (131)

Wells makes Polly seem feminized and comical because that is traditionally how the lower-middle-class fictional character appears. But he does so in order to break down that tradition. The other side of Polly's life revealed in this passage, a desperate, grey, incredibly sad and yearning side of his life, puts Polly on a different literary plane altogether.

It is this side of him that makes Polly far more than the comic, stereotypical lower-middle-class character seen in previous novels. Polly's actions in his botched suicide attempt put him squarely outside of previous expectations of literary depictions of the lower middle class. His suicide plan is perfect and heroic. In order to escape from his hopeless grey life he is going to set the house and shop on fire, cutting his own throat with a razor before he burns. In this way, he calculates, he will be rid of his unhappy life, his wife Miriam will be rid of the bankrupt shop and the husband she sees as a failure, and yet she will reap the benefits of his life and fire insurance and so will not suffer from want. But the plan goes awry specifically because of Polly's heroism. He suddenly remembers his neighbor's deaf mother-in-law at home alone in the shop next door and, unlike any comic lower-middle-class stereotype, Polly rescues the old lady by climbing over roof tops. He does so not simply at the risk of his own life, but conversely—and ironically—by sacrificing his own chance at suicide and therefore escape.

While Mr. Polly appears as a hero to the people in his town, he is faced with the ineluctable result that he must now resume his life with Miriam. But the fire has been a baptism for Polly; he is born again:

> [W]hen a man has once broken through the paper walls of everyday circumstance, those unsubstantial walls that hold so many of us securely prisoned from the cradle to the grave, he has made a discovery. If the world does not please you, *you can change it*. (172)

So Mr. Polly realizes that he can "clear out," and clear out he does, going on to even more brave deeds. The problem with his new abode at the Potwell Inn, an idyllic place by the river run by "the plumpest woman Mr. Polly had ever seen," is that it is visited on a regular basis by Uncle Jim, a large and brutish man whose main characteristic is violence (178). While Uncle Jim is not at all a psychologically well-developed character (he seems in fact simply to incarnate the brutality and violence common in the world), what he represents for Mr. Polly is far more important. For he at first flees the inn because he fears Uncle Jim, but then decides to return and face his attacker. With some wile, a bit of clumsiness and a lot of good luck, Polly manages to defeat him. Even though the battle with Uncle Jim is described by the narrator in much the same ironical tone as the rescue of the deaf old woman from the fire, the fact is that both of these incidents suggest a lower-middle-class world that is not as comical as one would like to imagine, for it contains desperation, violence and danger. And, in the figure of the feminized nobody—Mr. Polly—it also contains courage and heroism. Wells, then, has taken the conventional lower-middle-class clown and given him a completely new aspect. In so doing, he helps to break the hold the middle-class world-view has on the English novel.

Mr. Lewisham is not a comic figure but a sad one. His story is one of frustrations and limitations that must have echoed familiarly for many an Edwardian reader. The slightly ironic tone of respect with which the narrator refers to him as Mr. Lewisham in this formal way suggests that, in Lewisham's mind, in Lewisham's own not entirely humble opinion, he deserves such respect but that the narrator has his doubts as to whether the world will be willing to comply. Like many a lower-middle-class man at the beginning of the new century, Mr. Lewisham is ambitious. His hopes are all pinned on education, on science, on learning languages, on earning honors at the university. It is one of the few ways out of the limited life of his class. He has a *Schema*, a detailed plan that will control his time during the years ahead, allowing him to maximize that time for educational purposes. "Where Mr. Lewisham will be at thirty stirs the imagination," we are told. "There will be modification of the *Schema*, of course, as experience widens. But the spirit of it—the spirit of it is a devouring flame!" (5). But Lewisham's ambitions in the shape of his poor *Schema* are eventually thrown in the wastebasket, defeated not by lack of talent, lack of energy or lack of ambition, but by a woman and Lewisham's unavoidable love for her—hence Wells's sub-title "The Story of a Very Young Couple." For they are a couple so young that they cannot understand that love will *not* conquer all. They live in the world of a new fictional realism, not the world of the Victorian novel. In their world they are beset by worries about small amounts of money, and Wells give us the details. In fact, at one point he gives us Mr. Lewisham's balance sheet, a list of his cash in hand, his income and his expenses. "These details are tiresome and disagreeable, no doubt, to the refined reader," the narrator wheedles coyly, "but just imagine how much more disagreeable they were to Mr. Lewisham" (130). In other words, if the reader cannot sympathize with the minutiae of Lewisham's accounts then she is part of the wealthy class who do not have to worry over every sixpence, and it is such people who are Lewisham's problem.

In this new fictional realism, Mr. Lewisham and his Ethel have to get married, not because of anything as dramatic as a pregnancy, but for financial reasons. Lewisham cannot bear for her to be involved in the chicanery of the fake séances conducted by Chaffery and Lagune, but without the money she earns working for them she cannot survive on her own. Their choices are few and Lewisham, still a believer in the power of True Love, bemoans the fate of the less than wealthy:

> The world is against us, against—us. To you it offers money to cheat—to be ignoble. For it *is* ignoble! It offers you no honest way, only a miserable drudgery. And it keeps you from me. And me too it bribes with the promise of success—if I will desert you … You don't know all…We have to wait for years—we may have to wait for ever, if we wait until life is safe. We may be separated … We may lose one another altogether … Let us fight against it. Why should we separate? Unless True Love is like the other things—an empty cant. This is the only way. We two—who belong to one another. (100)

Of course, unlike the love portrayed in the traditional Victorian novel, True Love does turn out to be an "empty cant" in this book. No sooner are they married than their meager circumstances force them to see each other more clearly, without the rose-colored glasses that unsatisfied physical desire perches on the nose. They find themselves disappointed each in his or her own way. In this new realism, marriage is not the telos that provides the happy ending. There is no happy ending as there would have been for Mr. Lewisham's middle-class counterpart in Victorian realism. There is no truly tragic ending for a lower-middle-class protagonist, either. The *Schema* ripped and thrown in the waste-basket is the most tragedy we can expect. But it is, perhaps, the wasted talent, wasted hopes, wasted dreams, depicted so touchingly in this novel, that Wells sees as the tragedy of the lower-middle-class man.

In these novels, Wells employs a new realism to depict the changing class system, one that takes issue with the traditional Victorian realism and its middle-class world-view. In order to do so, he uses lower-middle-class protagonists who manage to retain some dignity despite being pathetic, and with whom the reader can sympathize because their creator treats them so tenderly. When Wells writes *Tono-Bungay*, the novel about which he would comment later "I shall never come as near to a deliberate attempt upon The Novel again as I did in *Tono-Bungay*," his protagonist/narrator is neither pathetic nor sympathetic (*Autobiography* 423). George Ponderevo is a disturbing character who pushes aside all preconceived notions about literary depictions of the lower middle class.

"Bladesover illuminates England"

Despite Wells's claim to have come "near to a deliberate attempt upon The Novel," *Tono-Bungay* is not a novel on the Jamesian plan, and it moves away from, perhaps even attacks, the traditional Victorian realistic novel in several ways. Traditional Victorian realism had masqueraded as history, tried silently to blur the distinction between history and fiction. The goal of the realist text is to approximate lived experience closely, to appear to be a window through which the reader can see her own physical world, the real world. It is the goal of the realist writer, then, to deflect attention from the constructed nature of the text. *Tono-Bungay*, by contrast, draws attention to its writing process and therefore to the boundaries between fact and fiction.

I have noted with Gissing, Hardy, and to some extent with James, the way in which similarities in their novels to incidents or elements in their own lives have caused some critics to equate the author's life with the novel. Wells encourages this comparison with regard to *Tono-Bungay* when he points out in his autobiography that he has "made a little picture of Up Park as 'Bladesover,'" and he goes on to explain that his own experience apprenticed to a pharmacist in Midhurst was drawn upon for his descriptions of Uncle Edward, his wife and his shop. Since *Tono-Bungay* is narrated by a figure belonging to exactly the shopkeeping class Wells himself grew up in, the voice of his narrator George Ponderevo could be considered the voice of Wells himself. But George Ponderevo, who writes, "I like to write, I am keenly interested in writing, but it is not my technique. I'm an engineer" (5), is clearly not H.G. Wells.[13] George's references to his inability to write well foreground the complicated relationship that always exists between author and narrator, or the real world and the fictional one.

The first-person narrator was a familiar technique in the nineteenth-century—especially in the Bildungsroman, the supposed story of a character's life. However, George Ponderevo's claim to autobiography is, from the first page, under erasure for he is writing what he describes as "something in the nature of a novel" (3). He says it is "my first novel and almost certainly my last" (5). Though the book is obviously a novel from the reader's viewpoint, why does the narrator insist that this is a novel from *his* point of view if he purports to tell us his life? Through this claim on his character's part, Wells exposes, in a rather Brechtian way, literary conventions and destroys our suspension of disbelief. It is an instance of what Wells describes as "the splintering frame," or "the frame getting into the picture" (*Autobiography* 416). Wells is pointing out here that to a large extent autobiography is fiction, but more importantly, so is realism—despite its ability to camouflage itself.

Through a series of awakenings, the protagonist of the traditional Bildungsroman matures and finds himself and his place in the world. It is as though there is an essence to the character—or a unity of the subject—that is finally uncovered, or as though the character finally finds the persona that fits him or her best—much like Cinderella trying on the glass slipper. The idea that this is patently *not* the case in real life is discussed by Wells in his autobiography. He writes: "For the normal man, as we have him to-day, his personal unity is a delusion" (349). And, so too, in Wells's anti-Bildungsroman. Even though the narrator begins, "[m]ost people in this world seem to live 'in character,' they have a beginning, a middle and an end, and the three are congruous one with another and true to the rules of their type" (3), the fact that he describes them as living "in character" suggests fiction as opposed to reality. The world the narrator references sounds more like that of the nineteenth-century realistic novel than the world of lived experience. For, of course, while purporting to represent the real, the realistic novel is highly constructed.

But even though it is true for "most people," this living "in character" does not apply, we find out, to George Ponderevo, the novel's first-person narrator. He says, "there is also another kind of life that is not so much living as a miscellaneous tasting of life. One gets hit by some unusual transverse force, one is jerked out of one's stratum and lives crosswise for the rest of the time, and, as it were, in a succession of samples. That has been my lot" (3). George is going to write about "unmanageable realities" (6), not construct a symmetrical "artistic" novel along Jamesian lines, nor a traditional Bildungsroman, and in so doing, George apparently finds neither himself nor his place in the world. For, of course, realities are always unmanageable, and the well-shaped, artistic novel cannot hope to reflect them.

The Victorian Bildungsroman is usually a novel about class in the sense that the place the protagonist finds for himself in society is a place within the class system, and often one on a higher level than the point at which he started. The point is, of course, that if he had "fit in" at that original level, there would be no narratable story. Pip may get his comeuppance for being such a snobbish prig, but he still does not belong back at the forge. These assumptions on the part of the Bildungsroman suggested to class-conscious, class-climbing Victorian readers that their true place in society was indeed, just as they had hoped and imagined, slightly *above* the place in which they began. They enjoyed the sense that they belonged at the next level of the social scale, the one they had been trying to reach. Wells's choice of the Bildungsroman form, then, is a significant one. His protagonist finds neither his essential self nor his destined place in society, despite his speedy rise up the class ladder, and so Wells debunks the class promise that the traditional Bildungsroman holds. George says of most people that "[t]hey have a class, they have a place, they know what is becoming in them and what is due to them, and their proper size of tombstone tells at least how properly they have played the part" (3). It is merely a "part" George notes, however, for they are "no more (and no less) than 'character actors'" (3), for class itself is merely a performance. Yet it is a powerful force for all that.

Tono-Bungay, then, is a novel about the changes that are taking place in England at the turn of the century,[14] especially those that affect issues of class. Indeed it is often described by critics as a condition-of-England novel, a sub-genre that in the past had dealt with the changing class system. David Lodge, in his seminal essay on this novel,[15] argues that England is its central character. But what much of the novel relates is the story of Edward Ponderevo, uncle of George the narrator, and a small-time shopkeeping chemist who has ambitions or, as was the case with Kipps, Mr. Polly and Mr. Lewisham, who yearns to be "better" than he is. Wells observes of Edward that, "[i]n a changing world there cannot be portraits without backgrounds and the source of the shifting reflected light upon the face has to be shown" (424). Context, in other words, is essential to one's understanding of literary characters, and to reading this character in particular. What may have led Lodge to make his claim about the novel is that Edward's character is so intimately entwined with his context that he could be said to embody the changing face of Edwardian England as it is depicted in Wells's novel. And George, as he narrates his distant, unemotional and often ironic reaction to Edward's story, expresses what might be described as the Edwardian *Zeitgeist*.

Edward Ponderevo is a product and producer of what was seen by some observers as the rampant commercialism of the Edwardian era. He represents the worst of capitalist immorality, for the product he markets, a "tonic" he has concocted called "Tono-Bungay," is, according to the advertisements, "the Secret of Vigour." But it is described by George, the narrator, as "mischievous trash, slightly stimulating, aromatic and attractive, likely to become a bad habit and train people in the habitual use of stronger tonics and insidiously dangerous to people with defective kidneys" (120). Despite this, Edward expands his product line to include hair stimulant, "Concentrated Tono-Bungay" for the eyes, "Tono-Bungay Lozenges," and "Tono-Bungay Chocolate." "You can GO for twenty-four hours," the advertisements claim, "on Tono-Bungay" (135). When Uncle Edward becomes immensely rich and attempts to repackage and market himself as higher in class, George describes him at the height of his success:

> There was, I seem to remember, a secular intensification of his features, his nose developed character, became aggressive, stuck out at the world more and more [...]. From the face that returns to my memory projects a long cigar that is sometimes cocked jauntily up from the higher corner, that sometimes droops from the lower; —it was as eloquent as a dog's tail, and he removed it only for the more emphatic modes of speech.[...] He preferred silk hats with ample rich brims, often a trifle large for him [...] and he wore them at various angels to his axis. (187-8)

In other words, Edward looks much like Edward VII in the photograph taken by Basano in 1871 when he was still the Prince of Wales. And just like Edward VII (whose heir was also named George), Edward Ponderevo is portly, overdressed and overfed, dying young from his too self-indulgent life-style.

"Le Steel Say Lum," he tells his nephew in an effort not only to impress upon him the importance of the performance of class, but to demonstrate his facility in that performance (217). But the very fact that Uncle Edward articulates this particular piece of worldly wisdom with an appallingly bad French accent reveals the fact that despite his success, despite his money and grand houses, poor Uncle Edward has no "steel" whatsoever. He is not, as he tells his nephew earlier, "Oh Fay"(215).[16]

Fig. 4.1 *King Edward VII*, c.1871 (at this time Prince of Wales). Photograph by Bassano (Reproduced with permission of the National Portrait Gallery, London)

(215). He is from the lower middle class and, consequently, as he rises up the class ladder, he soon runs into problems because he does not fit in with the protectors of the *old* class system. The notion that the nouveau riche have no class is a cliché, an often-used comedic scenario. We as readers are able to laugh knowingly at Edward's bad French. As with Hardy's poem "The Ruined Maid," the humor in this scene depends on our ability to feel, in fact, our enjoyment of feeling superior to Edward, and the same would have been true of Wells's readers nearly one hundred years ago.

These pseudo-French quotations are reported to us, even spelled for us with emphasis on the bad French accent, in a rather patronizing way, by George Ponderevo, the novel's narrator. Yet George himself is the son of a housekeeper, and his own ability to climb the social ladder depends entirely upon his uncle. George comes from the same class as his uncle and would not have enjoyed such a privileged lifestyle— he says he has "been a native in many social countries" (3)—without said uncle's successful marketing endeavors. "I was hanging on to his coat-tails all the way through," says George. "I was, you might say, the stick of his rocket" (4). George is educated, but it is his ambitious uncle who has sales and marketing acumen and is therefore financially successful. But while comical, Edward is conscious that he is not *au fait* and wants to change that—"We aren't going to be laughed at as Poovenoos, see!" he says (215). George's relation to his class status is a little more duplicitous: he mocks those at the same level as himself who aspire to social superiority. Yet his purpose in doing so is the same as Edward's: to appear to be above the lower middle class into which he was born. Hence, while George wants to think of himself as outside of this class climbing, his ironic and distanced description of his uncle's attempts constitute the same class-consciousness and class ideology, expressed in a different way. The class system is alive and well—both in Edward's psyche and in George's—in a novel that purportedly describes an Edwardian English society remade by the democratizing effects of commerce and the passing of the old order embodied in the country-house system.

This system, embodied in *Tono-Bungay* by Bladesover House, is depicted in the novel as it breaks down at the end of the nineteenth century, a time when many land owners sold off their land and lost their power and privilege. George Ponderevo tells us that when he was a child Bladesover House seemed to him "a complete authentic microcosm." "I believed," he says, "that the Bladesover system was a little working model [. . .] of the whole world" (7). The house and park represent more to George than merely an upper-class estate. He writes:

> [T]hat wide park and that fair large house, dominating church, village and the countryside [. . .] represented the thing that mattered supremely in the world, and [. . .] all other things had significance only in relation to them. They represented the Gentry, the Quality, by and through and for whom the rest of the world, the farming folk and the labouring folk, the tradespeople of Ashborough, and the upper servants and the lower servants and the servants of the estate, breathed and lived and were permitted. (7-8)

Bladesover represents, then, not only for the small boy George, but also in a metaphorical way for the novel, the country house system as it not only structured society, but structured society's thinking as well. "It seemed to be," says George, "in the divine order" (8). And although George points out to his readers that "[t]he hand of change rests on it all, unfelt, unseen," even George himself continues to think in the Bladesover mode. At the time of his writing, Bladesover house has been let to people who are decidedly not part of the English aristocracy; a certain Sir Reuben Lichtenstein now holds the lease (an allusion, perhaps, to the Jewish financiers who were part of King Edward's inner circle.) But despite this change, George admits that "the Bladesover theory [. . .] dominates our minds" (76). Even when George is in London, the Bladesover system still structures his thoughts:

> And as I have gone to and fro in London, in certain regions constantly the thought has recurred, this is Bladesover House, this answers to Bladesover House. The fine gentry may have gone; they have indeed largely gone, I think: rich merchants may have replaced them, financial adventurers or what not. That does not matter; the shape is still Bladesover. (86)

For Bladesover is, he says, "the best explanation, not simply of London, but of all England" (87).

So despite the fact that George often tells us that things are changing, and that he claims "to question the final rightness of the gentlefolks, their primary necessity in the scheme of things," his own constant reference to the Bladesover system suggests that the changes are external, not internal (8). George writes, "in a sense Bladesover has never left me; it is, as I said at the outset, one of those dominant explanatory impressions that make the framework of my mind. Bladesover illuminates England [. . .]. It is my social datum" (54). According to Wells, then, the country-house system—Bladesovery as the narrator labels it—lived on in the English consciousness. Far from disappearing, the class system that constitutes Bladesovery has become more pernicious because, while ostensibly unacknowledged, it is supported by those like Uncle Edward who are lower on the ladder and who see their opportunity to climb. Bladesovery—appropriately—has given birth to a new version of itself.

In seeing that the real power of the English class system now comes from within, Wells is anticipating a Foucauldian view of power. For, writes Foucault, "[p]ower is everywhere; not because it embraces everything, but because it comes from everywhere" (*Sexuality* 93). This idea is supported by George himself when he declares, "Every one was in the system, every one—except my uncle. He stood out and complained" (56). He goes on, "My uncle was the first real breach I found in the great front of Bladesovery the world had presented me. [. . .] my uncle had no respect for Bladesover and Eastry—none whatever" (56). Uncle Edward has found out that Bladesovery has no power if you don't believe in it. Yet, as we have seen, once he becomes successful, Uncle Edward wants to be back in the system with himself placed higher up the social ladder.

George claims that "Everybody who is not actually in the shadow of a Bladesover is as it were perpetually seeking after lost orientations"(13). Everyone seems to need the internalized social system in order to cope with the world. This could be a key to understanding George's life. For once George tries to break away from the Bladesover system he grew up with and that was instilled in him strongly by his mother "who knew with inflexible decision her place and the place of everyone in the world" (13), things start to go awry. He tries to find his orientation through education, through love, through moneymaking, through flying machines, and finally by building a destroyer. Bladesover seems still to be his chief yardstick, and it is as though his own amoral behaviour and that of his Uncle suggest that no replacement has been found. For despite his constant protests, George continues to work in a business he knows to be fraudulent; he is willing to exchange whatever notion he thinks he has of morality for enough money on which to marry. And his comment at the beginning of the novel that he once murdered a man "though it is the most incidental thing in [his] life" (4), is chilling. We find out later in his narrative that this happened when he had taken a ship to Africa in order to steal "quap" to raise the money to save his uncle's financial empire, one built on smoke and mirrors and on convincing people that what is bad for them is actually good for them. The analogy with the national colonial enterprise and its willingness to steal from other lands and take life in order to save a sinking empire is a striking one, suggesting that the old Bladesover system, the system of Victorian class and values, has been merely self-serving and commercial at best, and at worst immoral.

But is it the failing of the old Bladesovery, the solid country house system that has caused this amoral trend in the English society of Wells's portrayal? When we look at George's descriptions of the Bladesover he remembers as a child, we realize that it was a hollow system; while there are books hidden away in the attic, there is not much life in the house. There are no men; there are only two old ladies upstairs who spend their time dozing and petting their dogs. George writes, "When I was a boy I used always to think of these two poor old creatures as superior beings living, like God, somewhere through the ceiling" (10). While the house itself appears to be solid and to embody the dignity and traditional values of the Victorian class system, there is, in fact, no power, only elderly ladies whose power—if they have any—comes from long-time retainers such as George's mother who believes in and clings to the old system. George's encounters there with the members of the upper classes suggest that they are effete weaklings who have no strength left. He describes Archie, half-brother to his beloved Beatrice and part of the Bladesover family, as "a fair-haired, supercilious-looking, weedily-lank boy" (27), and of the fight he has with Archie, he writes, "I hadn't fought ten seconds before I felt this softness in him, realized all that quality of modern upper-class England that never goes to the quick" (31). The old Bladesovery, suggests Wells, was a false symbol of rectitude and certitude, watched over by elderly ladies, and it spawned the amoral behaviour of the new generation, embodied in George and Edward Ponderevo—and perhaps Edward VII as well.

Just as the country-house system, then, is shown to be a false symbol of solid values, so is its counterpart, the Victorian novel. Wells claims that the "social panorama" novel is "too often crude or conventional in interpretation, superficial in motivation and smeary and wholesale in treatment" (*Autobiography* 423-4). In other words, there is nothing very solid about the Victorian realism's depiction of life or its claim to promote morality.

Nor is George the wise, authoritative narrator that we have come to expect from the Victorian novel. Even those first-person narrators like Pip, whose attitude is flawed when they are young, demonstrate to us through their mature view of their younger selves that they are now mature and wise. Now that Pip had found himself and his place, he can look back on his former self and recognize his own priggishness. While George has reached a certain maturity which he refers to as that "criticizing, novel-writing age," he freely admits his shortcomings: "here I am writing [. . .] my own novel—without having any of the discipline to refrain and omit that I suppose the regular novel-writer acquires" (5). Again we find the foregrounding of the writing process, and he adds, "I fail to see how I can be other than a lax, undisciplined storyteller. I must sprawl and founder, comment and theorize, if I am to get the thing out I have in my mind" (5). In the end, George seems to tire of the process: "All this writing is grey now and dead and trite and unmeaning to me" (346). He goes on: "As I turn over the big pile of manuscript before me, certain things become clearer to me, and particularly the immense inconsequence of my experiences. [. . .] I have called it *Tono-Bungay*, but I had far better have called it *Waste*" (346). He has succeeded, though, inasmuch as the process of writing his so-called novel has enabled him to, as he said, "get the thing out I have on my mind." But George is an engineer by calling, not a novelist. And so, as critics have pointed out, his writing is flawed, his tale is disjointed.

George's narrative describes and, at the same time, embodies the restless and contradictory spirit of the Edwardian era. It eschews Victorian values and the conventions of the Victorian novel as well as the pompousness of James's idea of the novel as Art. Wells pulls the Victorian literary enterprise—in the form of an aptly named periodical *The Sacred Grove*, that "representative organ of British intellectual culture"—not only into the new world of the twentieth century, but into the modern age of advertising and commercialism. Edward buys *The Sacred Grove: A Weekly Magazine of Art, Philosophy, Science and Belles Lettres* for eight hundred pounds. But, George notes, Edward's "sound business instincts jarred with the exalted pretensions of a vanishing age" (205).

Wells shows the cover of one issue of *The Sacred Grove* whose contents include such works as "A Hitherto Unpublished Letter from Walter Pater," "Charlotte Brontë's Maternal Great Aunt" and "The Genius of Shakespeare." Surrounding the listing of these provocative items are advertisements for "the best pill in the world for an irregular liver" (206). Wells is having great fun here in his irreverence for the literary establishment. He confirms that the pretentiousness of the Jamesian project and other nineteenth-century literary sacred cows—symbolized here by the *The Sacred Grove*—cannot separate themselves from the world of commercialism. Those who see a split between commercialism and literature are deluded, Wells implies, for literature must be published to be read, and publication brings the sacred into direct collision with, and finally collusion with, the profane.

The section describing *The Sacred Grove* is followed immediately by a description of "a procession of the London unemployed" on a "drizzling November day" (206). George and his uncle look down from the windows of their luxurious hotel suite on this dreary procession. He says it was "like looking down a well into some momentarily revealed *nether world*. Some thousands of needy ineffectual men had been raked together to trail their spiritless misery through the West End" (206, my italics). The allusion to Gissing's novel here is no accident, for it brings into juxtaposition with *The Sacred Grove* that fictional bastion of Victorian culture, the *product* of Victorian values: that is, the poor. George writes,

> [W]e stood high out of it all, as high as if we looked godlike from another world, standing in a room beautifully lit and furnished, skilfully warmed, filled with costly things.
> "There," thought I, "but for the grace of God, go George and Edward Ponderevo." (207)[17]

For one moment, then, George can see himself as one of those men. He recognizes that his godlike status is nothing but "the Accident of Birth. It always is in England" (4).

The juxtaposition of the procession of the unemployed immediately following the listing of contents of *The Sacred Grove* is an example of the splintering frame breaking into the picture, the historical context shedding light on the story. It suggests why Wells sees the need for novels that break the frame, new novels that focus on the reality of social problems—as Gissing and Hardy had done and, ironically, so had James in *The Princess Casamassima*—so that literature is not a tool of the class system, and fiction is not merely a sham reality for it acknowledges its own constructedness.

Unlike the typical hero of a Bildungsroman, George does not end up finding his place or what it is he is looking for in the world. "All my life," he says, "has been at bottom, *seeking*, disbelieving always, dissatisfied always with the thing seen and the thing believed, seeking something in toil, in force, in danger, something whose name and nature I do not clearly understand, something beautiful, worshipful, enduring, mine profoundly and fundamentally, [...] all I can tell is that it is something I have ever failed to find" (182)—"And now I build destroyers" (346). We last see George heading down the Thames on the X2, a destroyer he has designed. The ship is the symbol for what he calls "the heart of life. It is the one enduring thing" (352). It is that elusive something that is "at once human achievement and the most inhuman of all existing things"—and so, certainly, a destroyer is an apt symbol. He says some "men serve it [. . .] in art, in literature" (352). It is a subtle irony to connect his destroyer with art, literature and eventually the empire. For, he tells us on the next page, the journalists who rode with him in his destroyer have "served [him] up to the public in turgid degenerate Kiplingese, as a modest button on the complacent stomach of the Empire" (353).

While I read much irony into Wells's use of the destroyer as the achievement from which George apparently finds some contentment at the end of this novel, it is also profoundly disturbing. For although Wells had had fun earlier in the novel in his merging of literature and profit, the sacred and the profane, here he seems to merge Art with Violence. He knowingly claims that he has become a man with a clearer vision. "I have come to see myself from the outside," he says, "my country from the outside—without illusions" (353). The objectivity he claims here is not the objectivity of the all-knowing Victorian narrator, but the cold, separate, hard objectivity of one who no longer finds comfort in illusion—illusion that surely used to include Bladesovery, and the English class system. Has George finally freed himself from Bladesover's influence? Enigmatically he ends his narrative by claiming, "We are all things that make and pass, striving upon a hidden mission, out to the open sea" (353). While we cannot discern the purpose of the "hidden mission," we know that the new century, with its new freedoms, holds both danger and promise.

The picture we get of Edwardian England in Wells's novel is one that not only looks back to the Victorian era and its system of class privilege and country houses, but one that looks forward, too. For George's destroyer is an ominous and prescient symbol of the violence that will explode across Europe just five years after Wells completes his novel.

While George's destroyer seems to foreshadow the coming clash of the Great War—a clash that will wipe away all lingering vestiges of the old class system—and the subsequent reshaping of Western society, George himself, has been formed by the changes taking place from the decline of Bladesover to the rise of commercialism. He is the product of that commercialism, despite his yearning to rise above it all in his flying machines.

Both George and Edward are overreachers of a kind. Edward is the ultimate class climber and the embodiment of rampant capitalism. But he could also be viewed as an example of what happens when the lower-middle-class man is given the opportunity to take advantage of the capitalist system. Despite all his achievement, he is in some ways still the lower-middle-class buffoon of Victorian literature and in the end he cannot exist in the new world order. George, on the other hand, is a different kind of lower-middle-class overreacher—a far more twentieth-century version. His technological skills place him in the future rather than the past; he is the coming face of his class.

One of the most extraordinary episodes in what is ultimately a rather bizarre novel is the rescue of Edward by George in the Lord Roberts Beta, a navigable balloon. George lifts Edward into the sky as though enacting some form of apotheosis, only to be blown off course. The melodramatic death scene in the Pyrenees is reminiscent of the days leading up to Gissing's death when Wells rushed to his bedside. George tries to keep alive the older generation, but to no avail. Edward has passed, just like the old century, the old Victorian rules and standards, and the old Victorian novel. Realism has changed as it goes into the twentieth century because much of what realism attempts to represent—the relationships between the classes—has also changed. The new writers of realism are not only describing a changed world, they themselves come from a different stratum of that world—their view is a different view.

If we compare the opening pages of *Tono-Bungay*—pages that focus a great deal on George's preoccupation with class, with Bladesover, and with novel writing—if we compare those first pages with the closing pages of the novel, we get a clear sense of Wells's dark vision. For novel writing has been replaced in the novel by the building of attack vessels; the only writers present in those last pages are journalists. And George heads out to the open sea, no longer involved or, indeed, attached to England. He is no longer a part of that changing class system, and yet, from his narrative we know, that Bladesover will always be with him. Whatever changes may be wrought, suggests Wells, that system cannot be exorcised.

Notes

[1] As the Prince of Wales, Edward was said to have donned workman's clothes and toured the slums of Clerkenwell, site of Gissing's *The Nether World* (Weintraub 287). Yet in 1900 the Prince made a speech in the East End confessing that he himself was a slum landlord (377).

[2] Exceptions to this generalization obviously existed. For example, sensation fiction was seen by some critics as not part of mainstream fiction, but even sensation fiction, while aiming some subversive barbs at society's hypocrisies, was written *in reaction to* the male, middle-class norm.

[3] That is, those writing from a middle-class intellectual point of view balked at the notion of themselves simply as workmen who deserved a fair wage (something Walter Besant was fighting for in founding the Society of Authors.) I'm asserting that they balked not because of their artistic stance alone, but because they saw the idea of being a workman as low-class and associated popular literature with low-class, low-quality writers and readers.

[4] See Patrick Brantlinger, *Bread & Circuses: Theories of Mass Culture as Social Decay* (Ithaca: Cornell UP) 1983.

[5] I use the term "mass-culture" here to denote the new commercialized culture, one associated eventually with mass-production, for example, a culture which was consumed by the "masses" as opposed to the elite few. As Raymond Williams points out, the term "mass" can be either negative or positive depending on whether one is a conservative or a revolutionary, an ambiguity which fits nicely with the debates I am trying to flesh out here (see *Keywords*).

[6] Wells writes of Gissing, "I thought him horribly mis-educated and he hardly troubled to hide from me his opinion that I was absolutely illiterate" (*Autobiography* 485).

[7] The debate over the true value of literacy for all had been raging all century and is thoroughly investigated in Patrick Brantlinger, *The Reading Lesson: The Threat of Mass Literacy in Nineteenth-Century British Fiction* (Bloomington: Indiana UP, 1998). The debate over public libraries was a similar, long-standing, class-based debate which also touched on the high vs. low culture issue: many in the middle classes didn't want to fund free lending libraries with local taxes—even when philanthropists such as Andrew Carnegie provided money for the

building—because they saw them as simply supplying worthless novels to low-class people, people who needed more moral, more "improving" reading matter.

[8] Wells writes, "Trotsky has recorded that Lenin, after his one conversation with me, said that I was incurably middle-class. So far Lenin was a sound observer. He, and Trotsky also, were of the same vital social stratum; they had indeed both started life from a far more advantageous level than I had" (69).

[9] See Christine DeVine, "Marginalized Maisie: Social Purity Discourse and *What Maisie Knew*", *The Victorian Newsletter* 99 (Spring 2001): 7-15.

[10] The "Later Phase" includes *The Sacred Fount* (1901), *The Wings of the Dove* (1902), *The Ambassadors* (1903) and *The Golden Bowl* (1904).

[11] See Arlene Young's *Culture, Class and Gender in the Victorian Novel* for a more extensive discussion of the fate of the lower middle classes in Victorian fiction.

[12] Arlene Young also notes this point.

[13] J.R. Hammond examines this question more closely in "The Narrative Voice in *Tono-Bungay*", *The Wellsian*, 1989: 16-21.

[14] The time-frame of *Tono-Bungay* takes us from 1871 when George is 10 years old to 1906 when he writes the book. Thus while he is describing class relations at the end of the nineteenth century, the view he gives us is a view from the first decade of the new century.

[15] See *Language of Fiction*.

[16] *Le style c'est l'homme* translates to something "like the style is the man," or as we might say in English, "the clothes make the man." *Au fait* is translated into English as "being informed," "knowing the latest." When used as a French phrase imported into English, it carries with it a sense of being conversant with manners, behaviors and other class-based knowledge.

[17] This event in *Tono-Bungay* could allude to the protest march of the unemployed in 1886 described in my second chapter.

Conclusion

> In recent decades, debates over the status of knowledge and our ability to know anything—others, the meaning of texts, past history, reality—have dominated theoretical debate in a wide range of academic disciplines. Epistemological skepticism has been pervasive, and the conception of truth that allows for the possibility of objective knowledge has come to be regarded as naïve and suspect. Debates on knowledge have taken on moral and political urgency, and skepticism and subjectivism are often assumed to be connected with radical leftist political positions. (Anger 1)

The above quotation from Suzy Anger's introduction to her recent collection of essays on the difficulties of knowing the past brings to the fore many of the problems and contradictions hovering over what we do as literary and cultural scholars, and especially as Victorianists. Many of us have come to question the possibility of knowing the "facts" of history. Yet, if we are teachers we often focus on the historical and social context of the works we teach. We read books by historians with the expectation that in doing so we will better understand literary texts written long ago. And we warn our students that modern-day usage and connotations cannot be applied to the language of nineteenth-century writers. Skeptical though we may be, we work on the assumption that something can be known and understood of the past, that nineteenth-century language usage can be grasped to some extent, and that we can convey this, at least in part, to students.

While we cannot hope to go back and recreate the mindset of the Victorian era— I should say, the many mindsets of the Victorian era—I believe there is a need nonetheless to garner all the knowledge we can about the period within which a text is written. However, we should do this while keeping in mind a healthy skepticism about the possibility of achieving that knowledge, and while recognizing that history comes to us also through a textual medium. As feminist and post-colonial criticism have shown, it is important to try to recognize the ideological forces at work in the historical context that surrounds a text of any kind, and indeed, that are at work within the text. If we do not, we risk always viewing the texts of past eras as unevolved and of seeing those who lived in the past so much through our own world-view that we validate Christopher Herbert's claim when he describes the Victorians as "those imaginary beings conjured out of nineteenth-century documents to enact twentieth-century imperatives" (33). Or, that the chief function of the Victorians is that of "ensuring for subsequent generations, by negative contrast, the role of bearers of enlightenment and sophistication" (34).

For these reasons, then, I think it important to examine the class context of nineteenth-century British literature, and to view texts through the lens of social class. Class, race and gender can seldom be entirely separated from each other, but while race and gender have become the focus, in recent years, of political, cultural and literary criticism, and deservedly so, the inequalities of the social class system—both fictional and real, past and present—have tended to be ignored. Yet what could be more morally and politically urgent than the issue of class? There is no arguing with the fact that much injustice of race and gender needed (and needs) to be addressed and redressed. However, class inequities—inequalities of monetary wealth and opportunity, and distortions of representation—must be exposed, too. And this is what I have attempted to do in this book, all the while being cognizant of Dominick LaCapra's warning that the "great temptation in recent 'political' readings has been to interpret all cultural artifacts predominantly if not exclusively as symptomatic expressions of dominant discourses and historical pressures and to mention forces that question or contest these discourses and pressures only *en passant*" (3). Indeed, I have tried in my readings to extract those voices questioning the dominant discourses, specifically those of class.

In Victorian England—and to some extent still in twenty-first-century England—class pervaded an individual's sense of identity. However, as I have tried to show in the preceding chapters, class affected not only the lived experience of Victorians at all levels of society, it affected how and why that lived experience was represented in discourse, both fictional and non-fictional. In the end, the point I am making about the changing approaches to realism in late-century fiction is that these approaches are tied to, react to and become part of changes in scientific, journalistic, moralistic, sociological, political and commercial discourse. Similarly, while a writer's biography cannot be allowed to dominate our reading of his or her fictional creations, as the ramifications of class identity demonstrate, a writer's personal history does affect his or her world-view and therefore his or her epistemology and ability to write from a certain perspective at a given moment in time.

This study has aimed at raising the awareness of the class issues at stake in late nineteenth-century realism, and in doing so has thrown into relief the importance of class in forming the work of earlier Victorian realists. It is hard for today's reader, especially the American reader, to appreciate the strength of class ties and class enmities, and the overwhelming power that class afforded in both Victorian life and literature. The distinction between rich and poor is easily recognizable, of course. In *Adam Bede* one can readily see that Hetty Sorrel is from a lower class than Arthur Donnithorne. In Gaskell's *Mary Barton*, it is clear that Mary and her father and those with whom they associate are poor, and that the Carsons are rich. However, it is not so easy for readers today to appreciate the overwhelming nature of this class differential, the kind of respect and even reverence a man like Henry Carson—a rather thoughtless if pleasant young man at best, a selfish and cruel one at worst—would have inspired in the community around him simply because he *is* a Carson. It is hard to appreciate the tremendous power differential—both of class and gender—that exists between himself and Mary. But, as Gaskell shows in her novel, to both the working people and to the rich, these power relations seemed the natural order of things—even if the poor resented it. From our own point in history, we can only with difficulty appreciate the kind of courage, or anger, or desperation or whatever it took for a John Barton to kill a Henry Carson. But today's reader must try to differentiate between the ideologically motivated depiction of the powerful nature of class relations and the life experience of Victorian factory workers in Manchester. Just how much effect does the ideological agenda of the writer, the world-view of the writer, have on his or her realistic depiction of the time and place? For while we cannot look for a window into history in a realistic novel, what we can hope to uncover, at least to some extent, is a reciprocal relationship between the history and the fiction. An examination of that relationship can be revealing of the ideological forces at work in both.

Looking at the changes in realism through the lens of class can help us to understand the parameters and conventions of realism itself, for the two go hand in hand. For example, as I have argued throughout this book, in late century, class is being written about as a cultural construction. This new attitude affects not only the representation of class relations, but the way in which characters conceive of their own identities. Earlier characters, such as Oliver Twist, Eliot's Hetty Sorrel, and Gaskell's Ruth and Margaret Hale may have been involved in class conflicts, but had not felt conflicted about their own class identity. Hetty, for example, had wanted to raise herself on the social ladder, but this is the fairly predictable, stereotypical desire of a working-class girl created by a middle-class writer. Dickens's Pip—writing his story at a time in his life when he can look back on his younger self and recognize his own priggishness—is perhaps the beginning of a new kind of class-conflicted character. At century's end, characters like Sidney Kirkwood, Hyacinth Robinson, Tess Durbeyfield and George Ponderevo have class conflicts going on within themselves. These new characters are the hallmark of late-century realism and serve to show the inextricable bond between realism and class relations.

The writers I examine are not the only ones that focus on class issues in a new way at the end of the nineteenth century, and novels are not the only relevant genre. A revolution was slowly taking place in the English theater, led by George Bernard Shaw and his support of Ibsenism, which brought a new realism to the stage. Theatergoing had changed along class lines during the century. Earlier in the period the "lower" classes had been catered to with melodramas, farces and burlesques. But after mid-century, the bourgeoisie began to show an enthusiasm for the theater and working-class audiences were more likely to spend an evening at the music hall. The plays that achieved success confirmed the attitudes and values of their audiences by "observing Victorian propriety, perhaps tweaking it a bit now and then, but usually just to tickle patrons or to make them thrill at their own liberality" (Berst 59). Then along came Shaw, the Fabian socialist, determined to wake up those audiences by combining Ibsenism and comedy. Like Gissing, James, Hardy and Wells, Shaw attacked bourgeois moral complacency by undermining two of the foundation stones of middle-class ideology: gender and class distinction.

The theater was an appropriate place to criticize the class system, for class is, to a great extent, a matter of performance. Class is often tangled with other identity components such as gender and race. But class is different. While gender and race have, in recent years, been seen to be culturally constructed, still there are some components of both gender and race—biological ones—that cannot be changed. Class, however, has no biological component; the components are all cultural, whether it be dress or speech differences, economic disparity, inequality in cultural capital, education or any of the other class markers used to represent class in novels, as in the real world. One can "pass" racially or in gender. One can even have an operation to change biological gender components. But some people are able to change classes, become a member of a different class without medical treatment, merely by changing their class performance. The theater often becomes a metaphor for the suggestion that there is, under the surface of things, more than meets the eye, and that the shiny exterior of Victorian middle-class life is merely that—a shiny exterior. Interestingly, Gissing uses the theater in *The Nether World* in a way that suggests that, for some people, performance of a better class is not possible. Clara Hewett's ambition is to become a great actress, to play the part of a beautiful romantic heroine on the stage, even if she cannot in real life. But her author disallows the dream; she ends up with vitriol thrown in her face on the night of her probable triumph. Gissing will not allow her to perform a better role successfully. By contrast, in *The Princess Casamassima*, James places his heroine in the theater for her first meeting with Hyacinth, to emphasize the fact that she is performing the role of "princess." And even Tess Durbeyfield (just like the ruined maid of Hardy's poem), once she concedes that she must live with Alec d'Urberville for the sake of her family, must perform the role of wife and dress like a "lady." But if class is merely a performance, one has to wonder at the power of class difference and the apparently ingrained nature of class. Again the essence of class seems to elude our grasp.

This study focuses on Gissing, James, Hardy and Wells because, as I began by pointing out in my introduction, these authors ask the question: What is class? In the few works examined here they have, of course, only begun to answer the question. But the very fact that they articulated it is innovative. Their facing the problems associated with class so squarely has paved the way for further questions in later writing. Other writers were coming to the fore with their own way of linking realism and class. For example, in early twentieth-century theater, J.M. Synge focused purposefully on lower-class life and speech in *The Playboy of the Western* World (1907), and Shaw conducted his trenchant examination of class issues in works such as *Mrs. Warrens Profession* (1898), *Widowers' Houses* (1898) and *Pygmalion* (1916). Arnold Bennett, among other novelists, continued the realistic genre, choosing to center his novels around life in industrial Staffordshire.[1] D.H. Lawrence, the son of a miner, foregrounded the working classes by giving his novel, *Sons and Lovers* (1913), a working-class hero. Such work could only be possible after the changes that had taken place in late nineteenth-century realism and through the efforts of Gissing, James, Hardy, Wells and other late Victorian writers who made class an issue that could be questioned and *de*classified.

Note

[1] Bennett's novels about the "Five Towns" include *Anna of the Five Towns* (1902), *The Old Wives' Tale* (1908), *Clayhanger* (1910), *Hilda Lessways* (1911), *and These Twain* (1916).

Bibliography

Abrams, M.H. et al., ed. *The Norton Anthology of English Literature*. Sixth ed. Vol. 2. New York: Norton, 1962.

"Alexander II." *Times* [London]. 14 Mar. 1881: 10-11

Alden, Patricia. *Social Mobility in the English Bildungsroman: Gissing, Hardy, Bennett, and Lawrence*. Ann Arbor, MI: UMI Research P, 1986.

Altick, Richard D. *The English Common Reader: A Social History of the Mass Reading Public 1800-1900*. Chicago: U of Chicago P, 1957.

Anderson, Amanda. *Tainted Souls and Painted Faces: The Rhetoric of Fallenness in Victorian Culture*. Ithaca, NY: Cornell UP, 1993.

Anger, Suzy, ed. *Knowing the Past: Victorian Literature and Culture*. Ithaca, NY: Cornell UP, 2002.

Armstrong, Nancy. *Desire and Domestic Fiction: A Political History of the Novel*. New York: Oxford UP, 1987.

"Assassination of Lord F. Cavendish and Mr. Burke." *Times* [London]. 8 May 1881: 7-8.

"The Assassination of the Czar." *Times* [London]. 14 Mar. 1881: 1.

"The Assassination of the Emperor of Russia." *Times* [London]. 15 Mar. 1881: 5.

"The Assassinations." *Pall Mall Gazette*. 8 May 1881: 1.

Auerbach, Nina. *Woman and the Demon: The Life of a Victorian Myth*. Cambridge, MA: Harvard UP, 1982.

Barthes, Roland. "The Death of the Author." *Image-Music-Text*. trans. Stephen Heath. New York: Hill and Wang, 1978. 142-8.

—. "The Reality Effect in Descriptions." *Realism*. Ed. Lilian R. Furst. Harlow, Essex: Longman, 1992. 135-41.

—. "What Is Criticism?" Trans. Richard Howard. *Contemporary Literary Criticism: Literary and Cultural Studies*. Ed. Robert Con Davis and Ronald Schleifer. Third ed. New York: Longman, 1986. 47-50.

Berst, Charles A. "New Theatres for Old." *The Cambridge Companion to George Bernard Shaw*. Ed. Christopher Innes. Cambridge: Cambridge UP, 1998. 55-75.

Besant, Walter. *All Sorts and Conditions of Men: An Impossible Story*. 1882. Oxford: Oxford UP, 1997.

—. *Children of Gibeon*. 1886. London: Chatto & Windus, 1895.

—. "The People's Palace." *Contemporary Review* [London] 51 (1887): 226-33.

Booth, Charles. *Descriptive Map of London Poverty, 1889*. London: Stanford's Geographical Establishment, 1889.

—. *Life and Labour of the People in London*. 5 vols. London: Macmillan, 1902. New York: Augustus M. Kelley, 1969.

Booth, William. *In Darkest England, and the Way Out*. London: Salvation Army, 1890.

Born, Daniel. *The Birth of Liberal Guilt in the English Novel: Charles Dickens to H.G. Wells*. Chapel Hill: U of North Carolina P, 1995.

Boumelha, Penny. *Thomas Hardy and Women: Sexual Ideology and Narrative Form*. Madison, WI: U of Wisconsin P, 1985.

Braddon, Mary Elizabeth. *Lady Audley's Secret*. 1862. London: Penguin, 1998.

Brantlinger, Patrick. *Bread and Circuses: Theories of Mass Culture as Social Decay*. Ithaca, NY: Cornell UP, 1983.

—. *The Reading Lesson: The Threat of Mass Literacy in Nineteenth-Century British Fiction*. Bloomington: Indiana UP, 1998.

Brewer, Derek. "Introduction." *The Princess Casamassima*. Henry James. London: Penguin, 1987.

Brontë, Anne. *The Tenant of Wildfell Hall*. 1848. Oxford: Oxford UP, 1998.

Brontë, Charlotte. *Jane Eyre*. 1847. London: Penguin, 2003.

Brown, Lucy. *Victorian News and Newspapers*. Oxford: Clarendon, 1985.

Bush, M.L., ed. *Social Orders and Social Classes in Europe since 1500: Studies in Social Stratification*. London: Longman, 1992.

Cannadine, David. *The Decline and Fall of the British Aristocracy*. New York: Vintage/Random House, 1999.

Casagrande, Peter J. "'Something More to be Said': Hardy's Creative Process and the Case of *Tess* and *Jude*." *New Perspectives on Thomas Hardy*. Ed. Charles P. C. Pettit. New York: St. Martin's, 1994. 16-40.

Caserio, Robert L. "The Novel as a Novel Experiment in Statement." *Decolonizing Tradition: New Views of Twentieth-Century "British" Literary Canons*. Ed. Karen R. Lawrence. Urbana, IL: U of Illinois P, 1992. 88-109.

Chialant, Maria Teresa. "George Gissing's Proletarian Novels." *The Gissing Journal* 12 (2) (1976): 1-13, 7-15.

Churchill, Randolph. "Elijah's Mantle." *Fortnightly Review*. May (1883): 613-21.

Collie, Michael. *George Gissing: A Bibliography*. Folkestone: Dawson's, 1975.

Collins, Philip. "Hardy and Education." *Thomas Hardy: The Writer and his Background*. Ed. Norman Page. New York: St. Martin's, 1980. 41-75.

Collins, Wilkie. *The Moonstone*. 1868. Oxford: Oxford UP, 2000.

—. *The Woman in White*. 1860. Oxford: Oxford UP, 2002.

Corfield, Penelope J., ed. *Language, History, and Class*. Cambridge, MA: B. Blackwell, 1991.

Coustillas, Pierre. *Gissing's Writings on Dickens*. London: Enitharmon Press, 1969.

—. ed. *London and the Life of Literature in Late Victorian England: The Diary of George_Gissing, Novelist*. Hassocks: Harvester, 1978.

—. and Colin Partridge, eds. *Gissing: The Critical Heritage*. London and Boston: Routledge, 1972.

Cox, R.G., ed. *Thomas Hardy: The Critical Heritage*. New York: Barnes & Noble, 1970.

Cross, Nigel. *The Common Writer: Life in Nineteenth-Century Grub Street*. Cambridge: Cambridge UP, 1985.

Curtis, L. Perry. *Apes and Angels: The Irishman in Victorian Caricature*. Washington: Smithsonian Institution Press, 1997.

D'Aeth, F. G. "Present Tendencies of Class Differentiation." *The Sociological Review* 3.4 (1910): 269-76.

Davis, William A., Jr. "The Rape of Tess: Hardy, English Law, and the Case for Sexual Assault." *Nineteenth Century Literature* 52. Sept. (1997): 221-31.

Dean, Michael P. "Henry James, Walter Besant, and 'The Art of Fiction'." *Publications of the Arkansas Philological Association* 10.2 Fall (1984): 13-24.

Dentith, Simon. *Society and Cultural Forms in Nineteenth Century England*. Basingstoke: Macmillan, 1998.

"The Desperate Revolutionists [. . .]" *Times* [London]. 14 Mar. 1881: 9.

DeVine, Christine. "Marginalized Maisie: Social Purity and *What Maisie Knew*." *The Victorian Newsletter*. 99 Spring (2001): 7-15.

Dickens, Charles. "Author's Preface to the Third Edition (1841)." *Oliver Twist*. New York: Norton, 1993.

—. *Bleak House*. 1853. Oxford: Oxford UP, 2004.

—. *Great Expectations*. 1861. London: Penguin, 1996.

—. *Hard Times*. 1854. Toronto: Broadview Press, 1996.

—. *Oliver Twist*. 1838. New York: Norton, 1993.

—. *Our Mutual Friend*. 1865. London: Penguin, 1997.

Dimock, Wai Chee and Michael T. Gilmore, eds. *Rethinking Class: Literary Studies and Social_Formations*. New York: Columbia UP, 1994.

Eagleton, Mary and David Pierce. *Attitudes to Class in the English Novel from Walter Scott to_David Storey*. London: Thames and Hudson, 1979.

Edel, Leon and H. Lyall eds. *The Complete Notebooks of Henry James*. New York: Oxford UP, 1987.

—. ed. *Henry James Letters*. 4 vols. Cambridge, MA: Harvard UP, 1974-84.

—. *The Life of Henry James*. Vol. 3 *The Middle Years (1882-1895)*. 5 vols. New York: Avon, 1978.

—. *The Life of Henry James*. Vol. 5 *The Master (1901-1916)*. 5 vols. New York: Avon, 1972.

—. and Gordon N. Ray, ed. *Henry James and H.G. Wells: A Record of Their Friendship, Their Debate on the Art of Fiction, and Their Quarrel*. Urbana, IL: U of Illinois P, 1958.

Eliot, George. *Adam Bede*. 1859. London: Penguin, 1980.

—. *Middlemarch*. 1872. Oxford: Oxford UP, 1998.

Englander, David and Rosemary O'Day. *Retrieved Riches: Social Investigation in Britain 1840-1914*. Aldershot: Ashgate, 1995.

Faber, Richard. *Proper Stations: Class in Victorian Fiction*. London: Faber, 1971.

Fairhall, James. *James Joyce and the Question of History*. Cambridge: Cambridge UP, 1995.

Feltes, N. N. *Literary Capital and the Late Victorian Novel*. Madison: U of Wisconsin P, 1993.

Fielding, Henry. *Tom Jones*. 1749. New York: Norton, 1973.

Foster, E.M. *Howards End*. 1910. London: Penguin, 2000.

Foucault, Michel. *The History of Sexuality: An Introduction*. Trans. Robert Hurley. Vol. 1. New York: Random House, 1990.

—. "What Is an Author?" (1969) *Contemporary Literary Criticism: Literary and Cultural Studies*. Ed. Robert Con Davis and Ronald Schleifer. New York: Longman, 1994. 341-53.

Gard, Roger, ed. *Henry James: the Critical Heritage*. New York: Barnes & Noble, 1968.

Gaskell, Elizabeth. *Mary Barton: A Tale of Manchester Life*. 1848. London: Penguin, 1996.

—. *North and South*. 1855. London: Everyman, 1993.

—. *Ruth*. 1853. London: Penguin, 1997.

"The Genesis of Nihilism." *Pall Mall Gazette* [London]. 9 May 1882: 4.

"The German Dynamitards." *Times* [London]. 18 Dec. 1884: 3.

"The German Dynamitards." *Times* [London]. 23 Dec. 1884: 3.

Gill, Stephen. "Introduction." *The Nether World*. George Gissing. Oxford: Oxford UP, 1992.

Gissing, George. *Charles Dickens: A Critical Study*. 1902. *Collected Works of George Gissing on Charles Dickens*. Vol. II. Ed. Simon J. James. Grayswood, Surrey: Grayswood Press, 2004.

—. *Demos: A Story of English Socialism*. 1886. Hassocks: Harvester, 1982.

—. *London and the Life of Literature in Late Victorian England: The Diary of George Gissing, Novelist*. Hassocks: Harvester, 1978.

—. *The Nether World*. 1889. Oxford: Oxford UP, 1999.

—. *New Grub Street*. 1891. Oxford: Oxford UP, 1992.

—. "Oliver Twist." *Collected Works of George Gissing on Charles Dickens*. Vol. 1, Ed. Pierre Coustillas. Grayswood, Surrey: Grayswood Press, 2004. 87-95.

—. *The Private Papers of Henry Ryecroft*. 1903. Hassocks: Harvester, 1982.

—. *Thyrza: A Tale*. 1887. Hassocks: Harvester, 1984.

—. *The Unclassed*. 1884. Hassocks: Harvester, 1983.

—. *Workers in the Dawn*. 1880. Hassocks: Harvester, 1985.

Goode, John. "The Art of Fiction: Walter Besant and Henry James." *Tradition and Tolerance in Nineteenth-Century Fiction*. Ed. David Howard, John Lucas, and John Goode. London: Routledge, 1966.

—. *George Gissing: Ideology and Fiction*. New York: Barnes and Noble, 1979.

—. "George Gissing's *The Nether World.*" *Tradition and Tolerance in Nineteenth Century Fiction*. Ed. David Howard, John Lucas, and John Goode. London: Routledge, 1966.

—. "Gissing, Morris, and English Socialism." *Victorian Studies*. Vol. XII. (Dec. 1968): 201-26.

Gorham, Deborah. "The 'Maiden Tribute to Modern Babylon' Re-examined: Child Prostitution and the Idea of Childhood in Late-Victorian England." *Victorian Studies* 21 (1978): 353-79.

Gross, John. *The Rise and Fall of the Man of Letters: Aspects of English Literary Life since 1800*. 1969. Chicago: Ivan R. Dee, 1991.

Grylls, David. *The Paradox of Gissing*. London: Allen & Unwin, 1986.

Halperin, John. *Gissing: A Life in Books*. Oxford: Oxford UP, 1982.

Hammond, J.R. "The Narrative Voice in *Tono-Bungay.*" *The Wellsian* 12. Summer (1989): 16-21.

—. "The Timescale of *Tono-Bungay*: A problem in literary detection." *The Wellsian* 14. Summer (1991): 34-6.

—. *A Preface to H.G. Wells*. Harlow, UK: Pearson Education/Longman, 2001.

Hardy, Thomas. "Candour in English Fiction." *Thomas Hardy's Personal Writings: Prefaces, Literary Opinions, Reminiscences*. Ed. Harold Orel. Lawrence, KS: U of Kansas P, 1966. 125-33.

—. "The Dorsetshire Labourer." *Longman's Magazine* [London]. July (1883): 252-69.

—. *Far from the Madding Crowd*. 1874. Ed. Robert C. Schweik. New York: Norton, 1986.

—. *The Hand of Ethelberta*. 1876. London: Penguin, 1996.

—. *The Life and Work of Thomas Hardy*. Ed. Michael Millgate. Athens, GA: U of Georgia P, 1985.

—. "On the Western Circuit." *Norton Anthology of English Literature*. Ed. M.H. Abrams et al. Seventh ed. Vol. 2. New York: Norton, 1962. 1918-34.

—. *A Pair of Blue Eyes*. 1873. Harmondsworth: Penguin, 1986.

—. *Tess of the d'Urbervilles*. 1891. New York: Norton, 1991.

—. *Under the Greenwood Tree*. 1872. Oxford: Oxford UP, 1985.

—. *The Woodlanders*. 1887. London: Macmillan, 1968.

Harlow, Virginia. *Thomas Sergeant Perry: A Biography and Letters to Perry from William, Henry and Garth Wilkinson James*. Durham, NC: Duke UP, 1950.

Harris, José. "Between Civic Virtue and Social Darwinism: The Concept of the Residuum." *Retrieved Riches: Social Investigation in Britain 1840-1914*. Ed. David Englander and Rosemary O'Day. Aldershot: Ashgate, 1995.

—. *Private Lives, Public Spirit: A Social History of Britain, 1870-1914*. Oxford: Oxford UP, 1993.

Harsh, Constance D. "Gissing's *The Unclassed* and the Perils of Naturalism." *ELH* 59 (1992): 911-38.

Hartsock, Mildred E. "*The Princess Casamassima*: The Politics of Power." *Studies in the Novel* 1 (1969): 297-309.

Herbert, Christopher. "The Golden Bough and the Unknowable." *Knowing the Past: Victorian Literature and Culture*. Ed. Suzy Anger. Ithaca, NY: Cornell UP, 2002. 32-51.

Herbert, Lucille. "*Tono-Bungay*: Tradition and Experiment." *H.G. Wells: A Collection of Critical Essays*. Ed. Bernard Bergonzi. Englewood Cliffs, NJ: Prentice-Hall, 1976. 140-56.

Higgins, Lynn A.and Brenda R. Silver, ed. *Rape and Representation*. New York: Columbia UP, 1991.

Himmelfarb, Gertrude. *Poverty and Compassion: The Moral Imagination of the Late Victorians*. New York: Knopf, 1991.

The History of The Times. 4 vols. New York: Macmillan, 1935-1952.

Hitchcock, Peter. "They Must Be Represented? Problems in Theories of Working-Class Representation." *PMLA* 115 (2000): 20-32.

Howard, David, John Lucas, John Goode, eds. *Tradition and Tolerance in Nineteenth-Century Fiction*. London: Routledge, 1966.

Huggett, Frank E. *Victorian England as Seen by* Punch. London: Sidgwick & Jackson, 1978.

Huntington, John. "Wells and Social Class." *The Wellsian*. 11 (1988): 25-32.

Hynes, Samuel. *The Edwardian Turn of Mind*. Princeton: Princeton UP, 1968.

Jacobson, Marcia. *Henry James and the Mass Market*. University, AL: U of Alabama P, 1983.

James, Henry. "The Art of Fiction." *Literary Criticism: Essays on Literature, American Writers, English Writers*. Ed. Leon Edel. Vol. One. New York: The Library of America, 1984. 44-65. First Published in *Longman's Magazine*, September 1884.

—. *The Princess Casamassima*. 1886. London: Penguin, 1987.

—. *Roderick Hudson*. 1875. London: Penguin, 1986.

—. *The Tragic Muse*. 1890. London: Penguin, 1995.

—. *What Maisie Knew*. 1897. London, Penguin, 1985.

—. "The Younger Generation." *Times Literary Supplement*. 19 Mar. and 2 Apr. 1914: 182-3

Jameson, Fredric. *The Political Unconscious: Narrative as a Socially Symbolic Act*. Ithaca, NY: Cornell UP, 1981.

Jann, Rosemary. "Hardy's Rustics and the Construction of Class." *Victorian Literature and Culture* (2000): 411-25.

Johnson, Warren. "Hyacinth Robinson or *The Princess Casamassima?*" *Texas Studies in Literature and Language* 28. Fall (1986): 296-323.

Jolly, Roslyn. *Henry James: History, Narrative, Fiction*. Oxford: Clarendon P, 1993.

Jones, Gareth Stedman. *Outcast London: A Study in the Relationship between Classes in Victorian Society*. Oxford: Clarendon, 1971.

Keating, P.J. *The Haunted Study: A Social History of the English Novel 1875-1914*.

London: Secker & Warburg, 1989.

—. *The Working Classes in Victorian Fiction*. London: Routledge, 1971.

Korg, Jacob. *George Gissing: A Critical Biography*. Hassocks: Harvester, 1980.

LaCapra, Dominick. *History, Politics, and the Novel*. Ithaca, NY: Cornell UP, 1987.

Laird, J.T. *The Shaping of* Tess of the d'Urbervilles. Oxford: Clarendon Press, 1975.

"The Late Emperor of Russia." *Times* [London]. 17 Mar 1881: 12.

Law, Jules. "A 'Passing Corporeal Blight': Political Bodies in *Tess of the d'Urbervilles*." *Victorian Studies* 40. Winter (1997): 245-70.

Ledger, Sally and Scott McCracken, eds. *Cultural Politics at the Fin de Siècle*. Cambridge: Cambridge UP, 1995.

Lodge, David. *Language of Fiction: Essays in Criticism and Verbal Analysis of the English Novel*. New York: Columbia UP, 1966.

Lucas, John. "Conservatism and Revolution in the 1880s." *Literature and Politics in the Nineteenth Century: Essays*. Ed. John Lucas. London: Methuen, 1971.

McDonald, Deborah. *Clara Collet 1860-1948: An Educated Working Woman*. London: Woburn Press, 2004.

McKibbin, Ross. *The Ideologies of Class: Social Relations in Britain, 1880-1950*. Oxford: Clarendon, 1990.

Marker, Frederick J. "Shaw's Early Plays." *The Cambridge Companion to George Bernard Shaw*. Ed. Christopher Innes. Cambridge: Cambridge UP, 1998. 103-23.

Masterman, C. F. G. *The Condition of England*. London: Methuen, 1909.

Mattheisen, Paul F., Arthur C. Young and Pierre Coustillas, eds. *The Collected Letters of George Gissing*. 9 vols. Athens, Ohio: Ohio U.P., 1990-97.

Melchiori, Barbara Arnett. *Terrorism in the late Victorian Novel*. London: Croom Helm, 1985.

Miller, D.A. *The Novel and the Police*. Berkeley: U of California P, 1988.

Millgate, Michael. ed. *The Life and Work of Thomas Hardy*. Athens, GA: U of Georgia P, 1985.

—. *Thomas Hardy, a Biography*. Oxford: Oxford UP, 1982.

Mitch, David F. *The Rise of Popular Literacy in Victorian England: The Influence of Private Choice and Public Policy*. Philadelphia: U of Pennsylvania P, 1992.

Mitchell, Sally. *The Fallen Angel: Chastity, Class and Women's Reading, 1835-1880*. Bowling Green, OH: Bowling Green U Popular P, 1981.

—. ed. *Victorian Britain: An Encyclopedia*. New York: Garland, 1988.

—. "William Thomas Stead (1849-1912)." *Victorian Britain: An Encyclopedia*. Ed. Sally Mitchell. New York: Garland, 1988.

Morris, Virginia B. *Double Jeopardy: Women Who Kill in Victorian Fiction*. Lexington: UP of Kentucky, 1990.

"New Number of the *Quarterly Review*." *Times* [London]. 15 Apr. 1885: 9.

Ong, Walter J. *Interfaces of the Word: Studies in the Evolution of Consciousness and Culture*. Ithaca, NY: Cornell UP, 1977.

Orel, Harold, ed. *Thomas Hardy's Personal Writings: Prefaces, Literary Opinions,*

Reminiscences. Lawrence, KS: U of Kansas P, 1966.

Page, Norman, ed. *Thomas Hardy: The Writer and his Background.* New York: St. Martin's, 1980.

Pettit, Charles P. C. "Hardy's Vision of the Individual in *Tess of the d'Urbervilles.*" *New Perspectives on Thomas Hardy.* Ed. Charles P.C. Pettit. New York: St. Martin's, 1994.

Pfautz, Harold W., ed. *Charles Booth. On the City: Physical Pattern and Social Structure, Selected Writings.* Chicago: U of Chicago P, 1967.

Pilgrim, Anne. "Gissing's Imagined Audience: A Note on Style." *The Gissing Newsletter* 10.2 (1974): 14-19.

Poole, Adrian. *Gissing in Context.* London: Macmillan, 1975.

Poovey, Mary. *Making a Social Body: British Cultural Formation 1830-1864.* Chicago: U of Chicago P, 1995.

Pykett, Lyn. "Reading the Periodical Press: Text and Context." *Victorian Periodicals Review* XXII.3 (1989): 101-8.

Rasor, Eugene L. "Purity Campaign." *Victorian Britain: An Encyclopedia.* Ed. Sally Mitchell. New York: Garland, 1988. 655-6.

Read, Donald. *The Age of Urban Democracy: England 1868-1914.* London: Longman, 1994.

Rochelson, Meri-Jane and Nikki Lee Manos, eds. *Transforming Genres: New Approaches to British Fiction of the 1890s.* New York: St. Martin's, 1994.

Rooney, Ellen. "'A little more than Persuading': Tess and the Subject of Sexual Violence." *Rape and Representation.* Ed. Brenda R. Silver and Lynn A. Higgins. New York: Columbia UP, 1991.

Rowe, John Carlos. *The Other Henry James.* Durham, NC: Duke UP, 1998.

Rubinstein, W. D. *Britain's Century: A Political and Social History, 1815-1905.* London: Arnold, 1998.

Scanlan, Margaret. "Terrorism and the Realistic Novel: Henry James and *The Princess Casamassima.*" *Texas Studies in Literature and Language* 34.3. Fall (1992): 380-402.

Schults, Raymond L. *Crusader in Babylon: W.T. Stead and the Pall Mall Gazette.* Lincoln: U of Nebraska P, 1972.

Seltzer, Mark. *Henry James and the Art of Power.* Ithaca, NY: Cornell UP, 1984.

Seton-Watson, Hugh. *The Decline of Imperial Russia, 1855-1914.* New York: Frederick A. Praeger, 1952.

Seymour-Smith, Martin. *Hardy.* London: Bloomsbury, 1994.

Shattock, Joanne and Michael Wolff. *The Victorian Periodical Press: Samplings and Soundings.* Leicester: Leicester UP, 1982.

Shaw, George Bernard. *Mrs. Warren's Profession. The Complete Plays of Bernard Shaw.* London: Odhams, 1937. 61-92.

—. *The Quintessence of Ibsenism.* New York: Dover, 1997.

—. *Widowers' Houses: The Complete Plays of Bernard Shaw.* London: Odhams, 1937. 1-28.

Skeggs, Beverly. *Formations of Class and Gender: Becoming Respectable*. London: Sage, 1997.

Stansky, Peter, ed. *The Victorian Revolution: Government and Society in Victoria's Britain*. New York: New Viewpoints, 1973.

Stoll, Rae Harris. "The Unthinkable Poor in Edwardian Writing." *Mosaic* 15.4 (1982): 23-45.

Thackeray, William Makepeace. *Vanity Fair: A Novel Without a Hero*. 1848. Oxford: Oxford UP, 1999.

Tilley, Wesley H. "The Background of *The Princess Casamassima*." *University of Florida Monographs. Humanities* 5. Fall (1960): Gainesville: U of Florida P. 1-61.

Tindall, Gillian. *The Born Exile: George Gissing*. New York: Harcourt Brace, 1974.

—. "The Haunted Books of George Gissing." *Essays by Divers Hands* 43 (1984): 62-74.

Tomlinson, T.B. *The English Middle-Class Novel*. London: Macmillan, 1976.

Toynton, Evelyn. "The Subversive George Gissing." *The American Scholar*. Winter 59.1 (1990): 126-38.

"Trial of the German Dynamitards." *Times* [London]. 16 Dec. 1884: 3.

"The Trial of the German Dynamite Conspirators [. . .]" *Times* [London]. 23 Dec. 1884:7.

Trilling, Lionel. *The Liberal Imagination: Essays on Literature and Society*. Garden City, NY: Doubleday, 1953.

Valverde, Mariana. "The Love of Finery: Fashion and the Fallen Woman in Nineteenth-Century Social Discourse." *Victorian Studies* 32. Winter (1989): 168-88.

Vincent, David. *Literacy and Popular Culture: England, 1750-1914*. Cambridge: Cambridge UP, 1989.

Walker, Brian Robert. "Gissing's Use of Irony." *The Gissing Newsletter* 19.4 (1983): 18-35.

Walkowitz, Judith R. *City of Dreadful Delight: Narratives of Sexual Danger in Late-Victorian London*. Chicago: U of Chicago P, 1992.

—. *Prostitution and Victorian Society: Women, Class and the State*. New York: Cambridge UP, 1980.

Watt, George. *The Fallen Woman in the Nineteenth-Century English Novel*. London: Croom Helm, 1984.

Weeks, Jeffrey. *Sex, Politics, and Society: the Regulation of Sexuality since 1800*. London: Longman, 1981.

Weintraub, Stanley. *Edward the Caresser: The Playboy Prince Who Became Edward VII*. New York: Free Press/Simon and Schuster, 2001.

Wells, H.G. *Boon*. London: Unwin, 1915.

—. *Experiment in Autobiography: Discoveries and Conclusions of a Very Ordinary Brain (Since 1866)*. New York: Macmillan, 1934.

—. *The History of Mr. Polly*. 1910. Boston: Houghton, 1960.

—. *Kipps: The Story of a Simple Soul.* 1905. London: Dent, 1993.

—. *Love and Mr. Lewisham: The Story of a Very Young Couple.* 1900. London: Dent, 1994.

—. *Tono-Bungay.* 1909. London: Dent, 1999.

—. *The Wheels of Chance: A Bicycling Idyll.* Guildford, CT: Lyons Press, 1997.

Widdowson, Peter. *Hardy in History: A Study in Literary Sociology.* London: Routledge, 1989.

—. *On Thomas Hardy: Late Essays and Earlier.* London/New York: Macmillan/St. Martin's, 1998.

Williams, Merryn. *Thomas Hardy and Rural England.* London: Macmillan, 1972.

—. and Raymond Williams. "Hardy and Social Class." *Thomas Hardy: The Writer and his Background.* Ed. Norman Page. New York: St. Martin's, 1980. 29-40.

Williams, Raymond. *The Country and the City.* Oxford: Oxford UP, 1973.

—. *Culture and Society, 1780-1950.* London: Chatto & Windus, 1958.

—. *The English Novel from Dickens to Lawrence.* London/New York: Chatto and Windus/Oxford UP, 1970.

—. *Keywords: A Vocabulary of Culture and Society.* London: Fontana, 1976.

Wood, Christopher. *Victorian Painting.* Boston: Bulfinch Press (Little, Brown), 1999.

Woolf, Virginia. "Mr. Bennett and Mrs. Brown." *The Virginia Woolf Reader.* Ed. Mitchell A. Leaska. New York: Harcourt Brace, 1984. 192-212.

Young, Arlene. *Culture, Class and Gender in the Victorian Novel: Gentlemen, Gents and Working Women.* New York: St. Martin's, 1999.

Zola, Émile. *Germinal.* London: Penguin, 1954.

Index